From Hagar to Rachel

Order this book online at www.trafford.com
or email orders@trafford.com

Most Trafford titles are also available at major online book retailers.

Printed in the United States of America.

ISBN: 978-1-5539-5339-5 (sc)

Trafford rev. 01/05/2015

www.trafford.com
North America & international
toll-free: 1 888 232 4444 (USA & Canada)
fax: 812 355 4082

This book is dedicated to:

My Friend Rev. Arthur Nurse,
Whose belief in my ability exceeded mine. I know you are thrilled with my accomplishment. Thank You.

My Sister and Friend Thea Spitz,
Who always understood my struggle and helped me to understand my own emotions. I hope you are proud of me, Thea.

My Sister and Friend Stephanie Tyndale,
Who has been a constant and devoted source of encouragement throughout the many crises of my life.

My Sister and Friend Dr. Betty Yanger,
Whose honesty and knowledge of human behavior let me know that I am quite normal. .

My Pastor and Friend Reverend Annette Rose,
Who agrees that the purpose of salvation is that we may be fully restored to God's image, understand our full potential, and realize our God-set purpose. Pastor, I hope you are pleased with my work, and find it useful, as you continue to minister to the people who need to be restored.

And To All Of Rachel's Family.

Table of Contents

Preface

As I sit down to write the foreword for my friend's book, *From Hagar to Rachel*, I am filled with a great sense of the honor bestowed upon me. Over the past twenty years, we have grown closer than sisters who were born of the same parents and raised in the same household, yet in actuality we could not be more different. My sister and friend is a native of Trinidad, a woman of color, born to a poor single parent, while I am a W.A.S.P. (White Anglo Saxon Protestant), born into a tightly knit middle class family. I was born in the City of New York, in a time when the structure of schools and neighborhoods prevented children of different racial backgrounds from coming into frequent contact with one another. My friend and I are so different on the surface, that we should have little in common, but year after year we discovered how similar were our experiences, our hurts, our joys, and our hearts. I am grateful to the Lord Jesus Christ who knit us together (an example of His sense of humor) and made us blood relatives (His Blood). Over the past twenty years I have discovered that my sister, Rachel Andrea Eden Palmer, is indeed, my spiritual twin sister.

In the fall of 1980, two newly saved women began attending a morning devotional meeting, which met during the time our jobs permitted for a coffee break. The devotional time was a better refresher than any brew of coffee, and soon the meeting grew large. I cannot say I specifically remember meeting my sister at the meetings; rather, a different circumstance in her life brought us together. At the time, I did not relate well to other women, and sought fellowship among the brothers in whose company I always felt comfortable and well accepted. My "twin" also related better to men and shared a problem with Leo, one of the brothers in the group. However, there are some things that a Christian woman cannot comfortably discuss with a brother. Since the problem had to do with resisting temptation, Leo introduced us to each other, and suggested that the two of us pray together. So, you might say that "temptation" is what brought us together.

Our fellowship together grew into a wonderful friendship, and we spent break-time and lunchtime in each other's company for many years. During that blessed time, God was fashioning us both and used us as support columns in each other's life. Whenever I'd hit a rough spot, my dear spiritual twin was there to pray with me and encourage me in more ways than she could ever realize. Through those times of honest sharing of our heart's concerns, we saw how alike we really were.

Leo, the same brother who introduced us to each other started a teaching fellowship at lunchtime. He spent all his free time in the Word of God, and it became apparent to both Rachel and myself that we needed to spend more time in the Word. It wasn't long before applied diligence and God's anointing bore fruit, and we both became teachers of the Word. We progressed from a small conference room, to teaching in an unused lunchroom in the basement catacombs of the Public Library at 42nd street and 5th Avenue in Manhattan. The growing numbers that attended made our presence obvious, and soon the room was no longer available to us for teaching the Bible. Unfortunately, this began a pattern that repeated often. First, the Lord would open a door for us for teaching, or for prayer. Next, the meetings would grow large and finally, we would be abruptly shut down. Each time this happened, our direction of service was changed, but our zeal and our heart for the things of the Lord only increased. Serving the Lord together in this fashion caused us to grow in understanding of His ways, and the bond of love we shared with each other.

There were fun times as well. Rachel has a wonderfully happy laugh and so became known as Chuckles, while my extra poundage caused me to be called, "Chubbs". Chuckles and Chubbs developed a "*frick and frack*" banter routine. Chuckles would relate stories of how poor her childhood circumstances were, that she had to walk miles to even fetch drinking water, and I would counter with concocted tales of my own poverty that forced us to use the same limousine on Sunday as we did during the week. This contrast amused a few of our acquaintances, but, I think, mostly it amused the two of us. In reality, our humor became unbearable. On one occasion, Leo was relating to us how he taught a group about those who put their trust in other things, and used the scripture in Matthew Chapter three where Jesus says: "*for I say unto you, that God is able of these stones to raise up children unto Abraham*". Chubbs commented that if that were to happen, they would be "stoned children of Abraham"….and Chuckles burst forth into ripples of laughter. Leo proceeded to admonish us in scripture about the eternal end of a fool. Rachel and I decided that Leo needed to 'lighten up'. We made him our first serious prayer project, and God answered by giving him a sense of humor more ridiculous than our own. We learned to be careful what we prayed for.

Those were the 'honey-moon' years of our walk with the Lord. We both went to Bible Colleges, and daily shared the knowledge and experiences gained. Trouble came in the form of a demonic attack against Rachel's eldest son. I watched a holy metamorphosis happen in my sister, as God raised her up - a mighty woman of prayer. Through much prayer, fasting, and spiritual warfare, her son was delivered. God performed on His promise to give her a "backbone of steel". Today, that backbone still causes her to stand tall and strong in God's service.

One morning at work, Rachel came into my office and stated

Preface

she felt her prayer life needed improvement. If my memory is correct, the descriptive word she used was “stinks”. I had to admit mine also was sadly lacking. We resolved to find an empty conference room at lunchtime and pray instead of eat. It wasn’t long before two other sisters joined us, and we were a four-some for prayer. God forged us together as a team, and prayer requests were given to us from all over the world. Rachel was anointed by God to articulate the requests, and I marveled as God always gave her the right words to pray in every situation. We learned so much about the Lord during this prayer time, and came to know each other in the spirit. If none of our prayers had been answered, we would praise God for having worked a miracle in our Christian development alone, but He is a God that answers prayer. Specific answers soon began to pour forth in response to the prayers of that group. We saw many come to know the Lord, and many were healed, and delivered from extreme circumstances. God gave us a flaming sword to use as a focus to direct our prayers toward the outcome of His will in each circumstance. Ministries grew out of that prayer meeting, and soon people from surrounding buildings began to join us.

Before long, the same pattern was repeated and word of the lunchtime prayer meeting spread. We moved from conference room to conference room in an effort to accommodate the size of the group. On two separate occasions, the floor actually shook (as if in an earthquake). A secretary seated outside the conference room did not feel the shaking, while all that prayed inside did. We investigated thoroughly, and could find no natural explanation for this phenomenon. It is hard to accept that a work of God like Rachel's prayer meeting should be only for a time and for a season, but that is frequently what happens. Soon, all the conference rooms were locked, and we started to meet on the stairwell, until that too was closed to us - and we were locked out.

The next stage in our development took us into street ministry. Having been brought up with maternal admonitions, "not to talk to strangers", I was really out of my element on the streets in New York City. Rachel too had to overcome intimidation, but she did so - and beautifully. Our first sermons were preached on the Promenade and Rockefeller Center. Rachel was used by the Lord also to preach in the subway trains, and at various locations throughout New York City. I marveled at her courage and her obedience to the call of the Lord in her life.

My sister Rachel Andrea Eden Palmer is a very courageous woman. She returned to school and earned her doctorate, she taught in Bible College, she counseled, she preached, she worshipped, and she prayed. Oh, did she pray! Together we prayed through unimaginable hardships, including the death of her son Allan, who was a decorated marine and veteran of the Gulf War. Allan died of cancer as his mother held him in her arms and together they sang 'Yes Jesus Loves Me". Rachel delivered Allan back into the arms of the Lord who had given him to her barely twenty-five years earlier.

Matthew.2:18

> *In Rama there was a voice heard, lamentation, and weeping, and great mourning, Rachel weeping for her children, and would not be comforted, because they are not.*

A year to the day after that event, Rachel returned home from work to find that her home had burned down. My sister is a very courageous woman.

In the Bible, there is a scripture that talks of the tribulations of the apostle Paul, and how his suffering enabled him to comfort others who also experience hardships. Rachel has been used in just such a manner. She has counseled families who have had to watch a loved one waste away from disease. She has comforted and counseled children who have been neglected and abandoned, and many couples who are struggling to keep their marriage together. She has comforted those who have lost everything, and kept them from despair. Rachel's training and life experience has also enabled her to encourage and advise young men and women in the ministry.

Preface

My sister Rachel is a very courageous woman. A few years ago, while worshiping the Lord in her church, she fell to the floor having had a massive stroke. The kind of cerebral event she suffered has an 80% mortality rate. The saints on several continents prayed diligently for her recovery, and God has answered our prayers. Her recovery has been complete, and I rejoice to still have my spiritual twin sister as a companion in this life. God has given her the opportunity to complete this book and to share with you her journey from Hagar to Rachel. Rachel once asked me if I was proud of her. The answer is a resounding yes!

At this writing, my sister is again stepping out in response to the leading of the Lord. She is moving her ministry headquarters to the island of her birth, Trinidad. Rachel is indeed a courageous woman. I have attempted to introduce you to her from the outside. In the pages of this book, you will come to know her from the inside, as you walk with her on her journey from Hagar to Rachel.

Reverend Thea Spitz

-1- The Truth Shall Make You Free.

I began writing this book early in 1999. It was my hope to have completed it by the end of that year. However, God knew that I needed to experience and learn more of his love before I could realize my own true value. So, although I had many facts written and knew in my mind how I wanted *"Keys"* to turn out, I was unable to meet my own dead line.

On December 26th, 1999 I was struck down and almost died from a ruptured aneurysm. Jesus touched and healed me. I am a miracle. For two years I was unable to return to my book, but it was during that time that my value appreciated in my own estimation. My life became precious; my purpose became extremely important; and the words, ***"Not by might, not by power, but by the Spirit of the LORD",*** became an experiential reality.

My life became precious to me, because by sparing my life, God declared that I was precious to Him. The importance of my purpose was heightened because God had given me a second opportunity to live and therefore it must be for ***His*** purpose. The words, ***"His Strength is made perfect in weakness,"*** which I had believed, had become my reality because I no longer had the vibrant physical strength and sharp intellect, to confidently approach any task. Whatever I do is by

His Spirit for His Honor and Glory.

I had not planned to write ***From Hagar To Rachel.*** However, as I returned to ***Keys*** in January 2002, this is how the Lord led me. God is amazing. In writing my journey I have discovered some lost keys that have brought me greater understanding of my previous self-defeating actions. I realize that only God who truly knows us can determine when the work is completed and that we must continually submit ourselves to him, so that ***He who has begun a good work in us will continue to perform it until the day of Jesus Christ.***

Hopefully you will read ***From Hagar to Rachel,*** before you get ***Keys to Unlock and Realize Your True Value,*** and having done those exercises, that you will continue to discover ***God's Truth About God and You.***

The Questionnaire in ***The Workbook*** was first prepared in miniature form as a guideline for a seminar on Self Esteem, entitled, **The Truth Shall Make You Free.** It was an impromptu assignment with a group of sixteen women, and I had no idea how it would turn out.

There were five sessions. During the first two sessions the search for honest answers unearthed layers of pain, shame, fear, guilt and anger. The third session addressed the subject of subjective, objective, and pathological guilt, which brought great sadness and depression. The fourth session dealt with forgiveness, being forgiven and forgiving, and the letting go of past abuses and guilt. After two days of intense heart-searching and emotional upheaval, the atmosphere at the retreat was heavy with exposed pain, grief, and gloom. It was awful and I did not know what to do.

That night my sleep was troubled. What could I say that would relieve the thick darkness that weighed the people down. I felt like a surgeon who had exposed an in-operable malignant cancer and had no hope to offer the patient. Early next morning, I awoke and said to the Lord, "I cannot leave the people the way they are, what shall I say to them." This is what the Lord spoke quietly to my spirit.

"Tell them that I am sorry that they had to go through the pain that has afflicted their lives. Tell them that it wasn't my plan and I am sorry. Tell them that I have a good plan for each life and that despite all the setbacks of their experiences, I have not changed my plan. I never have a plan 'B'. My plan 'A' is still in effect. In my omniscience I factored in all the circumstances of their lives and they can still walk into my plan. It is a good plan. *"For I know the thoughts that I think toward you, says the LORD, thoughts of peace, and not of evil, to give you an expected end. Then shall you call upon me, and you shall go and*

pray unto me, and I will hearken unto you. And you shall seek me, and find me, when you shall search for me with all your heart." " Jeremiah. 29:11-13.

He showed me how his plans for Abraham, Jacob, Joseph, Moses, and David did not change. Despite Abraham's initial lack of faith and subsequent fathering of Ishmael, Isaac was conceived as promised, in the womb of Sarah, Abraham's post-menopausal childless wife. Despite Jacob's characteristic deception and the harvest of deception, which he reaped, Jacob became Israel, the father of the Jewish nation. Despite Joseph being sold, enslaved, and imprisoned, he still became the Prime Minister of Egypt and Savior of the Jewish race. Despite Moses' crime of murder and subsequent forty years of obscurity, Moses became the deliverer of Israel, and the greatest prophet of God. Despite the abuse that David suffered so unjustly at the hands of Saul, David still became the greatest king Israel ever had.

When I told the women what the Lord had said, a miracle happened. They received the word whole-heartedly. It was as if the sun suddenly appeared in all its strength and dismissed all the gloom. That the Lord was sorry for what they had gone through amazed and gladdened them. That He hadn't changed His good plan was the encouragement that they needed. Chains were broken, shame was dispelled, and they began to share their hopes and future plans with joyful expectation that the good things that they dared to dream and envision, could and would come to past. The truth had set them free to love, to work, to serve, to fulfill God's purpose.

Since then I have gained much insight and the little questionnaire has developed into ***Keys to Unlock and Realize Your True Value.*** It is my sincere desire that you who read my story ***From Hagar to Rachel*** will be encouraged and seek to discover God's Plan A for your lives. Be Blessed.

Andrea Eden Rachel Palmer

-2- How Value Is Established And Determined

Everybody's talking about self-esteem. It seems to be the greatest psychological discovery of the twentieth century. Well it is a big deal and God agrees. He first said, *For as a man thinks in his heart, so is he:* Proverbs 23:7.

Self-esteem, simply put, is how a person evaluates himself. It is his overall judgment of himself. It is how much he likes being who he is and how much he respects himself. One can fake respectability, but it is very difficult for a respectable person, who thinks well of himself, whose measure of respectability is a sound moral value system, to fake disreputable behavior.

One may be a successful statesman, a billionaire, and a well-loved philanthropist, yet in the privacy of one's mind and heart, despise one's self. One may be a poor washerwoman, yet harbor a feeling of well-being and satisfaction that a monarch might envy. Just as some very wealthy people suffer from a poverty complex so that they hoard their money, worry about it, and never truly enjoy it; so it is that some well-admired people hide themselves, worry about themselves, and never truly enjoy life. They suffer from poverty of soul, commonly known as inferiority complex or low self-esteem. At some point in time these people were devalued.

The one who creates or makes a thing establishes its intrinsic value. The proven moral integrity, artistic excellence, and intelligence of the creator give credence to his claims of the worth of his creation. For example, a painting or sculpture by Michael Angelo has greater value, beyond the value derived from its artistic excellence. It becomes a desired and more valuable treasure simply because, Michael Angelo has been acclaimed as a master of art, and his signature is on it.

Value is also assessed by the appraised worth of the materials that are used to make or create a thing. A marble sculpture inlayed with gold and precious stones is obviously more valuable than a clay sculpture. An oil canvas by Michael Angelo is of greater value than a similar watercolor painting by him, even though his watercolor painting is exceedingly more valuable than an oil painting by me.

Apart from the intrinsic value that the creator's integrity, skill and choice of material give to a thing, there is an acquired value which is established by its usage and determined by its purchase price. A painting or sculpture that is made to grace the Sistine Chapel and blesses millions is of much greater value than one that is made to adorn a bathroom, even when M. Angelo's signature is on both creations. And finally, the price that the highest credentialed bidder is willing to pay to possess a thing decides its ultimate acquired value.

A thing or person is devalued by the lack of integrity or questionable character of the one who creates, makes, or owns it or him. A golden sculpture made by an unscrupulous rascal would be suspected of having only an overlay of gold, despite the claims by the owner that it is solid gold. Simply because a thing belongs to a person of questionable character, it would be of questionable value.

A thing or person is further devalued by defacement or defilement. A slave who appeared in good physical health was considered more valuable than one who was sickly, emaciated, deformed, or handicapped. A virgin is always more desirable and therefore more valuable than a woman who has been raped, or one who has been promiscuous.

So we understand that there is an intrinsic value and there is an acquired value. Intrinsic value is fixed firstly, by the integrity and expertise of the maker or creator; and secondly, by the value of the materials of which a thing is made. The acquired value comes from the integrity and expertise of the possessor or secondary owner of the thing; with the use or abuse of the thing; but more specifically by the redemption price that a person of worth is willing to pay for the thing, after it has been abused and marred.

When the creator is willing to redeem a masterpiece that has completely lost its intrinsic value, and is helplessly enslaved to one whose only plan is its ultimate destruction; when the creator gives that which is priceless for that which is worthless, and having repossessed the worthless, set forth to restore it beyond its original beauty and potential, he establishes its ultimate appreciated value. The ultimate depreciated value is determined when a thing or person remains un-redeemed.

What then can we say of man's value?The Almighty God who is incapable of lies or imperfection is man's creator. The essence of man is his soul, which was created by the breath of the Almighty and endowed with attributes like those, which God possesses. Divinity created humanity; humanity must then have been very good.

While the spirit of man was fed and ordered by the Spirit of God, man retained his created goodness, and was able also to acquire goodness by his decisions and actions. When man fell into the unscrupulous and wicked hands of the devil, he was defiled, defaced, and devalued. His subsequent decisions and actions declared him to be so. When God paid the redemption price with the blood of His own Son, He made it possible for man to acquire unimaginably priceless value.

A river flows into a lake. The lake's volume of water is therefore controlled by the river's flow. There are fishes in the lake. The water in the lake controls their lives. If the river is diverted, the lake does not immediately become empty. In fact it may never become empty. It might be fed by rain or underground springs. However it would not be able to sustain the fish that it supported when it was fed by the river. Nevertheless, it may sustain mud-fishes, crabs, and other such creatures. The good thing is, that unless the lake dries up completely, and is filled in with dirt and debris completely, it retains the potential to become a lake, if at any time the river's course is restored.

Man's deliberate rejection of the Creator-God and the knowledge of God-created man, in spite of the scientific evidence of an intelligent mind and design in creation, has resulted not only in the scientific elevation of animal life to the level of human life, but also the subsequent devaluation of human life. This is obviously demonstrated by the inordinate amounts of money, time, and energy spent to ensure the safety and longevity of birds, fishes, reptiles and mammals; and the comparatively slight attention given to the plight of unborn babies, abused children, delinquent teenagers, confused young people, overwhelmed single parents, battered spouses, lonely and infirm elders, and broken families. I have nothing against protection of animals. It is our responsibility as guardians of the earth to protect our environment and all that live in it; but since man, because of sin, has become the destroyer, he is the problem that needs to be solved.

Let me here declare that there are powerful differences between man and the lower creation. The Power of Choice, which belongs to no other created being, is one significant difference. The power of choice attests to the presence of intellect, as opposed to blind instinct. The power of choice is complimented by the power to change. This is why man has changed and progressed scientifically, while all lower creatures, even though they can be tamed and bent to satisfy man's needs and pleasures, continue to exist as in the beginning, doing by created instinct only what they were created to do.

The function of thinking, whether consciously or sub-consciously, whether previous to, or concurrent with circumstances, usually precedes our attitudes and actions. However, when the consistency of our thoughts continually results in the same attitudes and actions, behavior patterns, which eventually appear as normal to the individual, emerge. Our behaviors may be constructive or destructive. They depend on our most prevalent thoughts, which form our self-concepts and ultimately our self-esteem. The negative or positive results are most evident in our relationships, because it is only in the interactions that are necessitated in relationships, that we are forced to expose and betray the truth about ourselves. It is therefore within the relationship circle that we grade our selves. When failing grades shame us continually we feel worthless and we respond by hiding our worthlessness in the only possible way. We deny ourselves the pain and pleasure of intimate relationships.

However we can never be satisfied, because we need relationships. It is therefore very important that we understand ourselves, and the building blocks that contributed to our personalities, as well as to our successes and failures in life and relationships, so that we may deliberately activate the powers of choice and change.

The natural need for significance and security asks the questions: *Who am I? What is my purpose? Am I important to anyone?* These questions are usually answered long before they are ever actually asked. The ways in which one is treated, spoken to, spoken about, disciplined, respected, appreciated, rejected, abandoned, abused, touched, and taught, answer these questions and define one's self-image, self-concept, and consequently one's self-esteem. This process of definition begins at birth, and the results are often pretty well established before puberty. The normal changes and emotional upheavals that accompany adolescence, young adulthood, career, marriage, and parenting, as well as any incident of crisis, become more or less stressful, based on the psychological infrastructure that was built in childhood.

It is through the eyes of the significant people in our lives that we usually view our selves. The value that those who we perceive as our superiors, whether by virtue of dependence, power, or position, place on us when our psychological profile is being formed, is usually the value we accept.

Parents and / or caregivers are the people of primary significance. These individuals affect our security at all levels and have the opportunity and potential to do the greatest good, or the damnedest evil. Our parents and immediate family break the ground and lay the foundation for our emotional and mental health. They give us our first thoughts of self. Since it is impossible to give that which one does not possess, it follows that parents with poor self-image and low self-esteem, cannot plant in their children the seeds of good self-image and positive self-concepts, whereby they may view themselves as worthwhile, useful and deserving people.

The building of our psychological selves is later reinforced or undermined by people of secondary significance such as teachers, friends, sweethearts, and spouses. Depending on the power that the significant person wields, and the corresponding lack of power that the subordinate possesses, the secondary significant persons may altar the self-concepts of the subordinate either negatively or positively. It should also be noted that spouses generally are upgraded to the role of primary significance after a while. In fact anyone may be thus upgraded, if the subordinate/dependant person considers that one's intelligence, credentials and worth, to be of greater worth than his own primary caregivers.

Many of us have felt like mud-holes with the limited ability to produce little that has any value. We have therefore felt worth-little or worthless. The river of God's life has been diverted from its course in our lives by original sin, by the sins and circumstances of others, and by our own sins and circumstances. But as long as we are not dead, God is ready to restore us and let His life flow though us, so that we may yet realize our true value and full potential. I believe it, because I am a living testimony to the truth that I write.

I have discovered that many "normal people" like me, have suffered emotional traumas that have devalued them, and prevented them from truly loving themselves, loving others, and enjoying the purposeful lives that they were intended to live. We, the normal people, are not dysfunctional enough to alarm our community and families, and therefore no attention is given us; no help is offered. Most of us have developed strategies to cope with the generalities of life, while hiding our fears and inadequacies from the world. Some of us, especially Born-again Christians, have successfully deceived ourselves into believing that we are satisfied with our lots, because we have a glorious heavenly future.

However, every now and then, circumstances arise that cause us to question our concepts, and dissatisfaction steps in. When we are forced to really re-evaluate our lives we discover many unanswered questions and unfulfilled desires. For a moment we yearn for answers and fulfillment, but we become afraid of facing the unknown, and since our lives are not that bad after all, we retreat to the comfort zone of doing the best we can and applauding our own efforts.

God, who desires that we ***have life, and have it more abundantly*** (John 10:10), allows us to experience more and more circumstances that nurture dissatisfaction. Eventually we become frustrated enough to journey through the chapters of the past, to excavate and examine our erroneous concepts. If we invite God on our journey and allow Him to schedule the stops, He will gently guide us to the places of personality crisis, and with the thoughtfulness of a tenderhearted lover, expose the damage and consequences. With God, we can face the facts and accept His truth, which frees us to make new choices based on His excellent evaluation and planned purpose, which He reveals.

I am on such a journey and it's been so liberating and empowering, that I'm inviting you to start your own journey, if you've become discontented with yourself, your relationships, and your life. It is a worthwhile adventure.

Before you begin the first leg of your journey by working through the questions in the ***Keys to Unlock and Realize Your***

True Value -Workbook, come with me and examine my journey thus far, so that through my testimony you may take courage and derive hope. My story is not a complete biography, nor is it a chronologically written narrative. It emphasizes the principal relationships, circumstances, experiences, and feelings that determined my self-concepts before I learned the truth, and the path of restoration through which I have come so far. It goes back and forth, back and forth, relating stories, connecting past and present, and drawing conclusions that I have reached.

As I went through the process of investigation and discovery, I had to learn to express myself so that I could understand me. It was very hard to explain myself to myself, because, in order to escape the Pains of Life, I had learned how to freeze emotions before they could touch me and demand expression. When I began to thaw, unlock my soul, and dared to peep in, I started writing in order to clarify my thoughts and feelings.

If you are like some people who like to know how a story ends before they start reading let me tell you.

A wonderful thing has happened. I like myself. I am able to understand that I am likeable and loveable. It's not that I had not known that a few people love me. I just didn't understand why. Now I am loved by me also. My self worth is appreciating. I am comfortable with myself. However, I have the distinct impression that it is time to continue on the journey from caterpillar to butterfly. I am somewhat apprehensive about going through any more changes. What if people who like me the way I am now, do not like the person I become? Father whispered to me. "Whatever I do will be an improvement."

-3- What My Mother Told Me

When I was thirty-eight, Mama had a long conversation with me, the longest that I remember. Perhaps I should not say it was a conversation, for that would imply that I also had something to say. No, it wasn't a conversation. Mama talked and I listened. And afterwards I wondered why she felt it was necessary to burden me with the information, which she had imparted so nonchalantly.

For some reason, Mama decided to tell me about the circumstances surrounding the conceptions and births of all her children. There were eight of us and it appeared that we were all unplanned and unwanted. As far as I know she did not tell any of the others what she told me. Although I do not intend to disclose any information about my maternal brothers and sisters, I shall have to mention them. Therefore I shall protect them and other people to whom I need to refer with new names, because they might be ashamed of some of the things that I shall reveal.

It was extremely embarrassing to sit there and listen to my mother talk about her sexual life. After all we had never had a personal conversation before. Not even when I had my first period at twelve and was ignorantly scared out of my mind; not even when I was about to be married at nineteen, and would have been happier if she had shown some interest in my wedding; not even when I experienced my first pregnancy and needed her so badly. Talking to her had been difficult at best, and impossible at worst.

I remember when my boyfriend asked me to marry him at age seventeen. I had just completed high school and had my first job as a clerk at the Treasury. I didn't want to be married so soon, but my boyfriend said he was going abroad and would not be back, if I didn't marry him. In desperation I went to Mama for advice. It took a whole day of mustering the courage to say, "Mama, Paul asked me to marry him and I don't know what to say." Do you know what she advised? "Woman, do whatever you want to do." I told him no. He didn't go away. A year later we got engaged and Mama stopped talking to me. Why? I still don't know.

Unwanted, Un-welcomed, Illegitimate

But there she sat talking quite casually, as if it was the most normal thing for her to explain to me, how all her children happened to be conceived. But only my conception is relevant here. This is my story not my siblings'.

When Mama met Daddy, he was only twenty-one and nothing in his behavior suggested that he was married and already the father of two children. Daddy seemed to have fallen in love with the pretty dark-skinned woman, who was nine years his senior. He was an accommodating and jovial man who made her laugh, took her to the movies, carried her basket from the market, did her grocery shopping, and fetched water for her from the standpipe down the street.

Mama had encouraged and enjoyed his company for two years, always putting him off when he suggested that they take their relationship to a deeper level. He wanted sex, but she was holding out for marriage. She already had four children and no husband and she didn't want another fatherless bastard. Mama never loved Daddy. So she said. However, he was tall, handsome and light-complexioned, with moderately wealthy half-Portuguese parents, and she would have married him if he was available.

Eventually he broke down her defenses and she agreed to let Daddy into her bed, provided that he used a condom. Not trusting him, she bought the condom herself and placed it on him. The following month she discovered that she was pregnant. When she confronted him, he confessed that he had removed the condom.

Daddy thought that Mama being pregnant was great. She was not of the same opinion and proceeded to do everything, short of an actual abortion, to miscarry me. She drank all kinds of potions that people said were guaranteed to destroy the fetus, that was me, but to no avail. She jumped and fell and participated in unnecessary laborious physical exercise and work, but I held tenaciously to life.

After a gestation period of only seven months, not waiting to be positioned head down, I was born prematurely. Being a breach presentation, the midwife forcibly pulled me out by my feet, and actually saved my life. However, in the process, I was severely injured, nerves were severed, muscles damaged, and ligaments torn. Those unseen and unsuspected injuries destined me to be a semi-cripple.

So unwanted and un-welcomed was I, that no name had been considered for me. No one had lovingly conversed about whether I should be given her name, or the name of a favorite relative, movie star, historical heroine, or a saint. Eventually, the midwife who attended my mother suggested that she might call me Andrea, and so I came to be called Andrea. Later Daddy said that I resembled his aunt Eden. Eventually, those names became mine. I liked my names especially after I discovered that Andrea meant beautiful woman or womanly, and of course Eden was the garden of Paradise. There is actually no name on my birth certificate. In the place of my name, the shame of my illegitimacy is documented. I am the "Illegitimate Girl Child." Neither is my father's name present.

The Story Of My Crippled Leg

I was nine months old, when my seven year old big sister pushed a large diaper pin into my right foot. Mama discovered her wickedness, but was more shocked by the fact that I never cried out in pain. She stuck my left foot with a pin and I flinched and screamed. My mother then realized that something was wrong, even though both my feet looked exactly alike and perfect.

She took me to the doctor, who having examined me and finding my right foot devoid of feeling, concluded that nerve damage had occurred at birth and prescribed electrical shock treatment to revive the nerves. Every day, Mama took me to the hospital. Whether the treatment had any measure of success, I do not know. However, through some carelessness, too much electric heat was applied. This caused burn damage that resulted in a deformed foot, the toes of which were shriveled and curled under. Miraculously, I was able to walk and run, but I walked with a limp.

I listened to my mother's story in amazement and anger. I felt that I did not need to know that which could only cause me pain. Why did she tell me? Was it because I had moved beyond her control and she wanted to shock and hurt me? Was it that she needed to confess her sins, and since I was the one most sinned against she unburdened herself on me? I don't know. Was I supposed to absolve her? I couldn't. I wished I hadn't been told. I didn't need to know that I had been an unplanned, unwanted, un-named, illegitimate cripple.

Limited By A Crippled Foot

I was never able either to wriggle my toes or feel the ground under my right foot. I used to take great pleasure in the amazed look on the faces of my friends, when I took needle and thread and sewed up the sole of my insensate foot. I remember once while climbing a tree, I became aware that there was blood on the tree trunk. It was only when I sat down and crossed my legs that I realized that I had sustained a very deep cut. I could feel no pain. So I learned to be always consciously aware of possible injury to my right foot.

I loved to run and kick. My right foot has always been a size smaller than the left and somewhat thinner. I was unable to keep a shoe on that damaged foot, unless it was laced up or buckled. Mama used to have my Sunday shoes custom made and it was very embarrassing to wear two obviously different size shoes. While I was a small child my school shoes were laced-up ankle high boots, which boys usually wore. After a while, however, we being poor, and boots being more expensive than the girl's "washekongs", I was saved the embarrassment of wearing them. Washekongs were flat canvas sneakers. Mama used to stuff the toe of the right side with paper or old socks, so that they would fit me. Very often while I was running, the right side washekong went flying off or I tripped over my own feet and fell. Sometimes Mama called me "Andrea the runner", but children called me "brokofoot", or "hop-and drop".

I now remember, I hadn't for many years, how Mama would take me to healing crusades and tell me to place my hands on my foot when the preacher was praying. She had asked for a miracle for me. Her prayer has not yet been answered.

When I first came to New York, I was twenty-two, pretty, shapely, and still petite. The agent at the employment office thought I was gorgeous. He said I reminded him of Lena Horne, and he suggested that I could have a successful career as a model. I explained about my limp. He told me that my limp didn't matter. He could make me a star. I think he was sincere, but I lacked confidence. It was a nice compliment; however, I did not for a moment entertain the thought.

I loved calisthenics and yoga, and before aerobics became the popular form of keep fit exercise I used to frequent the gyms. Aerobics called for fast movement and balance. I could not participate in any activity that necessitated balancing. So I never rode a bike; I never roller-skated; and I knew better than to desire to ice-skate or ski. I loved to dance, but some turns I just couldn't do. Were it not for my handicap, I would have excelled at sports, dance, and drama. All activity was stressful to my right side, but I did what I could. Once I even ran and won a half-mile race.

I never learned to drive a car. With no ability to feel with my right foot, I have no way of knowing when my foot is touching an object. Sometimes my slipper would have come off my foot and I would be walking around the yard without realizing that I was no longer wearing one side of my slippers. The first time I tried to drive, I found that I had no way of judging the pressure of my foot on the accelerator. That's dangerous. I decided that the road could do without me. People would be safer.

Shoes that draw attention to beautiful feet are not for me. I need shoes that fit my right foot snugly and lend support to my ankle, especially now that I have become pleasingly plump. I am unable to wear sandals because of my deformed toes, or high heels because of my lack of balance There are times when I desire to purchase a beautiful formal gown, but my second thought is always, "What shoes would I wear with it." To get a comfortable fit, I must always purchase two pairs of the same style shoes, size seven for my right foot and size eight for my left. This has become very expensive, and yet the styles leave me without comfortable and pretty shoes. Purchasing shoes continues to be a frustrating and depressing chore. I continually remind myself that I am a miracle created by God for purpose and I am grateful that I can walk and run.

In 1973, after I'd been living in New York for three years, the winter cold had a very bad effect on my foot. The toes, which I could not move for myself, were curling under my foot, much like how a dry leaf curls, and I had to have surgery to stop it. It was then that I understood how extensive my birth injury was. There was nerve and muscle damage from my hip to my toe. At times a deep, cold, demobilizing pain starts in my buttocks and travels down my leg, testifying to damage to the sciatic nerve. My having always walked with a limp has resulted in a curved spine, and bones that have become misshapen and subject to arthritis. In the winter my skin, which is usually dry due to bad circulation, cracks and bleeds. No amount of moisturizing lotion helps.

The surgeon broke my toes, removed the cartilage, and pinned the bones together so that they would fuse. I had hoped that I would have had straight toes, but they were too deformed to be straightened.

At the time of my foot surgery, my father's oldest daughter and I became quite close. Being alone in New York, except for my husband, and not having the knack for making new friends, I was glad to get in touch with my father's wife and children, who had migrated to America a few years before I did. It was then that my sister revealed how Daddy had wanted her mother to adopt me. She said that when I was a baby, my mother used to pick me up and throw me across the room when she was angry with Daddy. Daddy was swift and caught me every time. After the talk, which Mama had with me, I asked Daddy about what my sister had alleged. He said that it was true. He was quite upset that she had told me. Of course I don't recall any of that.

-4- What My Father God Told Me

One afternoon, when I was forty seven years old, having been saved sixteen years previously, I knelt at the altar, at Pentecostal Circle Tabernacle in Brooklyn, New York, with the few who had special requests for strength, help, healing, or deliverance. I was blessed beyond my asking.

On that fateful Sunday in August 1995, Pastor Annette Rose had a word for me, a word from my heavenly Father. It was not very often that I was singled out for such blessing. In fact there were many years that I attended church services and conventions, when it seemed that God had something to say to everyone except me. How many were the prayer lines in which I had stood, hardly daring to hope that I would receive some word of encouragement, or some prophecy of a great future. How many were the times that I had walked away disappointed, discouraged, and depressed, until I began to say silently to the Lord, “Just say something, anything. Tell me I’m no good, but just let me know that you are aware of me.” At long last, there was a word for Andrea Eden Palmer.

“This is what the Lord says to tell you,” said Pastor Rose, “Your name is no longer Hagar. Your name is Rachel.”

So that’s who I had been. Hagar. Biblical names are usually

descriptive of birth circumstances, personality, character, and life conditions. So who was Hagar? She was an Egyptian woman, a slave to Abraham's wife, and Abraham's concubine by his wife, Sarah's design. Hagar was unloved, used, abused, and discarded. Hagar means flight. When life became difficult for her, she ran away. This unplanned, unwanted, un-named, illegitimate cripple called Andrea, had often felt like an unloved, used, abused, discarded Hagar. I had always run away from life's pain. And life had been full of pain.

I accepted the name change as from God my Father and my journey took a new turn. Before I go forward I must go backward in order to understand the making of Andrea, who God had called Hagar.

-5- My Sister, My Friend Forever

It's strange, but I suppose one cannot know one's self except in relation to someone, some place, or some circumstance. I have a little sister. I have other younger sisters, but she was my first little sister and I have always thought of her that way. I actually have been blessed with seven brothers and ten sisters. Daddy sired five sons and seven daughters, having loved and lived with three different women at different times and at the same time. Mama gave birth to three sons and seven daughters. Of Mama's children, only Deborah and I belonged to Mr. Maurice.

The fact of our half brothers and sisters, and our "step-mothers" was never hidden. We all knew each other, and accepted each other. Our parents never allowed their differences to prevent their children from forming relationships, and Daddy was especially proud of his twelve offspring.

My earliest memories place me at about four years old. I do not remember any event that did not include my younger sister, and I am three years older than she. I remember playing with her. I believe that life was pleasant then, but the absence of earlier memories may have resulted from the subconscious suppression of unbearably unpleasant or painful things, which may have happened during my infancy and very early childhood.

So my first memory is of my little sister. She was my baby, my sister, my friend. Mama said it was I who asked to have her named Deborah, after my cherished doll. After she came I didn't want my doll anymore. She was mine, my living doll. It was me who introduced her to the people inside the radio and the children in the mirror. At first she couldn't understand that we were looking at our reflections. She believed everything I told her. I taught her all my games and told her stories. When the hurricane came, and we were forced to stay inside the little house I frightened her with tales of bad witches, which I imagined were clawing at the windows, shaking the wooden shutters, and trying to come in. Together we hid under the sheets, hugging each other protectively.

Deborah was very small and thin. We called her Bones, (children can be so cruel), but Mama said that she was healthier than I. Whenever there was an outbreak of the flu, I was the one who became ill. Mama declared that I only looked healthy, but that I was as weak as filth. She said that my foundation was weak because I was premature and she could not afford good Klim milk when I was a baby. I was fed the cheap sweetened condensed milk. My sister Deborah was fortunate. Her godmother who had no children of her own, loved her very much, and was moderately well off. Mrs. Cynthia helped considerably so that Deborah fared much better than I; but I was never envious of her.

As Deborah grew, her godmother used to purchase lovely pieces of material, which the seamstress made into beautiful, wide, frilly dresses for her. At Christmas and on her birthday, she received more clothes and toys. Mama tried her best to give me similar things. Even at age six, I understood that I couldn't have many things, and truly appreciated what I was given. Every Christmas, I received a pair of shorts, which my godfather's wife sent me. We were always given new dresses, shoes, and ribbons to wear to church on Holy Innocents' Day, when children took their toys to be blessed. Each year we were given a different toy. One year a dolly tea set, the next year a dolly kitchen set, then a dolly bedroom set, and finally a dolly living room set. We took good care of all our toys and eventually had enough furniture for a whole house, which we set up in a cardboard box or under the high-back chairs in the living room.

One Christmas, when I was probably seven, Deborah's godmother gave her a beautiful doll with curly hair and clothes. All Mama could afford to give me was a plain naked hairless doll. That evening Daddy turned up with presents. It is the only time I remember receiving anything from him. He gave me a beautiful doll, bigger and better than Deborah's, and he gave her an Indian doll with feathers stuck in the head. She was so angry. She wanted mine. She pulled all the feathers out of her doll. I was so happy. It was the first really beautiful thing I had received and it said that Daddy loved me. I remember thinking that my doll would be taken away and given to her. That would have meant that she mattered more than I did.

Mama and Daddy explained that everyone was financially broken after Christmas. That meant that I was to expect no presents from anyone for my birthday, which is in January. If I did get something, it was a new school-bag, but I could not show it off, since everyone got a new school bag to start off the year. In those days, the school year began in January.

When Deborah was six, she started to have Asthma. As she grew, it worsened. It was very painful for me to watch her suffering. Even today when I hear of children with asthma, I get very upset. I thank God that none of my children suffered from asthma, although it runs in the family. Deborah suffered from asthma most of her life. As a child and well into her late teens, she was given all types of conventional as well as some really dreadful folk medicines. Shark oil, whale oil, cod-liver oil, olive oil, snail slime, lizard, just to name a few. But she took it all, wanting so badly to be better. Many were the nights when she could not lie down. Instead she had to sit upright just to draw a wheezing breath. I couldn't sleep well during those times.

The hospital staff knew her well. When it became almost impossible for her to breathe we took her to the hospital where she was given a pump and pills called Tedrol. Once, when I had a slight but frightening case of shortness of breath, Deborah gave me a half of one Tedrol. Immediately my heart began to race like a pay-train. It was scarier than the shortness of breath from which I was quickly relieved. When I thought that my sister sometimes took two pills in the extremities of asthma, I became fearful that her heart would burst and that she would die from the medication if the asthma didn't kill her.

Deborah missed school a lot, and very often was relieved from chores, because of her asthma. But she never let it get her down. Whenever she was well, she made the most of the time, participating in every activity, until the next attack grounded her. I really admired her tenacity.

Being closest in age, (we were three years apart), I had to take her everywhere I went. I didn't mind. It was quite normal for big sisters to be accompanied by their younger siblings. She was my principal chaperone and knew everything I did, and even though I never told her to, she kept my secrets. There was another sister who was nine years younger than me. She eventually became a part of my Sunday evening walks. She didn't have enough sense to keep her mouth shut. Like when I tried to convince Mama that I had been sucking on a cigarette-shaped candy. Janice insisted that smoke came out of it.

I loved poetry and I loved to sing. Whenever I was assigned homework to memorize a poem, I walked around the yard reciting it over and over, with appropriate actions and expressions. When I wasn't dramatizing my poems, I was singing. I sang nursery rhymes, school songs, love songs, hymns, gospel choruses, and calypsos. Some I learned in school, some in church, some from listening to the radio, and from listening to my mother, father, big sister, and big brother. They all loved to sing.

On Mother's day I sang every appropriate song all day long. "M Is For the Million Things She Gave Me", "Pal of My Cradle days"; and "Mother Mc Cree". At Christmas, I sang carols from dawn to bed-time. At carnival, I sang the calypsos. Mama said I was always making noise, but she didn't say it in an offensive or discouraging tone of voice. And as young as she was, my little sister learned all my poems and songs, and recited and sang them exactly like I did. Even now, decades later, if I start a poem she can join in. She amazed me.

As she became a teenager and acquired her own friends, we had some disagreements. Deborah's friends seemed to believe that we were very well off, because she was very generous and loved to supply her friends with anything that they wanted from our house. The problem was that she and I shared things and clothes, for by the time she was fifteen we were about the same height, I being a size bigger than her. By that time I was employed and was able to provide myself with a few nice things. Some of the things, for instance, like the two-piece bathing suit that her friend wanted, were mine. But Deborah, who always gave the impression of wealth, had no problem giving away what was not hers. I used to be so angry, but instead of supporting my right, Mama accused me of being uncharitable.

The Futility Of Anger And Tears

I soon learned that it was futile and even dangerous to display anger in Mama's household. Once, when someone stole my garters, I threw an angry fit. I was about eleven then, and had the audacity to declare, "It looks like a person cannot put down anything in this house and expect to find it again." I really don't know what was wrong with my statement, or my tone of voice, but I was slapped for being insolent. I think that is when I began to decide that I would not waste my time exhibiting anger, since no good results came from it. Eventually, I lost the ability to express anger or to be angry.

Another expression I began to lose was the ability to cry. Crying was a no-no. Looking back I don't understand why

Mama did not let us cry. She used to cry. But she felt that we had no reason to cry, and if we cried, we were looking for something to cry for. We all knew what that meant and since I was utterly terrified of being beaten, I learned how not to cry. But when I became very angry and couldn't or didn't express it, the anger would seem to strangle me, hurting my head and neck It wasn't until the hot tears came that I would be relieved from the choking pain.

Mama Divided Us With Her Tongue

Deborah and I were quite close until Mama starting cussing her. You see we all had turns of being ripped to pieces by Mama's mouth. Perhaps it was her way to keep us on the straight and narrow path.

A terrible and negatively successful strategy, which Mama employed, was that of exalting one child and debasing the other. But she did not do it in the presence of the one she exalted. For example, she told the rest of us how our big brother was always so obedient, and bright, and how he did everything perfectly, and how blessed he was, and what a blessing he was, but she never told him. To the rest of us she said, "If I put all of you in a bag, I don't know which will come out first." I don't know what that meant. I doubt if any of us knew; but we knew that we could never be as good and dutiful as our big brother. Yet, many years later when Gregory seemed so indifferent to Mama and I asked him why, he explained that he felt that Mama had never liked him. He said he'd got the most and worst beatings, and once Mama told him, "So you black, so your heart black."

Mama divided all of us with her tongue. It was only after she died that we found out the things she used to say that turned us against each other. To Deborah and I who had light complexions she said, "I could disown you two anytime because I am black and you are too red to be my children." To my darker sisters she said, "Andrea and Deborah have their light skin to recommend them, you all have nothing."

To Deborah, she talked about how brilliant I was, and what a great future I had, implying that my sisters were dumb and hopeless. But she never told me. This underhanded favoritism that Mama displayed drove a wedge between my little sister and I. She told me later when we became best friends again, that she felt that I was a "goody two shoes" and that she could never be like me. Mama seemed to imply that I was her favorite. That was a joke, if I ever heard one.

In those days I could no longer understand Deborah. She seemed totally unfeeling and uncaring. She did what she pleased, in spite of punishment, in spite of Mama's voice. But she was neither unfeeling nor uncaring. She was just struggling to protect herself with rebellion, as I protected myself with dutiful obedience. I don't think that she was as successful at freezing as I was. Later in life, when I realized all I had missed by my cowardly obedience and the perfected art of freezing pain before it hurt, I wished I had had her courage to rebel.

You've Got Your Troubles, I've Got Mine

One day when Deborah was eighteen we were walking through the city. I noticed that she stopped at every phone booth and made a call. She was very tense and I asked her what was wrong. She said to me, "You've got your troubles, I've got mine." I felt that I'd been pushed away and I said nothing more. I think that was when I walked away from her emotionally. But I always wondered what was wrong.

Many years later she told me that she was supposed to get married on that day, but she had chickened out, because Mama had disapproved of the fellow. You see, even though she decided to rebel, Mama's influence was still predominant. Mama put her through hell and I think she eventually learned that "we were damned if we did, and damned if we didn't". So she just did her own thing, letting Mama's abusive words fall off her as water off a duck's back.

Mama disapproved of everybody. We weren't good enough, or they weren't good enough. She used to say, "I make no match, and I break no match". But any time she sat down to converse with any of our suitors, she'd make some remark that caused the man to question our integrity or suitability. Each one of us has a story to tell, but I can only tell my own.

Actually, after we became adults, none of my mother's children had time for each other. It was survival of the fittest. As soon as we could, we each got away from home. By the time I was married, all my older siblings had gone. Eventually I moved away. Two years later opportunity presented itself and Deborah moved away. We lived on different continents.

I had frozen all my love for her, so I went about my business of survival and almost lost her. We all had learned how to be independent. We asked no one for help and expected help from no one. I wish we had known how to put our arms around each other and say those three important words: I NEED YOU or I LOVE YOU. We didn't know how. It hadn't been a part of our experience or education. We had learned to need no one; not Mama, not each other, not even God. Now we can express needing and loving. I learned first.

My Sister, My Friend, Again, Forever

After becoming a Christian I met and began to socialize with people who loved to hug and express feelings vocally and openly. Eventually, after a long time, I was able to hug my beloved sister and say I love you. She tried, but could not get the words out. So she sent me a stuffed teddy bear that wore a bib with the words, "I LOVE YOU," with a note that said, "There, I've said it."

We now have a wonderful relationship. When Deborah was about to get married the second time, (I knew nothing of her first marriage or her life for that matter), she phoned and asked me to come and be with her. I decided to go. It was the most important decision of our relationship. She was so happy to have me there. We were sisters again. She proudly showed me off to her friends and we talked. She described her life. I told her about mine. We laughed at the past, spoke ill of Mama in a good natured sort of way, criticized our brothers and sisters, and agreed that Daddy was quite ridiculous, and that the character of both of them had rubbed off on us.

Actually we now laugh a lot at the things Mama used to say, and find that some of the expressions with which she lambasted us, and some of the things she used to do, quite clever.

Deborah once said that she would like to die before me because she couldn't handle the anticipated grief of my death. I have put my sister through so much grief because she identifies so closely with me. My sorrow is hers, and it seems that I've had some profound sorrows. She has ground her teeth down fifteen thousand pounds worth over my pain. I learned to protect her from my traumas and only let her know what was necessary. Like when my son was terminally ill. I did not let her know how ill he was until the day I thought he would die. Only then did I call her and said three words, "Deborah, please come." I didn't have to explain. She didn't ask why. She came.

My other sisters would have come if I had asked, but it never occurred to me to ask them.

I do not know how I would handle her dying. Now that my emotions have been normalized, by the power of God and my willingness, the thought scares me. A decade ago she was very ill and the doctors could not determine what the problem was. Something seemed to be wrong with every vital organ in her body, and she thought that she would be hooked up to a life support system and allowed to vegetate. She asked me to promise that should it come to that, I would come and pull the plug. I loved her so much. I promised. Thank God, she recovered.

We are different. At times I think I am still avoiding punishment and she is still daring life to stop her. Recently she sent me a plaque that stated, "I'M SMILING BECAUSE YOU'RE MY SISTER; I'M LAUGHING BECAUSE YOU CAN'T DO ANYTHING ABOUT IT." That's my Deborah, my sister, my friend forever.

-6- In My Beginning

Another event, that puts things into proper dated sequence, is moving. We moved from the first home I knew when I was eight. There were things that never happened after that time.

My First Home - The Neighbors

When I began to know them, Mama and Daddy lived together, at #6 Suffolk Road, although he always had his room at his mother's house where he stayed sometimes, and I believe that he was always welcome at his wife's home.

Our house was one of five small wooden houses in a very large yard. Each house consisted of one very large room with two doors and three windows. The occupants divided it into smaller living areas with screens, which we called blinds.

I remember the neighbors. There was mother Hushum who was always old, with a pale complexion and wrinkled skin. She had no children. She reminded me of the witch in Hansel and Gretel. Her next-door neighbor was Mrs Ena who had a grown son, another boy and a girl. I think she had a husband. I remember the younger son's name was Harold. I believe that he was the first boy who liked me. When I made my first communion and had to wear a white dress with a veil and crown, Harold looked at me and exclaimed in amazement

"You look like a bride!!" I was seven.

Then there was Miss Iris who had two adult sons, three adult daughters, one teenager, a granddaughter and grandson. Miss Iris died from tuberculosis and everybody who lived in the yard had to go to the Medical Center to be X-rayed. All of her children and her granddaughter had contracted it. Three of them died, including the granddaughter. One had surgery to remove a lung, and one survived with treatment. It was a miracle that no one else had the disease, for it is very contagious. Mama was very upset and concerned because Miss Iris used to love to hug Deborah.

Up in the yard, next door to us, were Mr. and Mrs. Beaufong, with two teenagers, a boy and a girl, and two smaller children. Mr. Beaufong was a sailor. When Daddy and Mama were happy together, they devised ways of terrorizing the Beaufongs. Like when they put frogs on their back steps and hid behind the bathroom to watch as Mrs. Theresa Beaufong stepped on the frog and started screaming hysterically. Once, Daddy and Mr. Beaufong had a fight. Mrs. Theresa, who was not on speaking terms with Mama at the time, began to cry and beg Mama to prevent Daddy from killing her husband. Mama was laughing and egging Daddy on. "Beat him Maurice, beat him." They didn't stop until the police were called. I have no idea what the fight was all about.

Mr. Beaufong accused Daddy of entering his home and destroying the contents of his china cabinet. He walked into the court with a bag of broken glasses and dishes. However, on being questioned the judge discovered the cabinet was undamaged and realized that Mr. Beaufong had false evidence. He dismissed the case, charged Mr. Beaufong with contempt, and fined him twenty-four shillings in lieu of one month in jail. Mrs. Beaufong borrowed the money from Mama and the four of them left the court as friends, laughing at Mr. Beaufong's stupidity. It's funny the things I remember.

My First Home

Our little house was screened off into four areas. As one entered the house from the front door, there was a small drawing room area in which there were three Bentwood straight back chairs and a rocking chair. In the middle was a small table that sported a vase with crepe paper flowers on a pretty crocheted doily. On the right was the wall, which attached our house to that of Mrs. Theresa and Mr. Beaufong. On the wall were pictures of the Sacred Heart of Jesus, pictures of us that Daddy had framed, and the Radiofusion, which we rented. The floor was covered with gaily-colored linoleum, while the window and front door were dressed in matching lace curtains.

This room was principally for company. However, on Thursday nights at eight o'clock, if we had behaved well, we were allowed to stay up to listen to "I'll tell you a story", by Wendy Price. The only other time we were allowed in that room was when it was raining so hard that we had to be indoors. The small children were allowed to play quietly on the floor, while the older siblings were expected to sit properly in the chairs and read a book. Not a comic book.

At the side of the drawing room, behind a pretty screen was the big bed, where Mama and Daddy slept with my sister and I. During the day, Mama's bed was always spread with white sheets. Under the bed were boxes with linens, and the suitcase with the clean pajamas, nightgowns and good underwear, just in case anyone had to be hospitalized. A shelf was constructed on the wall high above the bed. On the shelf were books and hats, while under the shelf was a rod, which held the hangers on which our Sunday clothes were hung. This homemade clothes closet was covered by a printed cotton curtain. Facing the foot of the bed was a six-drawer dressing table with a large mirror. Deborah and I shared a drawer. A jalousie Jamaican window, which opened upward and was held open by a long stick, which settled in the window-jam, looked out on the side of the house over that bed. The window stick was often a weapon of punishment, and sometimes a bat with which the boys played cricket.

A screen behind the dresser gave privacy to another bed, where my bigger sister and one brother slept. Next to it stood an enamel basin and a jug of water, which was used only when someone was sick and had to have a sponge bath. In the space between the bed and the back wall, there was another screen that blocked off a little dining area, consisting of a small table and two benches. It was at this table that we had our meals and did our homework. Mama also used that table to knead dough for bread. From the dining area we looked out of the back window and could see Mama in the kitchen, or Daddy's head topping the opened roofed bathroom when he was bathing.

The back door was directly opposite the front door so that if both doors were open you could see straight through the house. A cabinet, which we called a "safe" was strategically placed to obstruct the view of anyone who looked through either door. It faced the front room. On its top shelf were the good drinking glasses, whiskey glasses, and decanters, which at Christmas were filled with wine and rum. On the second shelf were the good plates, cups, saucers, and teapot. At Christmas the ham, sweet bread, cookies, and apples, grapes, dates and fancy nuts were put in there. There was a key that prevented us from stealing the goodies, but sometimes Mama forgot the key in the door. There was a drawer for the good cutlery, which only visitors were privileged to use. In the bottom part of the safe were bottles of mauby, which was the beverage that we drank most of the time; but at Christmas there would be sorrel and ginger beer, as well as sodas, which we called sweet drinks, Carib beers and Guinness stouts.

Each Christmas, the curtains from the front door and windows replaced those that were at the back door and windows.

Life In The Yard

Nobody spent much time inside the house. The kitchen, bathroom, and lavatory were separate from the house. There was therefore little need to be in the house unless one was ill, it was time for meals, bed, homework, or rain was falling heavily.

Women were usually in the kitchen cooking or ironing, or at the tub washing. However, between eleven-thirty in the morning and one in the afternoon, the women gathered at our house, or at Mother Hushum's to listen to "Second Spring" and "Doctor Paul". Sometimes when Mama had to go out and she wasn't sure she would return in time to hear the story, she would say, "Andrea, listen to Doctor Paul for me." I felt so grown up. I would join the ladies at mid-day and listen and report back to Mama that someone said this, and someone said that. I didn't know who the characters were. It didn't occur to me that the neighbors would bring her up to date on the stories.

Men went to work and sometimes Daddy worked at home.

He was a candy maker by trade. But Daddy was the greatest marble player, slingshot shooter, kite flyer, comic book reader, joker and trickster; and children loved him. Sometimes he would take his false teeth out and make funny faces. He didn't laugh. He guffawed.

The large yard was a great place to play all kinds of games. The girls skipped and played such games as "Oliver Twist", "One, two, three lavay", and "Ring a Ring a Rosy", while the boys played cricket, pitched marbles, spun tops, and when it rained, the water in the drains were perfect for racing little wooden boats.

There was an extremely tall coconut tree near our house. We had to be careful of dry coconuts falling when it was windy. When the tree was full of nuts, a man who we knew as Mankibo, came with his rope and cutlass to climb the tree, pick the coconuts, and cut off the dry branches. The children would then be employed in making cocoyea brooms, with which we swept the dirt yard, from the stems of the dry branches. The fibers, which grew between the outer covering and the inner shell of the coconut, were washed and used to stuff mattresses.

The coconut water made a delicious and nourishing drink. When the coconut was young or medium, the meat inside it was soft and sweet and could be spooned out of the shell and eaten. We called it coconut jelly. When the coconut was dry, the meat formed a firm nut and was cut into small pieces or grated to make coconut bread and candies. Mama made the best sugar cakes with grated coconut, sugar, and spices, and toolum, which was made with molasses instead of sugar. The coconut milk, which was squeezed out of the grated nut, was used to flavor delicious ice-cream.

In the middle of the yard was a large breadfruit tree, which provided food when there was no money for other staples. Poor people are so proud. No one wanted the neighbors to know that the breadfruit was a necessity. So it was, "I feel like eating breadfruit today." The young, full breadfruits were boiled in soup, especially fish broth, while the full-ripened ones were roasted. Sometimes the men from the yard would get together and make a meal with breadfruit boiled in coconut milk with pickled pig's feet, salted beef, pepper and green seasonings. It was usually cooked in a large pan over four stones of fire. Then every man, woman, and child got a little bit. It was excellent. I liked breadfruit and I wished we had it more often.

In the front of the yard, as one came through the gate, was a guava tree. This was the children's delight. It was low enough to the ground for us to climb. The fruit could be eaten green or ripe. But when we ate it green, we were likely to become constipated. When we ate it ripe, we were likely to consume worms, which seemed to like ripe guavas. Green or ripe, eventually we were given castor oil. Mama made delicious guava jelly.

Routine Life In Mama's Family

Life was very structured. Mama awoke at five, or by the second cock's crow, to get the fire in the coal-pot started for breakfast. The children's day began about six o'clock with the sun rising and Mama's voice intruding on our dreams. It was considered the height of laziness to let the sun meet you sleeping unless you were ill. We were mindful to be outside by the time Mama gave her second call. Pajamas and nightgowns were special sleeping garments that were kept clean in an old suitcase, just in case we had to go to the hospital. We generally slept in some comfortable old garment, so we had to take off our sleeping clothes, before we went outside, so that the neighbors wouldn't see our shame.

We were expected to bathe, brush our teeth, and dress before we could have breakfast. We couldn't afford toothpaste, but I didn't even know that there was such a thing as toothpaste. I thought that everybody used salt or soap as we did. Mama would give each of us a little salt to put on our toothbrushes, or else we rubbed our tooth brushes across the bar of blue or brown soap. We waited in line to brush our teeth, and wash our faces at the standpipe that was conveniently located next to the kitchen. The younger children, those that had no pubic hairs or breasts, were bathed or should I say scrubbed, by Mama at the standpipe, while the older children took turns in the bathroom. After which we lined up to have our hair combed. After breakfast was eaten, and book bags checked, those who went to school were sent off.

If there was a baby, she was then given her bath, cod liver oil, and orange juice and put to sleep. Small children were also given cod liver oil and half of an orange to suck, then set to play. Lunch was at noon, then nap for those at home; even Mama, if it wasn't her ironing day, took a nap, while the school age children went back to school. When I began to go to school with my big sister, Mama packed lunch for us to carry to school, because the walk home and back to school at midday was too great for me. That meant that we could play in school during the lunch hour.

When we arrived home from school at three-thirty, we were given a snack. It might be some fruit or left over food. We had no junk food. Then homework had to be done. Even children who didn't go to school had to be taught the alphabet and primary numbers by Mama. At six we had tea. Children went to bed at seven, except on Thursday nights when we were allowed to stay up and listen to the radio program: "I'll Tell You a Story by Wendy Price." We tried to be especially well behaved on Thursdays. Punishment meant being sent to bed before the story. As we grew older and had more homework, our bedtimes moved from seven, to eight, to nine to ten.

Saturday morning meant "purge". Before we were given our breakfast, we had to drink either Senna tea or Epsom salts, and at least once a year, at the end of the summer vacation, we were given Castor oil. Half of an orange removed the awful taste of the purges and a hot cup of milkless "bush tea", hastened the results. We were not allowed to eat anything else until Mama was satisfied that we had had a good bowel movement. Whenever she caught us scratching our rectums or picking our noses she declared that we were probably infested with worms. We were supposed to have ingested worms from eating guava. We were then given worm oil and had to use the chamber pot so that Mama could examine our stools.

On Saturdays everybody worked. The dirt yard had to be swept clean of leaves. The concrete area between the back of the house and the kitchen, as well as the bathroom floor, had to be scrubbed to prevent moss from growing. The chicken coop had to be cleaned out. The dog had to be bathed. Those chores were considered boy's work. The furniture had to be dusted. The linoleum had to be mopped. The floor had to be swept. Thc lampshade had to be cleaned and the lamp filled with oil. The doilies had to be washed, ironed, and replaced. Those chores were considered girl's work. Sometimes we also had to pluck the chicken, which Daddy killed for Sunday dinner.

Mama went to early morning market to get fresh produce and fish, and Daddy did the grocery shopping. When Mama returned she set to work making fish broth and baking bread. When the chores were done, Mama washed the girls' hair and scrubbed us clean. During the week we had showers, but on Saturday she sometimes filled the oversized aluminum tub with warm water to which she added certain cleansing herbs and leaves. These were to keep our skin free from pimples and eczemas, and our hair free from dandruff.

Sundays were great fun. We were up early and sent off to the seven o'clock children's mass. Mass was very boring and there was a time when my older sister, who was in charge of us younger ones, instead of taking us to church, took us to her friend's house. There were a few mango trees in her friend's yard, so we spent the time happily enjoying mangoes. I don't know who told Mama, but she eventually found out and grounded us indefinitely. She actually prevented us from attending Mass for two years, until it was time for me to receive the sacrament of confirmation. But we still went to Gospel Hall Sunday school in the evenings.

Sunday meals were always better than weekday fare. During the week, breakfast consisted of hot cocoa with bread and butter, or bread and guava jelly, if the guava tree was bearing fruit. On Sundays we might have eggs, or sausages, cheese, and sometimes, black pudding. This tasty treat was made from bread soaked in cows' blood, seasoned with hot spices, scallions, thyme, and such like, stuffed in the animal intestines and boiled. It was one of the things I had to give up as a Christian, since the eating of blood is prohibited.

Lunch during the week was usually rice, some type of peas or beans, and fish, liver, chicken back, salted codfish, or salted pig's feet; except when we had split peas soup or fish broth with ground provisions and dumplings. On Sundays we feasted on stewed chicken, pelau, calaloo, potato salad, macaroni pie and green salad.

After lunch it was siesta time. Everyone had to take a nap, even Mama. Napping was difficult for me, but it was a pre-requisite for going to the park on Sunday evenings. There were times when I spent the whole nap-hour wrestling with the temptation to sleep, while pretending to be asleep. As a child I had a dread of death. I still wonder how I acquired such a knowledge and fear of death at such an early age. I couldn't have been more than four years old when, I became aware that sleep could lead to death and death was a terrifying unknown. At nights, the mental energy expended in the fierce fight to remain awake coupled with the tiredness from the day's activity, would put me to sleep while I was still unaware that sleep was overtaking me.

Before that unprecedented two-year grounding, Mama used to allow Marcia and Gregory to take Gerald and I for walks on Sunday evenings. Sometimes we went to the Rock Gardens, the Botanical Gardens or the Emperor Valley Zoo. On occasions, we visited the Museum or the grounds of the Princess Building. But mostly, we walked around the Savannah for a while, finally settling on a savannah bench opposite the police band stand to listen to the music, and watch the wedding parties drive slowly by in convertible vehicles, with their horns blaring to attract the bystanders attention. During these walks boys and girls met and many romances got started.

When we were on vacation from school, the children who lived in the lane spent most of their time in the dry river, or in our yard. Mama didn't let us play with the other children. She said we had each other. Mama was very strict. She just had to look at us in a certain way and we knew if we were doing something wrong and if we were in big trouble. A quick look meant, "fix what is wrong" A sustained look meant, "you are going to get punished". We learnt to be afraid of her eye, her voice and her whip.

Nevertheless, we watched for the times when she was busy entertaining visitors in the drawing room. We, the children, were called into the drawing room to say "good afternoon" to her visitors and answer questions about our behavior and progress in school. Then we sat quietly waiting for Mama to "give us the eye', that meant we could ask to be excused and go outside. On those occasions, knowing that her visitor would stay awhile, we would steal down the yard to play, until her voice would ring out, calling us back. If she had to come and get us, she came with a belt or a stick, and we knew what that meant.

During the summer vacation, on weekdays, Mama took us for walks to the park, or to visit her friends in the evenings, after the sun went down. This prevented us from socializing too much with the neighborhood children. Were it for Daddy alone, we could have played our lives away. Whenever Mama went out and left Daddy to watch us, he took us to the dry river, or let us join in the fun and games down in the yard. However, as soon as someone exclaimed, "Miss Alice coming!" We sped away to sit quietly on the front steps with a book, as if we'd been reading for hours. Mama made us feel that we were different and better than the other children.

In time I became aware of the ways in which we were different.

Different, Worse And Better

Daddy and Mama were never married to each other. Of course I became aware of their common law relationship when I started to attend school, and realized that it was not normal for mothers and fathers to have different surnames; for children within the same family to have different surnames; and for children to have a different surname than their fathers. My sister and I, Daddy's children carried our mother's surname.

Although it was not uncommon for children of the same family to have different features and complexions, we were the only family in the yard, or in the street, for that matter, where the differences were so pronounced. We ranged from the almost Caucasoid to the positively Negroid; from the almost straight to kinky hair; and from very dark chocolate to light milky coffee skin color.

The other thing was the fighting. If there were fights in the other families, I never knew. In my family the fighting was so terrible that several times the police had to be called, and Daddy and Mama were taken away, leaving us children weeping, terrified, and as we gained understanding, very much ashamed. Mama brought charges of assault and battery against Daddy. Of course, by the time the case was called, my parents were once more on friendly terms, so the charges were dropped.

Not only were we different from the others by virtue of the previously mentioned conditions and situations, Mama was determined that we would know how to become better than the neighbors. In spite of all the negatives that shamed us,

Mama was resolved that we would get the best education our brains could receive. She knew that that was the way out of poverty. She had served in the white people's kitchens, and she would see to it that none of us did likewise. Consequently, Mama paid for us to go to better schools. We were the only children in the yard who went to Providence RC, Intermediate Boys RC, or Queen's Royal College.

Mama also insisted that we attend Gospel Hall Sunday School because she believed that Bible knowledge was essential to our religious/spiritual development.

-7- The End Of My Beginning

Children were not allowed in adult company and we were never given any information that did not concern school or chores. So why Mama and Daddy started fighting was a frightful and shameful mystery. I don't know if it had any thing to do with the new brother and sister that Daddy brought to see us after church, on Holy Innocence day.

Fights, Fear, and Shame

I remember the fights and the fear: Mama cussing Daddy; Daddy beating Mama; us children, crying; neighbors calling the police; Mama and Daddy hauled off to the police station. Sometimes I arrived at home to find my mother very badly beaten. Once, Daddy beat Mama so severely that there were welts over every area of her body, except for her face, which she shielded with her hands, so that her hands were terribly bruised. She couldn't sit; she couldn't lie down. It was the worst I had ever seen. He had used a whale-bone to beat her, which it appeared, he had bought and kept for that precise purpose. I don't recall if that was the time that she deliberately punctured the tires of Daddy's bicycle by driving tacks into them, or the time she had spoiled the batch of candies that was boiling by adding soap to the mixture. Why did she do that? I never knew. I can only guess that he had angered or exasperated her somehow.

During the last two years of this phase of my life I used to roam the streets of our village, afraid to go home, afraid of what would be awaiting me there. And because of the shame of these and similar happenings, I never invited any of my school-friends to my house to play. I believe this was the beginning of my Hagar behavior. I always wondered if the next incident was a dream, but it was real.

This most terrifying episode happened one night while we were asleep. I think that at that time Daddy no longer slept at home. Children were not very wise or curious in those days, so I did not understand the reason that Daddy was not there at nights. However, the doors were never locked and he had the freedom to come and go as he pleased.

That night we, and all the neighbors, were awakened by Mama's blood-curdling scream. I woke up to see Daddy with a sharpened cutlass standing over Mama and to hear him say menacingly to her, "If you didn't wake up I would have sliced you like a fish." It seemed that he had intended to kill her, and maybe us too. I don't know. Every body came out of their houses. The male neighbors held Daddy and somebody called the police.

Mama told them what had happened. Daddy said she was lying, that Mama had had a nightmare. I knew that she was telling the truth, but I was afraid to say. Daddy dared them to produce the weapon. The police and the neighbors searched, but the cutlass was nowhere to be found, and the conclusion was that Mama could come to the police station the next day to file charges, but without the weapon there was no case. I think that the law officers were just tired of being called, taking statements, filing charges, and having the charges dropped. So, despite the many reports of domestic violence, Daddy had never been found guilty.

The neighbors went back to sleep, but of course no one in our house could sleep. After the yard was quiet, Daddy very deftly removed the large radio from the wall, where it had been for so long, I didn't know it could be moved, and from the back of it he pulled out the cutlass, and walked out laughing. From that time Mama locked the doors and as she said, slept with one eye open.

Then Daddy started acting strange. Even though he didn't live with us anymore, he came by often. One night he filled a large twenty-gallon pan of water and took a shower in the drawing room. Another night while we were sleeping, he poured tar all over the floor.

I think now, that he wanted to scare Mama into leaving. Maybe he wanted to bring his new children and their mother to live in our house. But where was she to go. She had four of us who were going to school. My big brother had started to work, but obviously, he couldn't support us. He didn't live at home anymore, because he worked in the country. It was too far for him to travel each day, so he stayed at someone's home and had to pay for room and board. He came home at end of each month and gave Mama some money. That helped to buy food. He gave us children nickels to shine his shoes. Sometimes Mama asked us for our nickels.

There were times when Mama didn't have any food to give us to carry to school for lunch and she would tell us that we shouldn't come home at lunch time. But she would say, "Meet me at the corner at lunch time, I will bring some thing for you all to eat." Her confidence was in the blessing of her grandmother, who, when she was dying, blessed my mother and said, "Alice, I will pray to God for you, that if you ever wake without breakfast, you will never go to bed without supper."

And so it was that at eleven-thirty we would stand on the corner near the school looking for Mama. She always came. She bought us juice and a heavy cake we called "a belly full." It was a cheap cake made from the previous day's leftover cakes. Many poor children survived on belly-full. When we arrived home in the evening, supper would be ready. Nobody ever asked where the money for food came from at those times.

When Mama could get no money at all, she would dress my

sister and I and we would go to visit her friends. She was too proud to beg, or borrow what she couldn't repay, but her friends would always give my sister and I, a dime or a quarter. And that is how Mama would have money for bread the next day.

Mama had a big sister. Tantie Pauline was very stern. We were all afraid of her. Daddy was afraid of her, so that when she came around Daddy behaved himself and treated Mama better. One day Tantie Pauline had a stroke and she died. Mama was devastated. Her protector was gone. Daddy was happy. The same day of the funeral, Daddy nailed a notice on the door. "48 HOURS TO LEAVE."

The Worst Shame

Mama cried and cried, and we cried, but two days later, I came home from school, not to find Mama beaten as before, but to find the house nailed shut and all our things thrown out in the yard. Daddy had left us suddenly homeless, having turned the keys over to the landlord.

Why did Daddy do that? I still don't know. How could he do that to his own children? I don't understand. I can't ask him. Both he and Mama died before my journey into my soul began.

It was the worst shame. The neighbors let the girls sleep on their floor. Mama broke open the kitchen, and slept on the cot in there while my brother Gerald, slept on the bench. Each morning we gathered around Mama and she made us tea and gave us bread. We went to school. Each evening she gave us something to eat. I don't remember what. We did our homework sitting on the bench in the yard. Mama helped us to memorize our tables and spelling and we waited for the neighbors to get tired enough to go to their beds, so we could sleep on their living room floor. Daddy didn't even come by to see what had become of us. I don't remember it ever raining during that time.

My Problem Of Being Freddy's Favorite

Then an elderly man took us in. We called him Uncle. Mama always said that he was a kind gentleman, and that we should always be grateful to him. I was to be especially grateful because he loved me best. Mama never knew how much he loved me because I never told. He said that if I did we would be homeless again. Mama trusted him so that when he objected to us girls sleeping on the floor and said that his bed was big enough so that we could sleep next to him, she was not suspicious of him having any ulterior motive.

I tried to avoid him, but Mama unwittingly encouraged me to respond to his affection. She had not idea how affectionate he was. At nights, he put his nasty tongue in my mouth, made me kiss his penis, which he rubbed up and down between my legs. He didn't penetrate me. But he did ejaculate on me. Sometimes when Mama was in the kitchen outside, he would call me to sit on his lap and put his finger in my vagina. Mama couldn't understand why Uncle Freddy's grand children who were the ages of her own children were not sent to visit him. I knew. I didn't understand what was happening. I knew it was bad. I didn't know the words to describe what was being done to me. Children were very ignorant.

Even after we moved from his house, he told Mama that she must send me to him, every fortnight when he got his pension, for pocket change. Mama used to be glad for the pocket change, so I went, but I would always ask a friend to accompany me. That way I wouldn't have to be alone with him. He wasn't pleased with me. But since he told Mama I was his favorite, he couldn't tell her not to send me, without giving an explanation and since we didn't live there anymore, he couldn't threaten to throw us out.

Some years later, Mama was talking about how she used to keep an eye on my father where Marcia was concerned. She had warned Marcia never to remain inside the house if Daddy alone was at home. She explained that she disliked the way Daddy eyed Marcia's chubby legs and that if he'd ever touched her she would have killed him. I wondered why she didn't have the same concern about me. Perhaps the stress of her situation had blinded her.

A few years ago, after Mama died, her friend, my youngest sisters father visited me in New York. I took the opportunity to thank him for rescuing me from Freddy's molestation. It was he who, after Mama became pregnant, found her an apartment to which we all moved. Mr. P told me that he had wanted to be a father to me. One day he had put me to sit on his lap as a fatherly gesture and Mama had made him put me down and had warned him never to touch me or she would kill him.

Mama had always accused me of ingratitude towards Freddy. She even apologized and made excuses for me when I didn't visit, write, or send him presents. Shouldn't she have known better than to let me sleep in the bed next to him? Years later after I moved to New York, he became very ill and penniless. Both his legs were amputated. He was put into a "poor house", where he was kept in just a shirt, with all his genitals exposed, because no one had the time to change his pampers. Grateful Mama was the only one who visited him, washed, fed, and tidied him. He had many children and grandchildren, but he died alone. I am glad that Mama was good to him. I hope that he repented and received God's forgiveness.

Did Mama love me? Did Daddy care? Was I important to either of them? What value did they put on me, by their actions? What value did they put on me by their words? As the illegitimate offspring of an unmarried woman and a married Catholic man, my grandparents did not want me. They were wealthy and always seem angry. They had everything. We had nothing. When we had no food, Mama said that Daddy didn't care because he ate at his mother's house. What value did I put on myself because of their treatment of me when I was a small child? How did I compare myself with other children?

Good Memories Of My Childhood

I remember Mama and Daddy taking us to the beach at Carenage. That was fun. I remember Daddy taking us to the park on moonlight nights when all the parents came with their children. We played till midnight, while the adults talked; but Daddy played with us. He was the pied piper of our street. I remember Daddy helping us and all the children of the neighborhood to construct kites, which we mounted on Saturday and Sunday afternoons in the Savannah, or in Robinsonville, where there was always a good breeze blowing.

And I remember the smell of bread being baked in the oven made out of zinc and mud that Daddy built. I remember Christmas with new linoleum and curtains, fruitcake and ham, a table-top Christmas tree, which Daddy decorated, and new shorts to wear. Those things never happened after we moved.

Before the fighting started, I believe that we were as happy as children can be. Life as a child was easy. For the most part, children were responsible to go to school, complete homework assignments, and do a few chores according to age and ability. Young children were given rags to wipe the dust off the furniture, older girls swept the floor, and made the beds, while older boys kept the yard clean. Every year in preparation for Christmas time we cleaned and varnished the furniture, and my big sister made new crepe paper flowers.

The very first time I experienced an earthquake was a Saturday afternoon, when I should have been in the back yard playing with Deborah. Instead I was in the house by myself, pulling out the drawers, curiously examining Mama's things. Suddenly the house began to shake violently. Frightened out of my wits, I ran out of the house and down the steps; I could hear Mama screaming out my name. I pelted down the yard and up the lane. I could not stop. I guess I would have run into the street if Daddy hadn't been coming home. He swooped me up in his arms. I had never felt so safe.

Most of the childhood good times, that I have related, had been shut up in my memory for decades. I seemed to have locked up the good and beautiful with the bad and the ugly. Deborah relates so many things of which I have no recollection that I used to wonder if her memories were fantasies. But for many years I used to have three beautiful recurring dreams, which stopped after my marriage became rocky and all my future plans and dreams became impossibilities. Then the dreams changed and in new dreams I struggled to get back to the place of the beautiful dreams, but couldn't. Then I stopped dreaming altogether. I had even forgotten the beautiful dreams until I began to unlock these doors. I really wish I could dream them again, but maybe I don't need them anymore.

Now I understand a little of how stressful Mama's life must have been. She wasn't even living in her birth country, and she couldn't go back there. They didn't know of her new shame. Besides, three of us belonged in Trinidad. What was she to do? She had left her small island, seeking a better life for herself and three children, and she had ended up with three more, and in worse shape than before. She was a strong woman, not to have gone insane. At the end of this chapter I will place the poems I wrote about Mama and Daddy. These were written after I had forgiven them and was healed of the emotional damage that they had caused.

-8- Education, The Way Out Of Poverty

Daddy was a Roman Catholic; therefore my younger sister and I had been christened in the Roman Catholic Church, and sent to Roman Catholic schools. My big sister Marcia, and second brother Gerald, had been christened in the Anglican Church, because our mother was Anglican. They were made to convert to Catholicism so that they could benefit from the better education, which the Catholic school system provided.

Government schools were free, and most children in our station of life went to government schools. As poor as we were, school fees, and schoolbooks were the most important expenses. Mama became very upset if the fees were due, and the money was not available; or if we had to go without a needed book. We sometimes bought second hand books, but we had to buy them from people who did not go to the same school as us, or lived in the same village. Nobody was supposed to know how poor we were. We didn't know how poor we were.

Actually, I didn't understand that we were poor and until I began to interact with children outside of the yard. We never went without shoes or clothes. We didn't have much, but we were always clean and well groomed. We had Sunday clothes, home clothes, and weekday going out clothes, and school uniforms. Maybe two sets of each. We were not supposed to even play barefooted like the other children. We must wear our slippers, which were mostly old shoes or washecongs, from which the back parts had been cut. I found it very hard to keep slippers on my crippled foot. Even today I seem to hear Mama's voice, "Put your slippers on your foot, or get inside the house".

Sometimes there was not enough food, and no money; but nobody was supposed to know that. At times breakfast was a cup of sweetened bush-tea and lunch was cornmeal porridge. We learned to stay in the house when the popsicle-man or snowball-man came by, and all the other children were buying the delicious treats. As children we never had much spending money. We learned not to look at the things we could not afford. Mama had a special look that told us that we should not even want that for which we couldn't pay. Except that education! We must be ambitious.

My First Feeling of Being Unwanted

I have no recollection of my first day at school, but I do remember being in Miss Wilson's first stage class. It was Mama's custom to send her children to a private Kindergarten school at age three. Children were not accepted in the Primary schools until age five. Two years of private school gave a child an excellent head start and ensured a solid foundation in Reading, Writing, and Arithmetic. Mrs. Benson, Deborah's

Godmother, had a private kindergarten school. Unfortunately for me, when I was three, Mrs. Benson said that her kindergarten was full. She had no room for me. Mama said Mrs. Benson did not make room for me because she knew that Daddy was an irresponsible playboy, and since Mama was not employed at the time, she had no confidence that her school fees would be paid. Gerald had attended Mrs. Benson's school, and so did Deborah when she became three.

I was convinced that Mrs. Benson did not like me. So what? I never liked her.

Attending Providence Girls Roman Catholic School

Mama did her best to give me a head start. It was she who taught me my first lessons and held my little hands to help me form the letters that spelt my names. And besides, I was tall for my age and Mama was a very convincing liar. I passed for five, and entered Providence Girls Roman Catholic School at age four. But my penmanship was never as beautiful as my sisters and brother.

We were encouraged to read. I really do not know what level of education Daddy had, but Mama, despite misfortune and bad choices that curtailed her formal education, never ceased to learn. Daddy's literature of choice was comic books. This infuriated Mama. That a grown man found such delight in comic books produced in her a great aversion to them. Nevertheless, we all developed Daddy's love for comics of all kinds. Mama did not appreciate that they had any value, but I think they helped to create in us that love for reading. She read everything, except comic books, and encouraged us to read. We had to join the library, and instead of playing down in the yard, we had to sit and read. We belonged to the large public library, the small Belmont library, and the school library. Our first library books were about "Teddy Robinson", and we progressed to the adventure books, then the career books, and on to the literary classics.

Knocked Down For Want Of A Reading Book

When I was six years old I needed a certain reading book. It was in the showcase of the store that we passed by every day on the way to and from school. Daddy had promised to purchase it for me. Every morning and every evening I ran to the store window to satisfy myself that the book was still there. I did not understand that the book in the window was only a display and that more books were available. I thought it was the only one.

One morning, my big sister crossed the street before we could go past the Semongul's store. I was frantic with worry. I had to know if the book was still there. So I pulled away from her hold and ran across the street straight into the path of an approaching taxi. My face hit the hood of the car, brakes screeched, and I fell. The taxi driver came out of the car, picked me up, and began running to and fro in a panic, before he caught himself and put me in his car and took me to the hospital. Every tooth was loose and I was bleeding profusely.

Of course, Mama blamed Daddy and so did I, because, if he had bought me the book, I would not have had to be keeping an eye on it every day. You can well imagine that he purchased the book that very day. Mama thought my zeal to obtain the book was a sign of great academic ambition.

I missed a lot of school because of that accident and other illnesses. Once I was very sick for what seemed like a very long time. I remember Daddy had bought peanut butter ice cream for us. I think it was my birthday. After enjoying the ice cream I started to vomit. I had a high fever. Mama and Daddy mixed some spices with rum and soft candle, which they heated until it melted and rubbed me from head to toe, pouring Bay-rum on my head. They worked on me all night and took me to the health office the next day. I think that was when I had been stung by a scorpion. I couldn't walk and had to be carried. My foot was so swollen. I really thought I would never walk again. But eventually, I was able to go back to school. For the first month Daddy took me to and from school.

Daddy rode a carrier-bike, which he used when he distributed candy to the neighborhood parlors (little shops) and school canteens. Grandfather made the most delicious variety of candies. People came from far and wide to buy from him. He was very successful and prosperous, but he was utterly disappointed in his only son, Maurice. Maurice was lazy and un-ambitious. He learned how to make peppermints, lollipops and caramels, enough to provide the very minimum for us, but he had no interest in his father's business.

In the carrier portion of the bike was a big sturdy cardboard box in which he placed the parcels of candy. However, sometimes Daddy put me in the box and rode with me to school. It was illegal to do so, therefore, whenever he spotted a police officer, Daddy made me crouch down in the box and he covered me over with a crocus bag. Sometimes when I was walking home from school with Marcia and her friends, Daddy would ride up, and swooping me up in his strong arms deposit me into the box, and ride off with me. That was wonderful.

Nevertheless, I also liked walking with my sister and her friends and their little sisters. Sometimes after school we stopped at the homes of her friends where the big sisters met with boys and talked, while the little sisters played. Mama would be quarreling when we got home. Marcia would fib (we were not allowed to say the word "lie") and say that she was detained in school for some good reason. She would promise me a penny to keep her confidence. Sometimes I forgot what I was supposed to say and she got into trouble.

I loved Providence. Assembly time was eight fifteen. Children generally began arriving at school at about seven thirty. It was time to play. The older children played hopscotch, skipping rope, and netball. The younger ones played the ring games, like Ring-a round-a Rosy, Brown girl in the Ring, In a Fine Castle, and, The Cat and the Mouse. We played Jane and Louisa, London Bridge, What is the time Mr. Wolf. Oh, it was so much fun. At lunchtime we gobbled down our food and ran back to the courts and the fields for more games.

Netball season was a most exciting time. We would stay after school to watch the netball practice as the teams trained for competition matches. My sister was on her house team. The first, second and third stage students did not belong to houses. The students in standards one through five belonged either to St. Joseph or Our lady Of Lourdes house. The students in forms one through five belonged to one of four houses. The competitions were among the four senior houses. The primary and intermediate students were generally not allowed to stay to watch the excitement, unless one had a big sister on the team. My big sister belonged to St. Roses.

Of greater interest than the matches for house championship, were the inter-school competitions. Each school had to play on the courts at the other schools. The two teams that made it to the finals had to play one game on each court. If there was a tie, the final game was played on the court of the team with the best score.

It seems to me that Providence R.C. and Tranquility E.C. were always the finalists. Both had excellent teams and so the games were tense and exciting. Invariably the champion won by a very slim margin. Tranquility girls were sore losers. There was almost certain to be a fight, especially if Providence won on Tranquility's court. Providence girls were more ladylike and were not permitted to be accompanied by boys, not even big brothers and cousins, while wearing their school uniforms. However, after a game with Tranquility, that rule was suspended, and their boyfriends and brothers were permitted to escort them home to protect them from the fierce and angry losers.

There were lots of fun activities at Providence. We had garden parties, bazaars, concerts and plays. Everyone could participate. Those were the days when girls dressed up according to age. Hairstyles were set according to age. And make up and jewelry were worn according to age. Uniforms were worn to school, and while in uniform we were expected to wear simple braids and white, black, or navy blue ribbons, to match our uniforms, which were navy blue overalls with pleated skirts, white blouses, navy blue ties, white shoes and socks. Our gym uniform was a green pleated overall, and our dress uniform was white with long sleeves and again pleated skirts. We had to wear knickers with our gym uniforms, and whole slips with our regular and dress uniforms.

The garden parties, plays and bazaars, afforded the students the opportunity to dress up and show off their Sunday best. Young ladies were allowed to loosen the braids, press and curl the hair, change from bobby socks to stockings, from uniforms to evening dresses, that reached mid calf, and from sneakers to high heeled shoes that encouraged them to walk with model-like grace. Children were dressed in widely flared, frilled, or tiered pastel colored nylon dresses that had huge sashes. They wore matching ribbons and socks with buckled shoes. We tried our best to keep the promises not to dirty the dresses, not to run wild. For those who were interested in boyfriends, these were special times when male relatives could be invited into the school, creating occasions for boys and girls to meet under the most respectable circumstances. They were grand times.

I Qualified For The Rich White High School

Even though the parochial schools at which we began our education went from kindergarten to form five, (The equivalent of the American twelfth grade), and provided an excellent and thorough education, Mama let us know that we were expected to get scholarships and enter the more prestigious high schools. And some of us, including yours truly, did.

When I was twelve, I was recommended for the scholarship preparation class. Only about thirty children from each school had the opportunity to write the "Exhibition Exam". The parents of such special children were required to send them to after school classes for extra tuition. The cost was three dollars a month. I don't know how she managed, but every month Mama handed me that three dollars to pay Mr. Julian or Mr. Smith. I was determined to make her proud, so that she wouldn't have wasted her money and she wouldn't have to kill me.

I passed the exam at a level high enough to be accepted into the Holy Name Convent. Apart from the threat of death by Mama, I honestly wished I had failed so that I could have remained in Providence Intermediate School with my best friend Cheryl. Cheryl had been very ill and had missed two months of school, and so she did not pass the exam. I believe I would have received a better education there at Providence, but to be accepted at HNC made my family very proud. I received a watch as a present. It was the most beautiful and expensive thing I ever owned. Mama pawned her bracelets to buy it for me. It was a gold watch with a tiny oval face and a thin band of interlocking tiny hearts.

Holy Name Convent had been known as the White High

School. Trinidad, the most cosmopolitan island of the West Indies had a population, which consisted principally of people of African and Indian descent. However there was (is still) also some Chinese, Syrians, Jews, Spaniards, as well as British, Canadian, and American Whites. The Chinese were the owners of grocery stores, laundries, and restaurants. The Syrians and Jews owned the fabric stores. The Whites owned the banks, hotels, and most large department stores. The few educated middle class Negroes and Indians were the civil servants, nurses, teachers, and oil field workers. The poor Indians were mostly farm workers, while the poor blacks were store clerks, seamstresses, hairdressers, peddlers of some kind, or servants to the whites.

Most of the country's money was in the hands of White, Syrian and Jewish people. However, a new government had opened wide the educational doors so that poor black children whose future would have been limited to being farm hands or store clerks, could fly as high as imagination could soar.

Until 1961, it used to cost a prohibitive sum to receive an education at the privately owned, and particularly, the parochial high schools. This ensured that only children of wealthy or influential parents would populate these schools. Therefore, except for a handful of blacks, and I mean about five out of five hundred, the children of Holy Name Convent belonged to the upper, white, money class of society.

In 1960, the Premier, Dr. Eric Williams, a black man, our first native born black political leader, declared that all high schools must accept anyone who was scholastically qualified. The government would pay the tuition, and give twenty-four dollars a year towards books for each scholarship recipient. Consequently, when I entered HNC high school, I was in the first class which had a majority of blacks, (Negroes and Indians). We were the cream of the crop. We were destined for greatness. Mama was right we came to be better than our social peers.

Prejudice And Poverty, The Scissors That Clipped My Wings

Providence Girls Roman Catholic had given me a wide view of my potential. There I had been introduced to English Grammar and Poetry, Health Science and Nature Study, Mathematics, Geography, History and Civics, Art, Singing, Sewing and Calisthenics, as well as Religious Instruction. I did well in all subjects. I loved them all. My sister who stayed in Providence until she graduated had also been taught Spanish, French, Typing, Shorthand, Book-keeping, and Cookery. I expected to do all that and more.

Imagine my great disappointment when I found myself in a class where for the next five years all I would be taught was English Grammar and Literature, Mathematics, Art, Spanish, Latin, Geography, Bible, and Art.

Holy Name Convent was my first experience of prejudice. We poor black scholars may have been the cream of the black crop, but we lacked two pre-requisites, white skin and blue money.

There were three types of classes in Holy Name Convent: The M-Classes, where students were told that they were being taught Modern Subjects. They majored in Art, Sewing and Cookery. I was a little better off. Mine was the A-class, we studied the Arts, and then, there were the S-classes. Yes, they studied the sciences. And guess who populated the S-classes, white skin and blue money. It was so very unfair.

Teachers Who Cared Versus Teachers Who Didn't

In Providence, the classes were over-crowded. It amazes me that the teachers could teach all of us. But somehow we were all pushed to do our very best and make our families and our school proud of us. Discipline went hand in hand with education, and it was not unusual be held in detention, or to feel the edge of a ruler on ones hands or legs. It all seemed very fair, and very few children dared to complain to their parents about corporal punishment. We knew that our teachers were not vindictive. They really cared. Even those that were feared, we discovered, cared greatly about our success. So we cared about succeeding. There was no expectation of failure.

At Holy Name that feeling that the teachers cared was missing. Holy Name's rules prohibited the beating of young ladies, nevertheless, corporal punishment was meted out, by vindictive and cruel nuns. I remember sister Mary Thomas, who sat in the shade and made us stand in the sun for a half an hour, with our hand straight up or straight out. We were threatened with longer periods in the sun if we dropped our hands. The crime was not being quick enough to observe her presence when she entered the classroom, or being sleepy or inattentive. I think she just didn't want to teach us.

Funny how I can remember all the names of my Primary School teachers but except for the principal, three nuns, and two teachers, I have forgotten my high school teachers' names.

In the first year my teacher was Sister Brigitte, a very unorthodox nun who would sail into the classroom, and if we were distracted and did not get to our feet immediately to say good-morning, she would throw a tantrum, fling the books which she carried at us, screaming, "So nobody would tell the dog good morning?" Then she would walk out, returning later very calm and ready to teach, as if there had been no outburst. We agreed that she was crazy. She introduced us to Shakespeare and had us act out *A Midsummer's Night Dream.* She also taught us how to tie-dye fabric. The walls of our classroom were decorated with squares of tie-dyed cloth. The children from the "S" class used to laugh at us.

The next year we were given teachers who specialized in their field. While most of my teachers were nuns, I remember Mrs G___, who taught geography, and Mr. M___ who taught math. Both affected me greatly.

In my opinion, Mrs. G did not teach or could not teach. She did her nails, fixed her hair. She gave us homework and did not ask for it. Eventually some of us stopped doing any work for her class. It seemed a waste of time. One day Mrs. G__ decided to receive the homework she had assigned the previous week. Very few of us had done it. We groaned. She asked, “All those who don’t wish to be in this class, please stand.” More than half of us stood, having no idea where she was going. The woman told us to leave and never come back. We were made to drop geography, and nobody could do anything about it. The Principal upheld Mrs. G——‘s decision.

Mr. M__ obviously thought very little of females. He should never have been allowed to teach in a girls’ school. The very first day of class, he introduced himself, letting us know that girls did not have the brains for mathematics, and he wasn’t expecting much from us. That made up my mind. I had to get a certificate in math. I would show the stupid arrogant man.

Eventually I dropped Latin. It seemed unnecessary, except that it helped with the root of English words. As you can see my education was quite limited.

In the absence of the teacher's interest it was necessary that our parents guide our educational and career path. But most of us exhibitioners had parents who were unlearned and intimidated by the "white school system" and who were not able to direct us. They were just thrilled that their children had the chance of being better than them.

There was one sixth former, Faustina Fraizer, who was the only real encouragement in my first year. She was our class prefect and she tried to help us to fit in. She was a black sixth former from an educated, middle class family. It was rumored that her father was an ambassador. She was extremely bright. Yet we could see that she didn't fit in. I never ceased to feel like a misfit.

I did participate in school as far as possible. I joined the choir. The choir participated in the National Music Festival and that was pretty exciting. We also sang at masses, both in Latin and English. When our school produced an operetta called, "The Royal Jester," as a member of the choir, I became a lady at the court of Prittania. It was wonderful, but after that first year, I didn't participate in anything anymore.

Everything cost money that we didn't have, even sports. Hockey and Lawn Tennis were the sports of choice. Hockey sticks and Tennis rackets were very costly. Only the moneyed girls played.

When I was fifteen, there was an advertisement for a debate competition. The topics were given out and I decided to try-out for the school team. Each evening we met in the library and I listened to the contestants as they auditioned. The subject I had chosen was 'Should Boxing Be Abolished?" No other person who had chosen that subject seemed to do justice to the affirmative answer. I had really worked hard and when my turn came, I knew I was the best. But I was disqualified. I was too young. I needed to be sixteen.

By this time the pressures at home were building up. The following year I was given a chance to take my GCE in the fourth form. I only succeeded in passing three subjects. I needed at least five to be able to get a decent job. Nobody was upset because they knew that I was not ready for the exam.

Facing The Undesirable Future Created A Mental Block

The following year, as we began our revisions in preparation for exams, we were all quite nervous. For poor ones like me, it was the last chance. I knew that Mama had no money and I needed to be employed. It was time to do my part for the family. I would have liked to continue into the sixth form to do my "A" level exams, which could lead to a college education, but I had no right to think of those things. Mama had done her best. She couldn't be asked to do any more.

At the beginning of May, we were given graduation information to take to our parents. When I read the letter, I knew that I could not participate in the graduation exercises. I didn't even show Mama the letter. All graduates were to bring $$ Xx for the material and sewing of their graduation dresses. We were all to wear dresses made of French Satin and Pearl du Soir Lace. School rings cost $$. The graduation ball costs $$. My family could eat for a year on the cost of my graduation.

The following day the principal, Mother Bernadette, called us one by one to answer three questions. Would you be returning to school next year? Would you be participating in the graduation exercises? I don't remember what the other question was. Suddenly I was weeping. My school days were ended and I couldn't even graduate.

I went back to class. The teacher was asking questions. I should have known the answers. It was literature. I loved literature. I adored Shakespeare. I had memorized every important speech. I could remember nothing. I ran crying from the class.

After three days I was scared enough to go to the principal. In tears I explained to her that I could remember nothing. Exams were a month away.

She sent for Mama and gave her a letter to take me to the doctor. Doctor Blanc said that I'd had a shock and I had developed a mental block. His advice was that I be allowed to do whatever I please. I should stay out of the classroom, and try not to worry. My memory would return but he couldn't tell when.

Some days I went to school. Some days I sat under the tree in the schoolyard. Sometimes I wasn't sure I knew my own name. Mostly, I cried. Time passed and I began to remember: Pythagoras Theorem, Mark Anthony's Speech, etc. Maybe it was good that I hadn't done chemistry, and biology, and geography. Who knows? Only God. And then it was time for the Cambridge General Certificate of Education Examination.

The day of the Spanish exam I hit a blank. I went walking about Port-of-Spain, just taking it easy, like the doctor had said. I decided to go and see my friend Margaret at her grandmother's house. When I got there she was on her way back to school. She didn't go to my school, and she hadn't known of my predicament. "Girl I have to run. I have Spanish exams today. Aren't you doing Spanish?

I ran all the way to school. When I got there the exams had begun. I had missed the dictation. I needed to write an essay. But I could remember nothing and all I did was break into big globs of cold sweat that fell on my paper. When I had calmed myself, I got up and walked away.

A couple months later the results were posted. I had distinguished myself with excellence in English Grammar and English literature, and credits in mathematics, art, and Bible study.

I wasn't very proud of myself because I had fallen so far short of the expectations I'd had when I had passed the exam that sent me to Holy Name Convent. Mama was satisfied. I had done well. I had passed both English and Math. Those were the minimal requirements for a decent job.

Later on, I did attempt to further my education but the trauma of the mental block, which I had suffered, plagued me with fear, which stole my confidence. I used to attend night classes at Queens Royal College, but it seemed to me that my brains could no longer receive and retrieve information. As time passed, instead of going to class on time, I would sit on the Savannah bench outside the school, making up my mind to go in. Sometimes it was half an hour before I did. Eventually, I stopped going altogether.

Giving Mama Her Dues

All in all, Mama tried to push us out of the poverty trap and to expose us to a better life than she enjoyed. She herself came from a family of property owners. In her youth, she had known a better life. She had been raised to believe herself better than others, and to expect great things for herself. As such Mama was somewhat of a snob. Her companions had been those who like herself, were ambitious, bright and beautiful, and she looked down her nose at the poorer and lower classes. The death of her mother and re-marriage of a cruel father changed her life, her perspective, and her future. Yet, even though circumstances had altered her state, no one and nothing could change her status and attitude.

The Embarrassment Of My High School Days

Although I was ashamed of being illegitimate, I was never ashamed of my mother. I was proud to have her meet my friends and visit my school on parents' day and on any occasion. However she only came when she had to. She attended no concerts or sports. Maybe she was ashamed of herself. But Mama had class. She carried her head high, always dressed well, and would keep her mouth shut when she was out of her depth. She was very wise.

I was ashamed of Daddy. He was an embarrassment. This was not because of the circumstances of my birth, but because Daddy was a flirt. Daddy flirted with anything in a dress. That included the nuns. He didn't mean anything by it. It was just a joke to him and he thought it gave them a thrill.

On occasion when Daddy made candies, he sold his product to the school canteens. I was mortified when he began delivering peppermints, lollipops, and caramels to my High School. It was acceptable when I went to Providence, where all the children, as well as the teachers, lived in the area and were already familiar with my father. I don't believe he used to flirt then. But he took a special delight in sweet-talking the nuns. Whenever I was aware that Daddy was on the school premises I hid in the toilet. Only the few friends, who used to attend Providence and my new friend Juliana, knew that the candy-man was my father.

-9- Religion: Spiritual And Moral Values

Gospel Hall Sunday School

At age three, I joined my brothers and big sister as, at two thirty every Sunday afternoon, we walked the half-mile to the Belmont Gospel Hall on Erthig Road. Mama thought this was necessary because the Bible was not part of Catholicism.

I liked the Gospel Hall Sunday school. We were placed in classes according to our ages. Children from three to ten were placed in classes in the rooms to the back of the building. Those from eleven to eighteen occupied classes in what we called, the big Sunday school. We sang and learned gospel choruses and heard stories about the love of God, Jonah who was swallowed by a whale, Daniel in the lions' den, Joseph and his wonderful coat, and Moses in the basket on the river. We were taught all the Bible stories and we had to learn Bible verses. Young children were given cards with pretty pictures that illustrated the texts to take home. Our mother made sure that we memorized our texts and were able to recite our verses before we left the house each Sunday. Each Sunday we received a different assignment, but if we were unable to recite our text by heart, we were shamed with the same assignment.

The smallest child may have to learn text like, "Jesus said, I am the good shepherd". The older children may have to learn,

"Jesus said, I am the good shepherd, the good shepherd gives his life for his sheep." When we graduated from primary Sunday school, we had to acquire a Bible and learn whole Bible verses. I always liked to learn. I remember when I was twelve there was a competition. The sixteen to eighteen year olds were challenged to memorize the whole of Isaiah chapter fifty-three. The rest of us were to learn verses five and six. I tried my best to learn the whole chapter. I didn't quite make it but I still remember all that I learned. We also had to memorize the books of the Bible in order.

Each year there was a Sunday school outing to Arima. This was very exciting. Whole families attended. Picnic baskets were packed with wonderful food and snacks. And there was the thrill of traveling by train. We were city folk and trains only took people from the country to the city limits and vice-versa. Arima was considered country. The scents and scenery of the country were more interesting, pleasant and serene than those of the city. The train skirted small picturesque towns and villages with animal farms and large vegetable gardens. The houses of the country people were very high buildings, with room enough below for hammocks, where the adults relaxed in the afternoons, when the sun's heat beat mercilessly down, sapping the energy of the farmers. The houses stood in the middle of large yards where chickens, ducks, dogs and cats lived peaceably with the children. The children grew in steps and there was always a baby present. A kaleidoscope of color arrested the eye as several varieties of croton, hibiscus, or lady of the night beautified the yards to the front of the houses, forming hedges that provided dividing lines of property.

The train rumbled through cane fields that grew taller than the windows of the train, momentarily shutting out the sun, causing some children to squeal with excitement, while others cried out in fear. People would board the train to sell the freshly cut sweet juicy cane to the travelers. I remember how, in my high school years, I used to wish that we lived in the country and had to take the train to Port-of-Spain, and the bus to Belmont, where I lived and went to school. The children were always full of stories of fun happenings on the train. There seemed to have been better opportunities to meet with boys, and there was talk of kissing as the train passed through the cane fields.

The Sunday school outing was held in a large Savannah. There was a covered grandstand where the parents set up the picnic things. Each child was made to memorize the place where his family was encamped, before running off to enjoy the wide-open grassy field, oblivious of the brilliantly burning sun. At one corner of the field was a cattle pen that housed bulls and cows. We were warned about the danger of antagonizing the bulls, but that only provided a better reason for the boys to dare each other to get into the bullpen. Parents and teachers had to be very vigilant to keep their charges out of trouble.

Sports were the anxiously awaited activity of the day. There were games and races for everyone. Three-legged races, sack races, egg-and-spoon races, obstacle course, hurdles, quarter mile, half mile, and the last race of the day, the mile. I remember the first time I participated in the sports. I was probably four years old. At the sound of the go-whistle, instead of running towards the finish line, I ran to my mother in tears. That was the year my big brother won the mile-race, and my big sister placed in the egg and spoon race. However, there were prizes for everyone, regardless of placement. I was happy to take home my prize. After the races, each child, from zero to eighteen was given an ice-cream cone, and a bag with candies and cake.

The other much-awaited Sunday school event was the Christmas program. Two children were chosen from each class to participate in it. The most talented were chosen for the Christmas play. Our parents, not intending to be shamed, saw to it that we studied our parts to perfection. The program usually took place on Boxing Day. We wore our new Christmas clothes and were on our best behavior as we sat with our parents and applauded as each student took the stage, bowed, and recited with great dramatic expressions and flourishes, making themselves, their parents, and teachers, proud. At the end of the program, each Sunday school student received a gift. Small children were given toys, but as we matured, we were given books with wonderful stories of great people. When I graduated from toys to books I was sad. I loved books but I was reluctant to leave childhood.

After we moved from Suffolk Road we continued to go to Sunday school for a while, but we never went to the picnic or the Christmas pageant again. Maybe it was because Daddy wasn't there.

I recall now how, between the ages of eleven and twelve, the Sunday school teacher used to encourage the students to become "Gospel lights". I believe that was about the time when we were taught about salvation, but as I grew in Catholicism, I deliberately prevented myself from hearing the message of the Gospel Hall teachers.

Catholic School Religious Education

My Catholic indoctrination began in First stage. That's how the first class in primary school was named. There was first, second, and third stage; then first, second, third, fourth, and fifth standards. The most important book was the little red catechism from which we were taught. It was written in question and answer form and parents cooperated with the teachers by helping their children to memorize both. So thorough were the lessons that I doubt that there is any question that I could be asked now, fifty years later, to which I would not give the precise answer. If the Christian Sunday school had such a thorough method of teaching scriptural truths, with the power of God's word to support their answers, I may have become a gospel light.

Nevertheless Catholicism gave me some good foundational knowledge.

Question:	Who made you?
Answer:	God made me.
Question:	Why did God make you?
Answer:	God made me to know him, to love him, to serve him, in this world and to be happy with him, forever in the next.
Question:	Is there only one God?
Answer:	There is only one God.
Question:	Are there three persons in one God?
Answer:	There are three persons in one God.
Question:	Are these three persons three Gods.
Answer:	These three persons are not three gods, the Father the Son and the Holy Ghost, are all, one and the same God.
Question:	How do you prove that you

love God?

Answer: You prove that you love God by keeping his commandments, for Christ had said, if you love me, keep my commandments.

And so, day-by-day, the truths of God and the traditions of Catholicism were indelibly impressed on our minds. Before I understood the meanings of the words, "adultery" and "covet", I knew the Ten Commandments. Before age seven when I "made my first communion", I had learned that a sacrament is an outward sign of inward grace, freely bestowed upon us for our sanctification and salvation.

I knew the evil of sin and the horror of hell. Original sin was the sin of disobedience, committed by Adam and Eve in the Garden of Eden. We are all born with the stain of original sin. Baptism is the sacrament, which removes the stain of original sin. Sin is an offence against God. Mortal sin is a grievous offence against God, which kills the soul and deserves hell. Venial sin is an offence, which does not kill the soul, yet displeases God and often leads to mortal sin. Those who die without baptism go to limbo. Those who die with venial sin on their souls, go to purgatory. Those who die with mortal sin, go to hell. Purgatory is a place where souls suffer for a time, after death, on account of their sins. Hell was eternal burning in a lake of fire from which there is no escape.

So well structured and presented were these questions and answers, that it was impossible in a society, where adults were always unquestionably correct, to think that anything I was taught was inaccurate or wrong.

Prayers were a very important part of the school day. Immediately after line up, at eight-fifteen, short prayers were said. One academic subject was taught, then at eight-forty-five we had morning prayers. Either a Nun or a senior student conducted prayers though the public address system. We began with the hymn "Come Holy Ghost, Creator Come". I don't remember the prayers although I used to know them so well, I could have conducted them myself. The whole exercise lasted twenty minutes and ended with a hymn to Mary, Jesus, or a saint, depending on what day it was. We sang hymns to St. Patrick because the clergy of the parish and the Catholic schools were Irish.

The importance of Mary and the saints was not actually taught. Praying to them was just an unquestionably natural part of the Catholic prayer-life. As situations arose one was advised to pray to such and such a saint, who was the patron of whatever cause. Of course there were very interesting stories to recommend and illustrate the efficacy of prayer to each particular Saint. Jude was the hope of helpless cases because the closeness of his name to Judas, made him understand hopelessness. Joseph was the patron saint of a happy death because Mary and Jesus attended him on his deathbed.

The many stories of Mary, the many names and titles she bore, were not taught in catechism, but were impressed on our souls through the prayers we said, the hymns we sang and the testimonies that were related and chronicled. Subtly and surely our brains were washed with her magnificence, authority and power, so that she became the main focus of our spiritual desire.

Before we went to lunch at eleven-thirty, the Dictaphone was turned on again, for us to say the "Grace before meals, bless us O lord and these thy gifts which we are about to receive from thy bounty through Christ our Lord Amen."

After lunch when the bell rang for the Angelus, we signed ourselves with the sign of the cross, formed ranks by class and filed into the classroom for afternoon prayers. First the Angelus was said, then, we recited five mysteries of the rosary. There were five sorrowful mysteries used during the Lenten season that put us in mind of the suffering of Christ. The five joyful mysteries accentuated the annunciation and birth of Jesus, while the glorious mysteries concentrated on His resurrection and ascension, as well as "Mary's assumption. Regardless of the targeted doctrines, we said six "Our Fathers", fifty three "Hail Marys" and six "Glory Be to God".

At three fifteen the Dictaphone called us to evening prayer.

At age seven, we were put in special religious instruction classes to be prepared for the sacraments of penance and the Holy Eucharist. We came to recognize the things that were sin. We understood that we sin by thought, word and deed, and that God knows and sees all things, even our most secret thoughts. We also understood that the day after we made our first confession, and did our first penance, we would receive Jesus into our hearts in first communion. It was an awesome, exciting time.

On that Friday when we were taken from school to the church, as I stood in line with the other girls, waiting my turn to go behind the curtain into the confessional box, I tried to remember every spoon of sugar I had stolen, every lie I had told, every time I had been disobedient, and every evil thought I had ever had. I wanted to be pure and sinless so Jesus would be pleased to dwell in my heart. With pounding heart I knelt, made the sign of the cross and said, "Bless me father for I have sinned. This is my first confession." "Now tell me your sins my child." "Father I stole the sugar and milk."

Soon it was over. I had said the act of contrition and was given some Hail Marys to say for penance. My soul was sinless and I would try my best to keep it so.

We were told to fast until we had received the Lord Jesus. The next morning I was afraid to let even a drop of the water I used to rinse out my mouth, slip down my throat.

Mama dressed me in the new white homemade satin panties, my white petticoat, and my white communion dress. I had new white socks, and shoes whitened with nugget polish. She combed my hair with new white ribbons, put some Ponds vanishing cream on my face and powdered me pretty. Then, Mama put the veil and crown on my head, handed me my satin communion bag, my new white mass missal and white rosary. I was an angel ready for heaven. I remained silent during the whole process too afraid that I might think of or say something to sin my soul. I was singing in my heart one of the two hymns we'd been taught for the occasion. "Come o come, sweet Jesus come, make this poor sad heart thy home, but before thou come prepare, for thyself a dwelling there."

As I walked through the yard and up the lane, the children and grownups came out to admire me, and with their compliments ringing in my ear, my big sister Marcia solemnly took me to the church. I don't believe that Mama ever entered the Catholic Church. She despised the idolatry of statues and the hypocritical Latin that few understood.

And there we were, hundreds of seven-year old boys and girls, from all the Catholic schools of the Belmont Parrish lined up in the yard of St. Francis R.C. Church, our arms placed piously across our breast, singing:

> "Who am I my Jesus, that thou comest to me?
> I have sinned against thee often grievously.
> I am very sorry I have caused thee pain,
> I will never, ever, grieve thy heart again.
> Come, o come sweet savior,
> Come to me and stay,
> For I want thee Jesus,
> More than I can say.
> Oh what gift or present, Jesus shall I bring?
> I have nothing worthy of my God and King,
> But thou art my shepherd I thy little lamb,
> Take myself dear Jesus, all I have and am.

I still love that hymn. I remember all the verses and still sing it sometimes. Solemnly we received the wafer, the body of Christ. I was so afraid that my teeth might touch it. I was absolutely positive that there on my tongue was the actual body of Christ that would bleed if I bit it.

Back at home an altar was set up. I was expected to pray all day. There was a cushion on which I knelt before the lighted cantles and pictures of the sacred heart. I didn't really know what to pray. I said the rosary. Being holy was beginning to bore me. Permission was granted to visit a school friend who had also received her first communion. She had her own room. At her house, we knelt before her altar and prayed the rosary, after which, we did what seven-year old girls do. We played with her toys.

From that time I went to confession every Saturday afternoon and received communion every Sunday. That is, until Marcia began skip church and go to her friend's home instead. When Mama found out and grounded us from the Catholic Church, my poor soul was in jeopardy. Missing mass on Sundays was the most grievous mortal sin that sent a person directly to hell. But Mama couldn't understand. She wasn't Catholic.

My religious instruction continued each day in school. We were given the blue catechism book, which taught some deeper lessons. I learned about the other sacraments of Confirmation, Marriage, Extreme Unction, and Ordination. I hoped desperately to receive Extreme Unction. It was the only fail-safe means of grace to escape both purgatory and hell. My friend Jacqueline was a lucky one. The priest was with her when she was dying. He heard her confession, absolved her from her sins, gave her the Eucharist, and she went to heaven.

The preparation for the sacrament of confirmation began at age eleven. By this time I was certain that the Holy Roman Catholic Church was the Only One True Church, founded by Jesus, who installed Peter as the first Pope, when he said, ***'Thou art Peter, and upon this rock, I will build my Church."*** I knew that only the Catholic Church had power to forgive sins because Christ had said to Peter, ***Whose sins you shall***

forgive they are forgiven, whose sins you shall retain they are retained. I learned that there was an unbroken succession of popes from the time of Peter, and that popes were granted infallibility when they sat Ex Cathedra.

I also understood the worth and influence of Mary, who I was taught, had been conceived without original sin, and remained a virgin all her life, never having any other children, and did not die, but was assumed up into heaven. We prayed to her because when, at the marriage feast at Cana, Jesus said that his hour had not yet come to perform a miracle, he, nevertheless, turned the water into wine because his mother had asked him. The implication being that if Mary asked anything on our behalf, Jesus would definitely grant her request, although he might refuse ours.

I learned how saints were first beatified and called blessed because their lives had given evidence of great piety, prayer, and good works. They were later canonized if there was proof that three miracles had been granted in their names. Then we could pray to them. I was grateful for the efficacious power of novenas and indulgences, in helping to defray the debt of sin, just in case I should not get Extreme Unction and went to purgatory.

I memorized the corporal and spiritual works of mercy; the sins that cry out to God for vengeance, the fruit and the gifts of the Holy Spirit.

I understood that when the bishop laid his hand on my head I would receive the Holy Ghost, who will strengthen me in my faith, and help me to live a holy life. We learned hymns that invited the Holy Ghost to come upon us. We even had to learn hymns in Latin, which made us feel quite holy. Eventually, we were tested to determine the level of our knowledge of Catholic doctrine, and subsequently, our readiness for confirmation. Then it was time for confession. Confession must precede the reception of every other sacrament, except of course, baptism, which was conferred on infants.

It had been almost two years since Mama had allowed us to go to the Catholic Church and I was frightened and ashamed of the many sins I had to confess, especially the mortal sin of missing mass. The priest, father Graham questioned me. I had to tell the truth about Mama. I understood that she was bound for hell, but I knew better. I would do my best to be a good Catholic so I could go to heaven.

Confirmation day was another momentous day. I recall how one of the very pious girls seemed to be having a fit when the bishop pronounced the words of confirmation. “Receive ye the Holy Ghost.” I think she really did.

By the time I turned thirteen I was a staunch Catholic. During my first year in Holy Name Convent High school, I was wracked with the guilt of participating in both the Gospel Hall, and the Anglican Church that Mama made us attend with her some Sunday nights. Catholics were not free to enter the church building of any other denomination, for any reason, not even a wedding or funeral. Consider then, the great sin I had committed in religiously attending Gospel Hall.

When I told Mama that I did not want to go there anymore, she said I was talking "chupidness". But when I told her that, if I was seen going there I would be expelled from Holy Name Convent High School, she gave in. She did not want to incur the wrath of the Catholics, and besides academic education was more important to my success in life, and therefore took precedence over my biblical instruction. She allowed me to quit Gospel Hall Sunday school.

At that time, I was the oldest child still attending Sunday school. My eldest brother and sister were past the age, and my older brother who had become rebelliously unmanageable, refused to go. It was up to me to take my three smaller sisters to Sunday school, so when I stopped going that was the end of the family's Bible based Christian education.

I joined the "Legion of Mary". Meetings were held weekly, which began with the leader declaring, "*Who is she that cometh forth as the morning rising, fair as the moon, bright as the sun and terrible as an army set in battle array?"* Then we recited the Magnificat and said the rosary. Each person reported on what spiritual and temporal works of mercy she had accomplished, new assignments were given and the meeting closed. Spiritual works were prayer and meditation. Temporal works were easier. One could visit the orphanage and help take care of the babies, comb the children's hair, or help them with their homework. One could visit the L'Hospice and chat with the elderly or take a plate of food to the poor in the St. Andrews' home. I enjoyed the legion of Mary.

Another exciting and interesting part of Catholic life in Trinidad was the pilgrimage on the thirteenth of every month from May to October.

Up on the Laventille Hill is a grotto. It is a duplicate of the shrine in Fatima, Portugal, where three children had had visions and received messages from "the Virgin Mary." Every month, Catholic children walked from their schools, to the Grotto to pray and sing hymns of devotion to the lady of Fatima. We wore the holy scapula medal, as a sign of our faith. Led by the Archbishop, we prayed all fifteen mysteries of the rosary. It was a spiritual work that gained great indulgences. It was also a time to meet and mingle with boys. Our schools were not mixed, and ordinarily, we were forbidden to talk to boys, while in our school uniforms, on pain of suspension from school.

In high school we no longer used catechisms. Our textbook of Catholic doctrine explained the reasons for the crusades and introduced us to the executed heretics such as Martin Luther and John Knox. And I believed it all. Bible Knowledge was a regular subject on the curriculum. Each student had a copy of the Douay Version of the Bible. However we only studied the gospels of Matthew, Mark, and Luke, and the Acts of the Apostles. We were required to learn the Beatitudes, the Sermon on the Mount, and the Parables and Miracles, and be able to trace the path of the three Missionary Journeys of Paul.

When I was about to graduate from Holy Name Convent, Mother Mary Petra called me aside and said, "Andrea we believe you have a vocation. Have you every considered becoming a nun?" "No, I hadn't". She advised me to prayerfully consider the idea. I never did.

But I did have a spiritual vocation. It is the High Calling of God in Jesus Christ.

-10- The Power And The Problem Of Older Siblings

In my youth, in my culture, older brothers and sisters had almost as much weight and authority as parents, and so their appraisal was very important. Approval or rejection by them evoked much emotion. But they were only children, and children are unwise and can be very unkind.

My Big Brother

I remember how I revered Gregory, my big brother, and how devastated I was the day he stopped talking to me. I was about eleven when for reasons which have eluded my memory, I had hit out at him in anger. Such an action was an outrageous display of impudence. Being twelve years older than me, Gregory was given all the authority of a father, and we accepted it as so. We all had to mind what he said. He would have been within his rights as big brother and wage earner to respond with a beating. Instead he did the worse thing possible. He stopped speaking to me.

When he became a teacher, he was assigned to a school far in the country and only came home at the end of each month when he got paid. We all looked forward to his coming. We knew that there would be money in the house. Besides that we had such fun with him. He used to bring us Cadburys' milk chocolate. Mama usually prepared a special dish of chicken and macaroni pie for him. Sometimes he wasn't hungry and he'd just pick at the food while we stood there waiting for his attention and leftovers. Even Mama shared in the leftovers.

After he had eaten, he would get very serious and ask us if we were behaving ourselves and enquire about our progress in school. I remember once the teacher had given us a mathematic problem to find an unknown quantity. It was the first of that type of problem. I could not understand it the way my teacher had explained it, but my big brother showed me a different way to work it out. When my teacher saw how I had done it, she asked me to explain it to the class and that is how we did those problems from that time. I was so proud. In my mind my big brother was a genius.

The best time was when, my little sister and I would sit on his knees while he sang folk songs; or we would sing while he strummed his guitar, which he had taught himself to play. He also wrote poems, which he would recite to us. I used to learn his poems, which I actually recited in school.

When he was all dressed up to go out, he would look in the mirror, flash himself a smile and say, "Mirror, mirror on the wall, who is the handsomest of us all?' Then in a fine voice, he would answer, "Gregory". And if we called him, "His Most handsome", he would put his hand in his pocket and reward us with some money. We played that game for years. It was grand when he came.

That day when I hit him the fun times stopped for me. I dared not complain to Mama about him. Firstly, he was my big brother who could do no wrong, and secondly, I had hit him. I used to be very sad and lonely when he came home and ignored me. When we moved from Uncle Freddie's house, he started coming home twice a month. I was miserable, figuring if Mama ever found out what was going on, I would be in big trouble. Everybody knew, but nobody told. We used to cover for each other, protecting each other from Mama's wrath. Eventually, after two years Mamma noticed that I was an outcast from Gregory's company and demanded to know what was going on between us. To my surprise, she rebuked him for holding malice against me. She said that as long as we were in her house she would not have any of us not speaking to another.

Maybe like me, he had even forgotten why I had hit him. Anyhow, we became friends again. I loved my big brother. I was growing up, learning to use make up, and he would examine my face and tell me that I must make sure that the foundation blended into the skin on my neck so that I did not appear to have on any. He tried to teach me to waltz, but that didn't work too well. He introduced me to Edgar Ellen Poe and used to read his stories with such dramatization that my imagination kept me awake for hours.

Eventually Gregory escaped to America, having obtained a scholarship to the University of Madison, Wisconsin. He had been pursuing his studies in agriculture at the University of the West Indies. By the time he returned, I was going crazy and needed to get out of Mama's house to keep my sanity. Perhaps if he had remained and mentored me I would have developed some dreams of importance, but I had had no guidance. I had completed high school and having worked at the treasury for a while, had then been accepted by the Catholic teacher's board as a primary school teacher. I was the breadwinner in my mother's house. That was not a problem. It was the quarreling and the accusations that made me unhappy.

Why I Went Against My Big Brother And Lost His Friendship

I went to stay at Gregory's house when he returned to Trinidad, only to discover that living in his house was tantamount to prison. He was still big brother, and although I was eighteen and employed, I had to adhere to his rules, some of which were ridiculous. For instance, it was vacation time, yet everyone in his household had to be up, showered, properly dressed (no dressing gowns), and be at the breakfast table, by 7:30am. Then we had to drink orange juice and take phospherine tonic. I know that there is nothing wrong with that, but one should have a choice. I was also not allowed to wear shorts nor go out without his permission, and I had to be home before dark

Dinner had to be waited for him, and after dinner I had to sit in the company of his friends who discussed subjects that did not interest me. My boyfriend could not visit. My brother said that there were two kinds of people, scientists and others. It was alright for me to socialize with his friends. My boyfriend was an "other". He was an electrician. The fact is, that I was a teenager, and I had no life.

Gregory friends, those brilliant minds with whom he associated were men of questionable character. I was acquainted with four of his friends. They used to visit our home. Mama accepted Gregory's friends and would never have suspected how lacking in integrity they were. One befriended me at a time when my boyfriend and I broke up. He attempted to rape me. You'll read about him later. Another planned a birthday party for me when I was eighteen. I felt so special. On the way to his house where the party was being held, he parked and locked his car on the Lady Young Road lookout, and reached for me. I threatened to scream and tell my big brother and he changed his mind. The other two proved very false to my brother, but they are not part of my story.

Before making the decision to live at my brother's, I had considered getting a furnished room and living on my own. It was not the normal thing to do. Good girls stayed at home until they got married. I had gone to see a room, but I couldn't afford the rent. I needed to be able to help Mama financially even if I wasn't living there. She depended on me. I paid her rent and I couldn't afford two rents. She had no other income besides mine, and the support she received for my two youngest sisters from their father. So it seemed a good plan, since Gregory had returned, and we had remained good friends, to stay with him and his wife. But I soon realized I was between a rock and a hard place.

One Friday afternoon, I told him that I had to go to the city for some good reason. I met my boyfriend and I complained to him, "I can't take living at my brother, it is a prison; and I can't take living at Mama, I've had enough of the verbal abuse." My boyfriend, who had proposed to me at sixteen when Mama had grounded me indefinitely and I had starved myself into malnutrition; at seventeen, when I first started to work and was exposed to more eligible men; now presented the same solution to my problem. "Let's get married." This time I said yes.

That same afternoon we pooled our resources and bought a diamond engagement ring. With the ring in the box I returned to my brother's house, while my boyfriend went home to write the appropriate letter asking for my hand in marriage, and to present it to Mama. He also had to acquaint his parents with our plans. That was a very courageous thing for him to do.

I confided to my sister-in-law that I was to be engaged on the Sunday. We had arranged for Paul, my boyfriend, to come to my brother's house on Saturday afternoon after he had spoken to Mama. If she reacted favorably towards our proposed engagement, he would then ask her to allow me to come back home. Depending on her response, he would take me home. At least he could visit me there. Linda, Gregory's wife, advised me to inform him of my plans. I was terrified to talk to my big brother, but I was desperate, and desperation gave me courage. So, on Saturday morning, at the breakfast table, I produced my engagement ring and told my brother the wonderful news.

He exploded. "That chupid boy you going to marry!!. You could do better than that!" Then he made me an offer he thought I couldn't refuse. He said that I had a good brain and could make something better out of my life; that I needed to go to university; that he would finance my college education, provide room, board, and necessities until I attained some degree. I needed to be exposed to a more educated, better class of people. All this he would do for me, if I would change my mind about marrying Paul.

Perhaps, if the offer had been made a year earlier when I left high school, I would have considered it. Perhaps if he had had a different tone of voice and had offered me a different reason for his very generous offer so that it didn't seem like a bribe, I would have considered it. If he had been able to impart a vision of what I could be, so that I could believe him, I might have accepted his offer and tolerated the prison he called a home. He could have said that if we were really in love Paul would want me to have the education and he would wait for me. That might have had some positive effect. You don't tell an eighteen year old who believes that the only person in the world who cares about her is her boyfriend, with whom she has been in love since fifteen, that she shouldn't marry that chupid boy because he is only an electrician.

That evening Paul came and I moved back to Mama's house. I think my brother lost respect for me that day. Since then, he has always treated me like a child of lesser intelligence and has always been of the opinion that I made a mess of my life. When I was thirty-two and divorced with two children, he came to visit me in New York, where I had been living for ten years. I had been through many changes, being divorced being the worst of them, and I had been paddling my own canoe with two children for several years, I had become a Christian, and had acquired new Christ-centered friends. He categorized all my friends as 'chupid' and asked me, "Now that you are getting to be a big girl, what plans do you have for your life?" I was incredulous. I was a great disappointment to him.

In 1988 when my mother was struck down by breast cancer, my brother thought that if Mama were not made aware of the truth of her condition, she would live longer. The doctor had said that she had cancer all over her body, except for her brain. Gregory who was with me when the diagnosis was rendered immediately decided that Mama was not to be told. He told her that her body's pains were caused by arthritis, and she grasped at the straw he handed her. A year previously she had had a mastectomy and had told us that the surgery had been completely successful. But she had lied. I later learned that she'd been given a year to live. However, she was in denial and so was he.

Eventually, seeing my mother deteriorating without proper pain medication because of my brother's stupidity, I told her the truth. I was concerned for her soul and wanted her to have opportunity to repent and make things right with whosoever and God, before she died. My brother was angry. He took me off her case, installed another sister in the house, and totally ostracized me. I went back to New York.

Two months later when Mama died, my brother, knowing that I was arriving at two o'clock in the afternoon on the day of the funeral, had the funeral service in the morning, and my mother was buried before the plane touched down. I was enraged. I was the one who knew what dress she had wanted to be buried in. She had talked to me about the hymns she wanted sung at her funeral. Nothing was done according to her request. Gregory didn't even church her in the Seventh day Adventist Church where she had been a member for twenty-two years.

I was enraged. I hated him. He had known nothing about her life. Until she was dying, he had avoided her. He was ashamed of her because of the manner in which she had lived her life. He was ashamed of her being Miss Palmer, and he being Dr.Gegory X. When someone in Trinidad, died, an announcement was usually made on the radio so that people would be informed and could attend the funeral. A normal announcement would say, "We've been asked to announce the death of Alice Palmer, who lived at such a place. She was the mother of (and all her children would be named), sister of—, friend of ——. The announcement that my brother requested made her appear to have neither family nor friends. And Mama was well-liked and well known for her kindness to others.

In the rage and wickedness of my heart, I had a notice placed in the newspaper publicizing her death and past funeral. I made sure to mention all her children, with all their names and aliases, with special emphasis given to her first son Dr. Gregory X, who was the director of XYZ. I wanted the world to know who she was and who he was. I didn't know how to express the rage of anger, but I knew how to get even.

Almost immediately the Lord began to discomfort me with the compulsion of forgiveness. For a couple of weeks I agonized over my Christian duty; and unable to enjoy any peace while I held my brother in hatred, I forgave him. Nevertheless, because of distance, lack of opportunity, and the knowledge that Gregory had promised to sic his dog on me if I ventured into his yard, I didn't seek him out for four years. When I returned to Trinidad four and a half years later my brother-in-law took me to Gregory's house. He did not sic the dogs on me, but entertained me with his condescending, Mr. All-wise-everybody-else-is-stupid attitude that I tolerated, while trying tactfully to express a contrary opinion. In response, he charged me with lack of knowledge and understanding. And so we were reconciled.

However his overbearing big brother attitude that continues to this day, makes a relationship with him impossible. Whenever I visited him, I tried not to be alone in his company. He seemed to always try to intimidate and overpower me. I respected him as my big brother, but I don't like him anymore.

Recently, I had a thanksgiving celebration to give thanks to God, in the midst of my family, for miraculously saving my life. I invited my brother, but he felt disrespected because I chose to stay at my best friend's home, where the celebration was held, rather than his. I am sorry he didn't attend my party. I think I still wanted him to see what God had done in my life and be proud of me. I'm sorry for him. If he could stop being the big know-it-all brother, recognize that the rest of us are adults for whom he is not responsible, and who have no responsibility of accountability to him, he could join the family. But I guess he has been that way too long.

Gregory wanted something from us that we didn't give him and we should have. He wanted recognition. He has achieved much but his family was too busy fighting to survive to notice and honor him. Besides I think we all just wanted the guitar strumming, folk song singing, poetry reading, His Most Handsome, who could participate in life at our level. The Scientist was beyond our reach.

He wants to give us what we do not want and can't understand that we cannot be bribed into his life.

The house in which Mama lived at the time of her death had been Gregory's; but more than that, it had become the family home. She had lived there for nineteen years and it was that home to which we all returned from time to time. He never liked that house. It didn't suit his elevated position. One of us, especially me, who had no other roots, would have bought that house and kept it in the family. But without informing anyone of his plans, and doing what he felt was best for us, my big brother sold the property and bought twenty-five acres of agricultural land in a remote area. We were expected to applaud his foresight because his purchase could provide food and shelter for all his brothers and sisters.

Looking back I realized that he had never reached out to me after my wedding day, when he took me to the church. Even twenty-five years later when my first son who idolized him died, Gregory did not phone to offer his condolences. Even when I almost died and everybody who loved me showed concern, Gregory did not phone. Why? Perhaps he doesn't know how to reach out to someone. Perhaps he has so much hurt that he can't afford to add my hurt to his pile. Perhaps he received the largest portion of the legacy of pride and independence, which Mama left us, and suffers from the same fears, the same damaged emotions, which had blinded me to truth and reality, and prevented me from embracing people in particular, and life in general, with passion.

It is obvious that he needs family, but none of us can live his life. What he fails to realize or believe is that we all love him, but we will not sacrifice ourselves on the tyrannical altar of his arrogance. His approval no longer matters to us. Right now he and I have no relationship. He still remains divorced from my life. I am sorry.

My Big Sister

My big sister nicknamed me "Clumsy". I was somewhat cubby as a pre-teen and due to my love for running and my problem foot, I bumped into things and fell quite often. Marcia said I would never have a figure, and I would never have a boyfriend. She had lots of handsome beaus. So I took her words to heart and set out to get a figure and lose my clumsiness. And I succeeded.

When I had the Asian flu at the age of ten, I was so sick for so long, that my baby fat melted away. At about age thirteen I started belting my waist so tightly that when I removed the belt my waist was swollen with welts. Even if the outfit I was wearing didn't need a belt, I put one on under my skirt. I don't know if the belt helped, but I did acquire a very attractive figure.

When I compared myself with Marcia, I never thought I could ever step into her shoes. In my eyes, my sister was outstanding. She was petite with a 32-22-32 figure; and she knew how to accentuate her best features to make herself more attractive. I thought she was as pretty as any princess in my library books. I was not jealous of her. I just admired her. I never thought that she was too short, therefore, when I realized that I was taller than her by about three inches, I felt rather awkward.

I was unaware that my height was just average and that I was prettier than her. I realized that I wasn't ugly, but even my boyfriend admired my brains more than my beauty. Not too long ago I met someone from my teenage years who remembers me as being petite. I had to smile. Petite was desirable. I never thought myself so. Actually I had maintained one hundred and twenty-five pounds on a five feet, six inches frame from about age thirteen to thirty five. With a twenty-three and a half inch waist, thirty-six inch hips, and thirty-four bust size, I guess I looked quite attractive.

I was precocious, and loved to pretend to be older than my age. It was Marcia's policy not to get ready for a date, until her beaus arrived. It became my happy privilege and interesting duty to sit in the drawing room and entertain her friends, while she got dressed. I took those opportunities to slip into my grown up role and discuss articles of interest in the newspapers, making intelligent comments in perfect English with proper diction. I think I amused her friends and they found me friendly and likable. But I did not set out to impress them. I just loved living my fantasies. My big sister had issue with me over her boyfriends, but I was never interested in any one of them. Handsome as they were, they were too old for me, and besides, I had my own boyfriends.

Some Sundays, Mama went to the country to visit a friend and she did not return until we were all in bed. Then, I was not allowed to go to the park or by the savannah, which was where I usually took a walk on Sunday evenings with my smaller sisters and my friends. With nothing to do when Mama was not at home (there was no television), I usually set about transforming myself into a femme fatale. I would put on my sister's hobble skirt and belt my waist painfully tight to accentuate my hips, pad my bra, comb my hair in a Carmen-Jones style with a French roll, apply red lipstick and rouge, and lengthen my eyebrow with eyeliner. Then I'd just stroll down the lane and up the street to chat with my friend Carol, feeling all of eighteen years, wanting to look like my big sister. Marcia did not appreciate my attitude, but she did not tell on me.

One way in which I was disappointed in her was this. I had expected and looked forward to the day when my big sister would take me and introduce me to the exciting world of parties in which she lived. And I had thought that when she started working she would see that I had a supply of money, a promise she had made when I used to steal Mama's money to give her. But neither of those things happened. I suppose she was saving to escape.

Marcia was a teacher but desired to be a nurse, so when I was fifteen, she set sail for London. We all went to the ship to see her off. The watch that Mama had presented me for winning the exhibition scholarship was my pride and joy. A few months before Marcia traveled, something had gone wrong with my watch, but Mama could not afford to have it fixed. However, even though it could not tell accurate time, I never stopped wearing it. On the morning of the day Marcia was leaving,

Mama asked me for my watch and took it to have it repaired. She said that she had no farewell gift for Marcia, therefore she would give her my watch, and one day, buy me another. I was not happy. It was not fair.

On the way to the ship from the repair shop, Mama lost the watch and I felt better. I preferred to know that neither of us had it.

It was about fourteen years before I visited London to attend Deborah's wedding and saw my sister again. I understood that she had been to New York several times but had never considered looking me up. The physical distance and lack of interest in each other's lives had put emotional mileage between us.

It gives me great pleasure to say that Marcia and I are now good friends and have a beautiful caring relationship. She has stepped up to the plate as a big sister, letting us know that she is there for us, caring for us unconditionally, willing to help if need be and if she can. If I had ever reached out to her for assistance, even during the years that we were not close, I know she would have helped me. Over the years we have communicated in the effort to resolve issues of our childhood. And we have. I know she loves me and I hope she knows that I love her.

Less Important Siblings

My brother Gerald, who was four years older than me, nicknamed me "Brokofoot." He wasn't that important to me. Maybe if he had stayed in school and acquired some decent friends (by Mama's standards), I would have looked to him as a source of boyfriends; but he became rebellious at about thirteen and his companions were the undesirables. I believe that I discounted him because he never behaved like a real big brother. He could not be depended upon for anything. He obviously cared about no one but himself. Gerald distressed me until I became indifferent to him. He used to find my piggy-bank and steal my money.

There was a time when I had no comfortable shoes. I had outgrown my shoes and the hand-me-down pair that I had to wear was so hard that my feet hurt to the point of tears. One day, seeing my obvious misery, my boyfriend took me to Bata's Shoe Store and bought me a very comfortable pair of shoes. Strange, but Mama never asked me where I got the money to buy such shoes. Perhaps, because she couldn't afford them and she knew how much I needed them, she just kept quiet.

Anyhow, on Carnival Sunday night my shoes disappeared and re-appeared caked with mud, on Ash Wednesday. Gerald had needed comfortable shoes to walk the streets, playing in the steel orchestra during the carnival and he had taken my best shoes.

This brother just did as he pleased; took what he wanted; always was up to some mischief, always had a scheme to outsmart somebody; always got himself in trouble and had to be bailed out. The policeman's knock on the door became a constant in our lives. Gerald shamed the family and Mama cried oceans over him. She went to the obeah woman to see if she could get some potion to take away his bad behavior. She even went to the Catholic Church to burn a candle for him. Nothing worked. Gregory paid to have him go to the Seven Day's Adventist boarding school away from the influence of vagabonds but that proved to be a very temporary respite for the family. But this is my story not his.

Gerald migrated to New York before I did and I had hoped that being strangers in a strange land we would have become close, but in the thirty years that we both lived on American soil, I didn't see my bother ten times. Throughout all the troubles of my life, he was never there. He only appeared when Mama or Deborah came to visit. At such times I had to put the word out that they were visiting, eventually the message reached him and he turned up. God knows I could have used a brother when I got divorced, when Ian turned rebellious, and especially when Allan died.

Nevertheless, I did try to help Gerald whenever he showed

signs of desiring positive change. I was always disappointed. I think Gerald is more family-oriented now. I hope his journey ends is peace and that he finds his purpose. I've also discovered that I do love him. I may never trust him, but he's my brother.

I have an older sister, one who wasn't raised with us. That's Precious. We didn't interact much except at vacation time. I was not a risk taker, and she was, and I was sure to get into trouble by following her example. Like the time when we were only allowed to go to the park but Precious wanted to visit a boyfriend in an area with which I was unfamiliar. It got late and I wanted to go home, but I couldn't leave her. I didn't want to tattle on her, and besides I didn't know my way home. When we finally arrived home I got into trouble, because Mama said she depended on me to let Precious know the rules of our house, and that included the time we should be home, before dark.

Then there was the time when Precious came to Mama and said that her adopted mother wanted Deborah and I to stay for a week at her home. To our joy, Mama allowed us to go. On the way there, Precious stopped to buy groceries, and advised me to tell her Mama, that our mother had visitors and asked could we stay for a week. I was to give her Mama the groceries that my Mama had sent. She knew that her mother was going to be busy at the Church that weekend and we would be on our own. Her mother trusted her. That's how I came to be kissed on the lips by Solomon or Leslie.

My main purpose in life at that time was to stay out of trouble. Precious was not the right companion for me.

By the time I was able to cultivate a relationship with her, I was struggling to survive Mama, getting married, and moving away. However, we were always aware of the bond between us. Now we are sisters twice, for we are sisters in Christ and we enjoy a beautiful relationship. We know that we love each other.

Mama had two daughters after we moved from Uncle Freddy's house, Janice and Jillian. I loved my sisters but by the time they were seven and ten, I was married and gone. However, we kept in touch, especially since my children were part of their lives for some time. At present we have truly loving relationships.

Sisters Bonded By Abuse

Four years after Mama died, Precious, Deborah, Janice, Jillian and I got together for the first time in years and began to open up our hearts to each other. We were each astonished to discover that each of us thought herself to have been most ill-treated and disliked by Mama. We each related stories of her cruel destructive tongue, and her beatings. Janice and Jillian had felt that Deborah and I were favored. We had believed that they were the favored ones. We were surprised to find that Precious, who had not had the dubious pleasure and the pain of actually living with us, had her own stories to tell. We had been separated by the illusion of Mama's favoritism. But it seems that she had no favorites. We wished that Marcia and Gerald were with us, because we knew that they also had stories to tell. We concluded that she hated all of us. Had a good laugh and started to build a closeness that she could no longer rip apart.

I used to say that I was glad that my mother died because, except for Gregory, my maternal siblings came together as a family, after her death.

-11- My Cousin

When I was eleven, Mama who had been away from her homeland for about fifteen years, decided to take her Trinidadian children to St. Vincent for a visit. That meant my brother Gerald, my sisters Deborah and Janice, and me. At that time Janice's father was able and willing to finance the trip and with the help of a "Sou Sou," Mama was able to prepare us to meet her family.

Preparation meant getting us some new clothes and buying presents to give to all and sundry. The story was that she had done well, so she had to prove it. She borrowed some beautiful dresses from her niece Catherine, and placed a plain gold band on the third finger of her left hand. Gerald, Deborah, and I were light complexioned, Janice was dark-skinned. But that was alright. So was Mama. We could all pass for being the children of her "husband".

We set sail on the Carib Clipper. Before it was out of the harbor, I was throwing up. We could only afford deck seats, but I was so sick that a family let me lie in their cabin. It was a rough twenty-four hours. Two days after I had set my foot back on terra firma, my head was still spinning and my stomach remained unsettled.

Everyone was glad to see us. Mama dressed us in our new clothes and we swept through the town looking very important and prosperous. She flaunted her wedding ring and informed her family and old acquaintances that her husband's business prevented him from coming. He would come next time. She distributed her presents with the air of royalty and promised to send other needed things when she returned. Mama's family didn't give us any presents, not even Uncle Mike who owned a grocery and liquor store. I guess we were just too rich to want anything that they could offer. Alice proved to her hometown that she had made good.

We stayed at my Aunt May's whose husband was a pastor. I liked it there in that big house where there was plenty to eat. At nights after supper, we sat on the floor with Uncle Harry and he told us wonderful stories of Brer Anancy and other folk tales. Best of all we had very few restrictions. We were allowed to play with all my cousins' friends.

My cousins were seven and thirteen year old boys. So their friends were boys. Like Deborah and I, the younger one was small for his age, the older one was big. His name was Charles. Sometimes his behavior was repulsive. He liked to talk about dissecting rats and frogs, especially at meal times.

One night at supper, he began his usual disgusting conversation about cutting up rats and eating them. My stomach was so upset that I asked to be excused from the table and went to lie down. I was dozing off when Charles came into the room and asked how I was feeling. He was laughing. My being squeamish was funny to him.

Then he got on top of me. As I began to struggle under him, my little cousin came in, saw what was happening and exclaimed so that Mama and Tantie, who were still in the dining room, could hear. "Charles is on top of Andra!!" With that, both mothers appeared in the room. My mother dragged me away, as if it was my fault. She didn't listen to anything I tried to say. I felt that it was a good thing I hadn't told about Uncle Freddie.

Of course, I was no longer allowed to play with Charles and his friends and had to stay where Mama could keep an eye on me.

Two other things that were important to me happened in my mother's hometown.

My cousin Lilly was a teenager with a little baby named Brian. I asked her how the baby came out of her stomach. I was not curious about how it got there. God made babies. Anyway she showed me a scar on her stomach and told me that the doctor had to cut her stomach to take the baby out. Not having a curious nature about such things, it wasn't until I was about to have my own child that I asked the question again. I was horrified when the midwife said, "same way it go in, same way it come out."

My cousin had a friend named Ronald who obviously liked me. I had liked Robert who was taller and better looking than Ronald, but he was a jerk. He told everybody that he was my boyfriend. He had no right to say those things, so I stopped talking to him. Ronald however was a quiet boy who seemed content to sit on the veranda in view of the grownups and talk to me.

When we were leaving, he asked Uncle Harry if he could come to the boat with us. While Mama and her family were saying their goodbyes Ronald and I walked around the boat to explore. In the middle of our conversation he asked if he could kiss me. I told him yes. I was expecting a kiss on my cheek. Instead he put his lips to mine and tried to get his tongue in my mouth. I was outraged. I hit him, pushed him away, stared at him in disbelief, and spat and spat. All he could say was, "I love you. I will never forget you."

-12- Significant Friends

Girl Friends

A precious moment in my emotional life was the day I asked my best friend Cheryl if she was not embarrassed to walk with me. We were about thirteen then, and physical attractiveness had become very important. She asked me why would I think that she might be. I replied, "Because of my limp." Her incredulous response was, "What limp?" And I knew she was sincere. Her love had blinded her to my defect. I have found that people who love me don't notice my physical imperfections, and even if they do initially, they soon forget them.

When I was in the third standard, Alison Fraiser and I were best friends. We both loved to draw. One day I messed up with her painting and she became very angry. She stopped talking to me and we were never friends again. Looking back I think that was a tragic thing to happen between two nine year olds.

Forever friends

In fourth standard, Cheryl and I became friends for life. She belonged to a very respectable family. Her mother and father were the best examples of parenting that I have ever known. They were a very close-knit family and from the start Cheryl's parents, as well as her two younger sisters and brother accepted me into their household. It was customary for close friends to address each other parents by the same generic parental names by which their own children addressed them. I called Cheryl's parents, Mummy and Daddy. My friends called my mother Mama.

Cheryl's Daddy was a police officer while her Mummy was a seamstress by profession and a jack-of-all-trades by practice. I became a part of their household, and I never heard them quarrel, curse, or fight. They watched over and guided their children into appropriate careers, and always showed affection to their children, appreciation for their achievements, support in their undertakings, and kindness, understanding and encouragements in their times of failure or trouble.

Cheryl's house was half way between the school and my house. Every morning and mid-day, I stopped by to meet her so we could walk to school together. Many mornings and middays when I arrived at their house, I met Cheryl and her sisters at the table groaning over the good delicious food they had been given. They didn't like to eat. I would offer to help Cheryl and I would be compelled to help Yolande and Pamela also, else they would squeal on Cheryl. It was my pleasure. I had a hearty appetite.

Ours was a very productive relationship. We both enjoyed

reading and sharing the stories, which we read. We both loved poetry as did our sisters and we had concerts in Cheryl's drawing room with her parents and grandmother as our audience. They were very supportive and applauded our efforts as if we had achieved Oscar winning performances. Mama never refused to allow me to go to their house or to go out with them. The very first party I attended was our friend Margaret's thirteenth birthday party. Cheryl's Daddy escorted us. It was the only way Mama would have permitted me to go.

In the period before Paul became a part of my life, Cheryl with her sisters and brother, and I with my sister Deborah, had great fun on Sunday evenings. There was a children's radio talent program and we regularly joined the audience. We even auditioned and were accepted to recite poetry. After the program was over, we took our siblings either to the grounds of the Princess Building or to the Rock Gardens.

On the grounds of the Princess Building were two fountains. We would climb up on the edge of the fountain and walk around holding each other as we tried to keep our balance. One day we all fell into the water. We had to get dry and respectable looking before we could go home, else, we were sure of a beating and we would probably be grounded for life. That day we ran for miles so that the wind and sun would dry nylon dresses, slips, socks, ribbons and hair. Our siblings were sworn to secrecy.

The Rock Gardens were situated in a hollow, at the north end of the savannah, the sides of which were grassy slopes. We enjoyed rolling down the slopes. We would lie at the top and start rolling, picking up velocity as we tumbled along laughing and getting our clothes and hair dirty with grass and sweetheart seeds. When it was time to go home, we inspected each other and after making ourselves as clean as possible, we invariably held hands and started running in order to arrive home before dark.

A couple of years after I started at Holy Name Convent, I discovered that Cheryl had another friend and I was jealous. The young woman was a proper lady and I thought that I had lost Cheryl as my best friend, because it was obvious to me that Ira was a more desirable person for her to have as a friend than me. I withdrew a bit from the family to give her space, but I was very sad. Of course I had other friends and by that time I was going steady. But I missed the closeness I'd had with Cheryl and I missed her whole family. Needless to say, it was just my insecurity rising up. We have never ever stopped being best friends. Cheryl became the godmother of my first son.

Margaret is another lifetime friend from primary school days. It was her thirteenth birthday party that we had attended.

Margaret and I were allowed to visit each other and I looked forward, once a year to spending a week at her house. Her Mama was strict, like all parents, but she was kind. (It was she who made my wedding dress). We didn't live close to each other, so most of our time together was during school hours. Margaret and I also shared a love for literature in particular and learning in general. We were in exhibition class together, and in the afternoons we enjoyed playing parliament. We used to listen to the government program broadcast each night, and the next day the students of the exhibition class staged the parliamentary proceedings, each of us portraying a particular member of parliament. It was a fun way to stay abreast of current events.

The next best thing to staying at Providence would have been going to St. Joseph's Convent with my friend Margaret. Sadly, we were sent to different high schools. However we kept the friendship going.

When I started to work, I did not visit Margaret as frequently as when I was just going to school. Life was busier, there were work related activities; and I needed time for courtship. One evening I went to visit her, and her mother pulled me aside and distressed me by suggesting that I didn't want Margaret for a friend because I was employed and she wasn't. I was so hurt that I cried. My boyfriend who had accompanied me to her house was very upset and wanted us to leave immediately. But I think Mama was just upset because it seemed like I was neglecting my friend. I spoke to Margaret about the confrontation, and she shrugged and said I shouldn't worry about what her mother said. She wasn't of the same opinion.

After I migrated to New York and she went to London we lost touch. Imagine how happy I was one day when my husband came home with the glad news that he had met Margaret's husband. She then lived in Canada. Paul had her phone number. I telephoned her immediately. She was as happy to hear from me and to learn that I had just had my second baby, as I was to hear that she was pregnant with her first. We chatted for hours catching up on each other's life. A few months later, she moved to New York and we resumed our close friendship to this present day.

My High School Best Friend

A new school meant a new best friend. Juliana was my high school best friend. She was a small, thin ambitious girl who understood the prejudice of the nuns and the bondage of Catholicism much more than I did. She was a dreamer like me, but a more realistic dreamer. My mother liked her and when there was much food in the house Mama would tell me to invite Juliana to stay with us a few days. She tried to fatten her, but some people were born to be small and thin. Juliana enjoyed the way my mother pampered her. Her parents were married, and her father was not poor, but he did not provide, as he should have and could have, for his family. She and I shared an understanding of poverty that bonded us together.

One day I told her that she would be my first baby's godmother. We were probably just chatting about what we expected our futures to be when I said that. Anyway I totally forgot ever making that promise and so I asked Cheryl to be my baby's godmother. If Juliana had reminded me of my promise to her, Allan would have had two wonderful godmothers, but she was hurt and offended and it was years before she told me what was wrong.

Juliana migrated to England to study Psychiatry. I used to tell her that she laid her own train tracks, built her own train and drove it all the way to success. She had no help or guidance. She just made up her mind and set out. We have visited each other over the years. When she became a Buddhist I figured that we couldn't be friends anymore. But praise God! I received a midnight call from her not too long ago. My friend received Jesus as her Savior and Lord. I am so grateful. We are even better friends now.

Other Girl Friends

I have had other friends like Margarita who I knew from primary school and high school, but our friendship developed later when we met as young adults. She is also a lifetime friend.

Of course there is Carol who was genuinely saddened and disappointed by the news that Paul and I had divorced. She too is a lifetime friend.

Over the years of my Christian pilgrimage, I have been blessed with genuine, caring, beautiful friends, both male and female. I believe that friendship is a priceless gift and I treasure these God-sent gifts that have blessed my life. If I do not elaborate on these friends it is only because they were not part of the years of emotional damage that disfigured and devalued me.

Boyfriends

I also had boyfriends, who chose me above the girls who had perfect feet and walked without limping. In those days having a boyfriend was simple and perhaps a little silly; but so important to a girl like me.

When we first moved to the Valley Road, before I was considered responsible enough to take the longer Savannah walks, my little sisters and I used to play in Belmont Park on Sunday evenings. Of course, that was with Mama's permission. The only stipulation was that we got home before darkness fell. We were never given a time. It was always, "before darkness fell, or it would be the last time you get to go to the park".

Immediately after Sunday school was over, we used to visit Deborah's godmother whose house was full of quaint ornaments and toys. She had a twenty-inch doll with which she permitted us to us play. Her name was Ardit and we loved her. Eventually Mrs. Benson gave her to us. Anyway, she used to fill our handbags with fancy candies. She and her husband, as well as her brother with whom she lived, always gave us pocket change, which we were not allowed to spend. We carried all money home to Mama. We would wait until we had our booty, then to show good manners as we were taught, we would stay fifteen minutes longer, before we said our goodbye and left for the park.

Even at twelve, I wanted to be considered grown-up, especially when I wore my big sister hand-me-downs which were styled for her age, not mine. Clothes usually told the story of one's maturity. Little children wore short dresses with sashes, that allowed their frilly panties to show when they bended over. Preteens wore dresses with sashes, which reached about six inches above the knee. But when one became a teenager the dresses had belts instead of sashes, and went a few inches below the knee. About age sixteen, girls were allowed to exchange bobby socks for stockings, and begin wearing lipstick. I was in transition.

Candies For A Boyfriend

Anyway, back to the park. One Sunday, I noticed five boys who I had seen on previous occasions as they rode through the park on their bicycles, watching me and talking. So I put on what I considered a no-interest attitude, I sat demurely on the bench, pretending not to notice them. They began to ride past me over and over again. Eventually, one of them stopped briefly and asked for a piece of the candy, which I was eating. Before I could reply he rode way. A few minutes later he came back smiling, and I reached into my handbag and handed him a candy. He rode off in triumph, returning a little later to tell me his name and ask me mine. Then the other boys, three were his brothers and one his friend, came and introduced themselves. Every Sunday after that I shared my candy with Beade, and that's how he became my boyfriend.

Puppy Love

I was thirteen plus, when I first fell in love. Puppy love was unbelievably exciting.

One Saturday afternoon, relieved of the company of my sisters because I was attending a school concert, I walked down the street, dressed in my favorite yellow dress. It had no sash, was fitted at the waist and flared at the hips. I was not usually observant, but I could not help but see the young man that was walking behind me. He was more handsome and older than Beade and I could not believe that he was really following me. Then he came into step with me and requested in a very quiet voice, "May I walk with you?"

Every girl knew that one cannot appear too anxious when approached by a boy, so although I was thrilled to my bobby socks, I said, "You may walk wherever you wish, this pavement is public property." He smiled and my heart tumbled over and began beating a tom-tom. He was all the stories that had nurtured my romantic soul. His presence at my side changed me into a beautiful alluring damsel. This was the moment of destiny. What should I do? He was telling me his name and asking me mine. He'd noticed me before and just had to get to know me better. I acted as if this was just an ordinary happening, but I was thinking, "Why me, the girl who walks with a limp? He could have any girl. I too had noticed him before, but did not even entertain the thought of him liking me. Well why not me? This wonderful boy could be mine".

His name was Anthony, and his voice so soft and sweet, fell like a kiss on my enraptured ear as he engaged me in conversation. I was aware of concentrating hard on walking straight. Perhaps he had not noticed my limp. He was seventeen, but he didn't seem to mind that I was only thirteen. "Could we be friends?" He asked. Inside my skin I jumped up and down with joy to the tom-tom of my heart, but demurely, with just enough disinterest, I said, "Yes, I'd like to be friends."

Everyday I saw him on my way home from school and we would talk. Now I wonder what we talked about. On Saturday mornings I was supposed to go to choir practice. He would walk me to the school gate and we would stand there, saying goodbye. But we lost track of time, and an hour later we were still saying goodbye. Then I'll just turn and we walk back the way we came. Eventually, I told the choir mistress that I had asthma and could no longer belong to the choir. But I never stopped going to choir practice.

Sometimes Anthony held my hand as we stood and talked. I don't know if young people today who are experimenting with adult physical intimacies can understand the thrill of holding hands. Once, as we stood near a hedge talking, he drew my attention to the fact that we were both picking the leaves. He said that it was significant. I had no idea what the significance was, but by the way he smiled, he seemed to imply something good. I was very happy loving him. On Christmas morning, after mass, I met Anthony at the corner store. He wished me a happy Christmas, and then kissed me on my cheek. My Christmas was complete. Then came the bad news. His aunt with whom he lived was moving to Diego Martin. He said he would only be able to visit Belmont once a month. I couldn't handle that. I was already jealous of any girl to whom he spoke.

There was a wealthy girl who liked him. She was about his age, and I thought she was quite pretty. She made it her business to be where he was. Once, I invited him to a concert at my school. He had to do some chores for his aunt and said that he couldn't attend. While sitting in the hall, I saw that girl, who was not a student at my school, walk in with him. I was livid. After the concert he waited to escort me home. When I had invited him, I had fantasized about us walking home by way of the savannah, holding hands, and just maybe, he would kiss me. However, anger and pride got in the way. I would neither walk nor talk with him.

It was a few days before I gave him the opportunity to explain. Having finished his chores, he had decided to come and meet me. The girl had also been invited by someone else to the concert. So she said. They just happened to arrive at the same time.

I did not want a once a month boyfriend who was drop dead handsome. I did not want to be wondering which girl was trying to take my place the other twenty-nine or thirty days of the month. It was not as if we were dating. I couldn't date, and older girls could. So very composed, not betraying the tears in my heart, I said goodbye, told him don't bother, out of sight, out of mind, absence makes the heart go wander, and I walked away.

I must have been quite desirable, because after Anthony left, his friend who was actually fourteen (I was then fourteen), asked if he could be my boyfriend. I looked at his baby checks, compared them with Anthony's manly looks, and said, "No, but we can be friends". He settled for that and we remained friends. Many years later, after we had both been married and divorced, we met, fell in love, and almost got married.

Mama knew nothing about Beade and Anthony. My sisters kept my confidence. There were other boys who liked me, such as Junior and Clyde and Iondes, but they were just friends.

-13- My Teenage Years

I came to believe that Mama didn't care about me. I came to feel that nobody cared. So I stopped loving and became indifferent. Actually, I know now that I probably felt loved in my pre-teen years and I did love my mother then. I had lost the memory of that good time. I unlocked it a few years ago. I remembered how I used to play in Mama's salt and pepper hair. Even as a young woman, most of her hair was gray. My sister and I used to try to braid her long hair as she sat on the stoop in the afternoon after she had bathed and tidied herself. She used to let us take out some of the gray.

I used to save every penny I was given or found, to buy her the best present for mothers' day. When I was seven, I managed to save two dollars and forty cents and I bought her a glass tray with a wine decanter and six wine glasses. (That was 1955). She couldn't believe I could save so much money, seeing that I never got more than two cents a day. But I must have loved her for I hardly ever spent a cent on myself.

I don't recall how long we lived at Uncle Freddie's house. Eventually, Mama got a boyfriend and before long she was pregnant. He helped her to rent an apartment and that is how we moved to the Valley Road. I was just glad to escape Freddie's sexual molestations. We were comfortable in the apartment, except for the fact that sometimes when the water in the reservoir was low, it did not reach the pipes in our street. Then we had to fetch water in buckets from the standpipe lower down in the valley. When my big sister started to work she considered it unbecoming for her to be seen fetching water. When Mama sent my brother Gerald to fetch water he didn't come back for hours. So it was, that Mama and I did most of the fetching.

On Saturdays I enjoyed going to the grocery with her. Eventually I took over that chore completely. I would write out a list of the things that were needed, Mama would approve the list, add this or delete that, and I would do the shopping. The shopkeeper, twisted-neck Edward was a Chinese man who knew everyone. He kept the lists of people who couldn't pay him until the end of the month. Unlike other shop keepers he gave correct weights and would rather add more than defraud his customers. Consequently, his well-stocked shop was always full and it might be an hour to an hour and a half before one could be served. It was customary to give Edward the list, and even though you were not present in the shop, when your turn came, he put your goods in bags and put them aside for you. This gave me adequate time to play, read comics, which were not permitted in my house, and talk with my friends.

These friends were: Junior and Clyde with whom I used to

play boy games of cops and robbers; Carol, with whom I used to chat; and Edward and Ahing, from whom I borrowed comic books.

Becoming A Young Woman: The Changes Begin

I guess that it was after I had my first menstrual period that the cussing and screaming began. I was scared stupid when my period came. I had absolutely no knowledge of my body or the natural processes that girls went through. I knew of one girl to whom this had happened. She was quite developed, and rumor had it that she had a boyfriend. How did having a boyfriend cause a period, I could not comprehend, but I understood that it was a bad thing. Consequently, that day in school when I went to the bathroom and discovered that my knickers were bloody, I almost fainted. I returned to the classroom white as a sheet. Mrs. Miller asked if I was ill. I didn't know what to say, so I said no, and felt like dying.

That evening I tried to wash my knickers, which we wore with our gym uniforms. The next morning I put on an extra pair of panties stuffed with toilet paper and went to school. Meanwhile, Mama discovered the still-soiled knickers. When I arrived home for lunch, (after we moved, we sometimes went home for lunch), she called me. "Andra come here.' Expecting to be questioned about having a boyfriend and knowing that I liked Beade, I went timidly into her bedroom. She asked, in what I felt was a sharp tone of voice, "Are these your knickers?" "Yes Mama." "When did this happen?" "Yesterday Mama." "Go and wash yourself and when you finish call me." So I washed and then she gave me some nappies, some elastic and two safety pins, and showed me how to take care of myself. Then she said, "You are a woman now." I did not know what that meant, and I didn't know what to ask her. So I was a woman.

I suppose I was blossoming into a beautiful desirable young woman. But I didn't know it. Anyway, she began the accusations. What was I doing with those young men? What young men? They were the boys with whom I played cops and robbers, cowboys and Indians. They were the guys whose comic books I borrowed. When did they become young men? And why should I stop playing with them? But I dared not ask her any questions. I was afraid of being accused of being rude. And that would be followed by a threat to knock my teeth out of my mouth. If I didn't say anything, I was accused of silent insolence. Mama seemed to love the word "insolence'. It was used to describe the whole gamut of our attitude sins. And that warranted a beating.

After a while I used to sneak my big sister's True Confessions magazines, and when everyone was asleep, I got my sexual education by the dim light of the kerosene lamp, which stayed lit at night. I enjoyed the feelings that I experienced as my imagination transported me into the romance of delinquent teenage girls and before long, not knowing what I was doing, I learned to masturbate. I began to get an idea about Mama's accusation, but I would not ever do the things of which I was accused. I would be too afraid.

A Failed Attempt To Make My Mother Proud

It was always my intention to make Mama proud of me. I understood that to achieve that I must do well in school and not get pregnant. I know that she felt proud when I was accepted into Holy Name Convent. Consequently, I worked very hard my first year in high school and had the pleasure and reward of achieving first place in a class of brilliant students. We were all scholarship material, so the competition was tough. Feeling proud and happy, I took my report home, expecting to be congratulated. My mother read my excellent report card and declared, "How did this happen? This must be a fluke." I was crushed. I never worked hard again. I was bright enough to get by without extra effort. As a result, I never did as well as I might have. Who cared anyway?

Bewildered By Mama's Behavior Towards Me

Little by little I reached the conclusion that Mama hated me. One time she threatened to put me out on the street. I was fourteen, and what had I done wrong? She had been sick for three weeks and I had been taking care of her and my three smaller sisters. I had had to stay home from school, by the edict of my big brother, because my big sister was a teacher and therefore she couldn't miss school. I was happy to do it. I felt so grown up and responsible. My younger sisters were two and five and eleven.

The doctor didn't know what was wrong with Mama. She just went in and out of consciousness for three whole weeks.

The day before she came out of it altogether, I thought she had died. Usually, at some point in the day she would wake up and complain about being starved. I would feed her and sometimes she would talk of things she seemed to have dreamt. On that Friday, after I had put the baby down for her afternoon nap, it dawned on me that Mama had not called out to complain about being starved. I went and stood over her and it seemed to me that she was not breathing. Then I touched her to shake her awake, and her skin was ice cold. I froze. I just stood there watching her, unable to move, not knowing what to do, afraid of what I was thinking.

Suddenly, she opened her eyes and said, "My grandmother send me back. She said I couldn't stay because I still have young children to care for." Then she related a story about going to a beautiful place across a river where she met her grandmother, mother and lots of people. She had wanted to stay with them but her grandmother took a cloth, cleaned out her mouth, and sent her back to us. Having related her story Mama closed her eyes and slept until the next morning.

It was Saturday morning, exactly like the day when she took ill. Mama awoke around eight o'clock, wanting to know why she had been allowed to sleep so late, why didn't we wake her to go to the market. It was difficult to make her believe her that she had been ill for three weeks, but the weakness that she felt when she tried to walk convinced her.

Word spread that Miss Palmer was better, and the neighbors, who used to inquire about her condition daily, came to visit. With the house full of people, I left and went to see my friend Carol with whom I had had no opportunity to chat since Mama became ill. We had three weeks of happenings to catch up on, and I didn't realize it had gotten late. All of a sudden there was my big sister ordering me home.

My whole family was angry at me because I upset Mama. Nobody commended me for the way I ran the house during her illness. I was really expecting some praise. Instead, Mama decided that since I thought I was a big woman and could stay out after dark, I must leave her house. It was a neighbor who pacified her and begged her to reconsider. Mrs. Wiggins related how I had been taking care of her, my sisters, and the house. Then Mama gave me a piece of the bread and ham she was eating. That meant she was sorry. I was hurt. I was confused and began to withdraw further into my make believe world. There was no pain or disappointment there.

I Never Asked For Anything That Was Not Absolutely Essential

I did my best to make things easy for Mama. Going to high school was not the most pleasant experience. I really liked school, but in order to fit in and make the most of high school, I needed things that Mama couldn't afford. HNC was a school for the rich. Mama did her best, and maybe if I had asked, she would have found a way to give me what I needed. But it was I who used to carry the rent money to Mrs. Plouden, and it was I who trusted the groceries at Edward's shop three weeks out of the month. So I was too well aware of the financial state of our house. I never asked for anything that was not absolutely essential.

Emotional Divorce

Daddy, who had not lived with us since he had thrown us out of the house when I was eight, did not support us adequately. As ridiculous as it sounds, the court had appointed him to pay two dollars per child, per week until we were sixteen. So regardless of the cost of living or the needs of growing children, because we were bastards, that was all the court decided, we were worth. And even that, Mama had to take him back to court ever so often to obtain. I would ask him for money if I had a particular need. He never had.

There came a day when I needed one lousy quarter. On my

way home from school I decided to stop at Daddy's house and ask him for it. He told me that I had been too slow. Both my sisters Jacqueline and Deborah had passed by before with their needs. He had given them all he had and was flat broke. I was silently enraged and quietly told him, "Daddy, one day I will get a job and I will have money and you will ask me for bread and I will spit in your hand." And I walked away. I never asked him for another dime.

Consequently, at fourteen I emotionally divorced my parents. You can do that you know. Once you are convinced that you are all alone and unloved, you either push everybody away, or become a pest in the effort to get people to love and want you. Some children become disobedient, disrespectful, difficult, and end up in all sorts of trouble in an attempt to gain the attention of a parent or caregiver who should love them but doesn't seem to. Some make themselves indispensable by becoming extremely obedient and helpful. Sacrificing play for work they become perfectionist, hoping to gain the admiration and approval of parents.

Obedience, Complacency, And Fantasy

I didn't become the troublesome child, because I was afraid of beatings, and I couldn't bear to hear Mama screaming and cursing at me. I tried being good and perfect, making sure that all my chores were always done, doing well in school. But that didn't seem to work. No one was good enough for her. If I came home late from school, she would sniff me and declare that I smelled as if I had been with a man. And I still didn't know what she meant.

So I stopped being bothered, or so I thought. I still did all my chores but it was not in an attempt to please her. It was just to shut her mouth and gain permission to go out.

O how I daydreamed. I read books and daydreamed. Some people said I was a snob. Now what did I have to be a snob about? I remember how adults used to complain to my mother that I passed them by "without so much as a good morning." That was a cardinal sin for a child to commit. But I didn't see them. I hid myself in fantasyland. It was the furthest I could run from the oppressing circumstances of my life. Even today I meet people who seem to have known me as a teenager, but I don't know them. They were unreal. My books and dreams were where I lived. Some people actually thought that I was an only child because of my behavior.

My Girlfriend's Boyfriend

It was just before Easter in 1962 that I met the guy I would marry. Precious, my sister, who had been given away as an infant, asked Mama if Deborah and I could spend the week at her house. Permission being granted, we set off for San Juan, but before we left, I made a detour to borrow some comic books from my friend Ahing. A young man was there, to whom

I gave no thought, until Ahing said, "Andrea, this is my cousin." We shook hands. I didn't even pay attention to his name, but noticed a large ugly scar that seemed to cover most of his left arm. Then, I went on my way and forgot all about him.

Some time afterwards, my girl friend Carol and I were hanging out at her gate, opposite Edward's shop where I had been sent for groceries. At this time of lives our main topic of conversation was boys. We especially admired a young man who was much older than us. We had no aspirations towards him, but just enjoyed drooling over his perfectly muscled physique, his smooth tight brown skin, and Adonis-like chiseled lips. At that time neither of us had a boyfriend, although Beade still thought I was his.

Carol began to tell me about a boy she had met and liked, who also liked her. His name was Paul. Suddenly she said, "Here he comes," and this handsome young man rode up on his bicycle and stopped to speak to her. She introduced me to him. "We've already met." he said softly, and shook my hand. And, there it was, the scar, jogging my recollection of that April afternoon, when I hadn't even glanced at his face. He was hers she had said. The interest in his eyes was mine.

"I've seen you in the street, and said hello to you". He seemed a trifle bit annoyed, but pleasant just the same, he continued,

"You looked right through me, and never said a word."

He could not know that I, fantasy child of literature, had begun to live in a world beyond the normal reach of less important men. I walked with kings and queens and millionaires. And in that sphere of affluence, forgot the world, except for brief interludes, when necessity put fantasy to flight, and compelled me to join the common folk.

We chatted a while. "What school do you attend?" That sort of thing; and then I went to take my groceries home.

Paul had a brother named Arthur and because Carol and I used to hang out together, the four of us became friends. Not being allowed to have boyfriends, far less date, we met on the way home from school, at the grocery store, and we walked to and from church together. That was really the extent of our involvement. However, it was enough time for lots of conversation.

Falling In Love And Making Choices

Carol planned to spend that carnival with her cousins and Paul asked if I would hang out with him. That meant taking my two sisters with me, because it was the only way to get Mama's permission to go to town. Paul didn't mind. Both carnival Monday and Tuesday we met at one o'clock. We took the children to Woodford Square, where we could watch the bands of masqueraders as they danced their way up Frederick Street on their way to the Competition at the Savannah.

Paul and I sat on the grass and talked. We enjoyed each other's company tremendously. At twilight, we joined a band that was going to Belmont. Like other couples, we put our arms around each other and swayed to the rhythm of the steelband music. I felt light and confused and happy. I had forgotten all about Carol. I was falling in love.

Carol was furious when she heard that we had been together. Someone told her that Paul and I were so close that there was no room for breeze to past between us. Another person had said that he and I were like "Chewing gum on hot iron".

I apologized, explaining that we had met by chance, a lie that pacified her. I assumed that things would return to normal. He was her boyfriend. I was her best friend.

We loved the Lenten season, which followed carnival, because we were compelled to attend church more often. Added to the usual Saturday afternoon confession and Sunday morning mass, there were the Stations of the Cross on Wednesday and Friday nights. That meant walking home in the dark. The only time it was allowed.

So it was that every Wednesday and Friday night, Carol, Paul, Arthur and I walked home conversing together. After a while it dawned on me that the conversations were almost exclusively between Paul and I. Somehow we would find ourselves walking next to each other, and talking as if Arthur and Carol did not exist. Carol did not seem to notice anything wrong. It turned out that both brothers liked me.

Eventually one night, Paul disclosed the fact that he and his brother had been discussing their feelings for me. They had decided that I would have to choose between them. Without hesitation, I said, "I choose you." His reply, "You have made me the happiest man in the world." Then, being very sensible and sensitive about the turn of events, I said, "I will walk with Arthur and tell him, you must walk with Carol and tell her." I wanted everything in the open and above board. It was never my intention to take away my girlfriend's boyfriend, and if I wasn't given the choice, I don't think I would have pursued him.

And so, I told Arthur and he responded, "Thanks for telling me, I hope you'd be very happy." But Paul chickened out and did not inform Carol of the way things were. Neither did he tell me that he didn't have the guts to tell her. So I went along quite happily confident that I had the best girlfriend and boyfriend in the whole wide world.

That is how at fifteen, I began to "go steady" with that wonderful young man who made me feel cherished and very secure. With him I was never aware of being undesirable. I needed no one else.

One evening, Carol came to my house. She was livid. She started to curse me out and I couldn't understand why. It turned out that she had overheard a conversation between two girls. They had been discussing Paul and I, and one remarked that she couldn't understand why Paul would choose Andrea instead of Carol, because Carol was prettier and more shapely than Andrea, and to boot, Andrea walked with a limp. The other replied that it didn't matter to Paul if Andrea's foot was twisted and crooked, and that it was obvious that he loved her.

I was truly distressed about the way things turned out, but I was too much in love by then, to give him up, which would have probably been the decent thing to do. The beautiful friendship that Carol and I had had was understandably strained for a long time. I had betrayed her. She no longer trusted me. But we still liked each other and it hurt that I couldn't share the most important part of my life with her. Eventually the small world in which we lived came to know that Andrea and Paul were more in love than anyone had ever been before. Our love was so bright and shining that even Carol was happy about us.

Experiencing Sexual Desire And Receiving A Promise

I remember the first time Paul and I went to the movies. It was Easter Sunday and my friend Judith and her sister Maureen had their parents' permission to go to the cinema. I asked them to come and beg Mama to allow me to go with them. It was never my habit to sneak out without permission. I didn't want the risk of being caught. Mama said I could go as long as I had my own money and Deborah and Janice accompanied me. I was fifteen. Mama knew that I used to save any money I was given, and that I had quite a sum in my piggy bank. She used to borrow from me when she was broke. I could afford to pay for my sisters.

We didn't have a phone, so I asked Judith to phone Paul and inform him that I would be going to the 4:30pm show at De Luxe Cinema and if he could make it, to meet me at the corner at half past three. He was waiting for me, but said he couldn't go to the movies because he had no money. I told him that I could pay for him. It wasn't the ladylike thing to do, but I didn't know when we would have that opportunity again. He gave in, promising to repay me as soon as possible.

The cinema was crowded. House and pit were full and we had to go to the balcony, the place where lovers make out.

Seated with Deborah on my left side, Janice on my lap, and Paul to my right, it was impossible to kiss, which is all we had ever done so far. Then I felt his hand on my leg. That was all, and suddenly I understood the danger of being in a private place with the man I love. Feelings that I never could have anticipated despite my nocturnal readings of romance magazine, hit me like a ton of bricks. I felt faint. I felt high. I couldn't talk. I wanted to scream, to run, to cry. I wanted to move his hand. I wanted to take his hand and move it in places it shouldn't go. It was wild. It was my first experience of real sexual desire. I don't believe that Paul had any idea what he was doing to me and I was glad about that. And I was also glad that I was in the cinema with Janice on my lap and Deborah on my left side.

I never saw the movie. It was called "GIANT'. But Paul had seen it before and he related it to me because I would be expected to talk about it when I went home.

That experience moved the boundaries from kissing to touching, but I always resisted the feelings, and ran away if they threatened to overcome my resistance.

In the evenings when I was sent to Edward's shop to buy bread, I would delay going until a prearranged time so that Paul and I could meet. We'd go to Ahing's house and kiss and sit and talk and kiss. I told him every minute detail of my life.

We would get pretty hot with all the kissing that eventually led to fondling, but we were two staunch Catholics, and besides that, society frowned on premarital sex and unwedded pregnant women. It may have occurred to him to do it, but we took it for granted that we would get married and were prepared to wait. He bought me a gold ring with my initial on it, and that sealed everything.

My chores had increased with age, so that I spent almost the whole Saturday out in the street. And I didn't have to bring along my sisters. In the morning, after grocery shopping, I went to the farm for chicken and eggs. In the afternoon, I took the clothes that Mama had laundered to Mrs. Benson and Mr. Forde, and collected the money and dirty clothes. There was no thought of taking a bus or taxi. I walked everywhere. I loved to walk. And besides, Paul went everywhere with me.

Saturday continued to be confession day. On our way to or from Mrs. Benson's house, Paul and I would stop in at St. Francis Church to make our confessions. We were always relieved when Father Lennon was there. He wasn't as stern as father Graham. As we grew older the priest asked leading questions such as, "Have you been kissing any boys? Where, how, what kind of kiss, and did you touch, and what else did you do?"

Somebody Loves Me And Mama is Mad

Mama used to administer some terrible beatings. Gerald received the worst beatings. He used to scream, "Mama you go kill me and they would hang you." This, of course, infuriated her more.

I remember the time I accidentally broke the cabinet. That night she got a piece of wood and came at me. After one blow, I ran out of the house. That night she locked her doors and left me outside. I sat on the back steps more afraid of Mama and the beating that was awaiting me, than the frogs that were in the yard. Eventually, about four in the morning, because it would be a shame for the neighbors to know that I slept outside, she opened the door and let me in. I lay in bed, afraid to sleep, expecting any moment to feel the wood across my back, and preparing to die. It didn't happen.

People grew accustomed to seeing Paul and I together and Mama heard about us. I tried to be invisible in her presence, but she picked on me for everything, terrorizing me with threats of beatings. "I don't have time right now, but I am keeping a record of every beating I promise you. God help you when I am ready."

But I was so much in love, I brooked Mama's wrath. As the lists of my punishments grew I realized that she wasn't going to carry out her threats. But as painful as the physical beatings had been, I think I would have preferred them to the verbal abuse. Beatings produce temporary grief, but painful words have a long life span. Mama cussed me at the top of her voice. She called me a whore. She supposed I was sexually active. (I was not). All the neighbors and anyone within half a block of the house could hear her piercing voice.

I was so ashamed. I thought if my own mother could say those things about me what would people say? Mama put me through hell because of Paul. But for once I had purposed to take her abuse, rather than give him up. I also determined that I would make a liar out of her. I would never do any of the sins of which she accused me.

I once met a young man at a wedding, which I had attended with my big brother. This fellow, to my horror, came to ask permission to visit, and to my amazement was allowed to court me in the drawing room on Sunday evenings. I decided to tolerate his attentions because it took the focus off Paul, and allowed me to have some peace. After a few months however, I could no longer endure his serenading and his kisses, which he planted on me the moment Mama left us alone.

One Sunday when he was expected to visit, I told Mama that he wasn't going to come and I asked permission to take my sisters for a walk around the Savannah. Permission granted, I met with Paul and told him what had been going on. Meanwhile, Mervin, that was his name, arrived at the house to Mama's surprise. Mama told him where to find me and that's how he and Paul met. I informed him that Paul was my boyfriend and that I didn't want to see him again. When he didn't turn up two weekends in a row, Mama questioned me about what I had done to chase him away. I said nothing. And so the peace ended, and she went back to her accusations.

Breaking Up

One day Paul and I fell out. We had got our signals crossed so that he was waiting for me at one place and I was expecting to see him at another. When we did meet, he was furious as if I had deliberately misled him, so we parted in anger. It turned out that as he rode out of sight, he met my little sister who knew all my secrets. She was very mischievous, and chose that time to tease him, telling him that I had a male visitor who had come in a red convertible, waiting at home for me.

Now, considering how strict Mama was, what would I be doing with a male visitor in a red convertible? Commonsense should have told him that it wasn't true, but to him that explained my supposed deception. He broke all the rules of my safety, turning up at my house with my prayer book and letters, which we had exchanged, asking for his prayer book and letters back; and his ring. Dismayed and knowing nothing of my sister's conversation with him, I proudly gave him back his belongings, without asking for an explanation, wanting him to leave before Mama could discover he had been there.

The next day was Saturday. As usual, Paul met me at Edward's shop. I was happy to see him, thinking that all was well and back to normal, but I was so wrong. He started whispering in my ear. People who loved the way we loved each other could never guess what he was saying to me. He said that I had destroyed him and that he would destroy me. He sounded so menacing. I was scared. Then as was our custom, he followed me all day, walking and holding my hand, appearing to the world that all was well, but threatening me all the while.

The next morning as I stepped out to go to church, there he was. He fell in step with me, and began his threats of destroying me once more. My sisters were not with me, because I no longer went to children's mass at seven o'clock. I went at six. Paul sat by my side in church, watching me with a grin. When mass was over, there he was walking me back home, threatening me all the way.

Suddenly I made up my mind. I would not allow this anymore. My friend Claire, whose house we had to pass on the way home, had a brother who was a policeman. When we got to their house, I pulled away from Paul and ran inside calling for Hugh. Paul stayed outside. He probably thought I was just visiting Claire. I explained to Hugh that Paul had threatened to kill me. He called Paul in and questioned him. Paul said that he never used that word 'kill'. That I couldn't decide what he meant by his use of the word 'destroy'. Hugh expressed how sad he was that young lovers like us should break up. He encouraged us to make up, but I was too afraid and Paul was still too angry.

When Hugh realized that we were at a stale mate, he advised me that since I was still a minor, if I wanted to press charges against my boyfriend, I would need my mother to go with me to the police station. Then he sent me home and kept Paul at his house for a while. Of course I couldn't say a word to Mama.

After a few days I realized that Paul had disappeared out of my life. For a whole month I never ran into him, neither by chance nor design. After a while I began to feel comfortable. I missed him like crazy but I could do nothing about that. Mama got wind of our breakup and I guess she rejoiced, because for a little while the diatribe of abusive words stopped, and I was free to go out if I wished.

Almost Raped By My Big Brother's Friend

About this time I met a friend of my big brother who invited me out. Being glad for the male attention I went. I even let him kiss me, but there were no sparks. One day he asked me to meet him at his office. He had to work a little late, but we would go out after. He was alone in the office and he asked me to go into the back room and close the windows. Suddenly he appeared behind me and held me in an embrace. Before I realized his intention, he had unzipped my dress, which fell to the floor leaving me standing in my underwear. He threw me on the table and was about to climb on me when I said, "Carl, would you like my brother to do this to your little sister? It was the right thing to say, for he seemed to come to his senses. He stood up laughing, saying, "Put on your dress." I put on my dress and ran from that place. I developed a great aversion to the color green and I never wore that dress again.

Only recently I exorcized that ghost and overcame my dislike of green.

Making Up: Together Again

A month later, while I was going about my usual Saturday rounds, Paul rode up on a Lambretta as if he would knock me down. He grinned, a friendly grin, and asked whose rings was I wearing. Since he had taken back his ring, I had borrowed one from my aunt, and I had found one on the street. I said, "That is for me to know and for you to find out." "Well," he replied, "The only ring I want to see you wearing is mine." Then he gave me back my ID ring and that is how we made up. I was happy again. And the truce at home ended.

Starving For Love

Mama grounded me for life. I mean, I was only allowed to go to school. No extra curricular activities. I was not even allowed to go to church.

I stopped eating the food she cooked, convinced that a person who hated me as much as Mama did might put poison in my food. My friend, Juliana used to share her sandwich with me. I threw away the lunch that Mama packed every day. When summer vacation came and I could not go out, I literally starved myself. I grew weak, lost weight and was so depressed that Mama had to take me to the doctor. Of course all she could think was that I was pregnant. She didn't understand that I was so afraid of her, God and hell, and had made up my mind not to be pregnant, that I dare not have sex. The doctor thought that I might have contracted tuberculosis, but after appropriate X-trays, it turned out that I was only suffering from mal-nutrition.

When, with the help of a neighbor, I had an opportunity to see my boyfriend, he thought we could solve my problem of Mama's ill treatment by getting married. But I was still in school, and besides, I told him, I was under age, and Mama would never agree to the marriage. He suggested that if I were pregnant, Mama would be happy to see me married, but I did not want to have sex. I did not want to get pregnant. I wanted to complete high school. So Paul decided to take the bull by the horns and request permission to visit me.

He was as afraid of Mama as I was. He used to acknowledge her with a mannerly greeting when they met on the street and her attitude intimidated him. However, his desire was greater than his fear. One night, after walking behind her as she went to church, waiting for her to come out of the church, following her to Mrs. Atwell's house, waiting for her to leave there, and following her back home, Paul worked up the courage to approach and speak to her. Expressing his love and honorable intentions, he asked permission to visit. Being caught off guard and taken aback by the tears in his eyes, she gave consent to his request. He might visit either Saturday or Sunday evenings about five o'clock. He could stay till seven.

Trying To Take Mama's Advice

That did not mean that Mama stopped harassing me. She changed her tune. Now it was that a young girl like me should have many friends. I shouldn't be stuck up under one man. I tried once more to please Mama.

One Sunday, being tired of her voice, I decided to take my sisters for the usual Sunday evening walk by the savannah. I made up my mind to make friends with every man who approached me that day. I would show Mama. She wanted me to have many friends. Okay. I would. So I parked my seductive self opposite the bandstand, and while my sisters played in the grass, I put on a friendly face to attract and invite company.

Eventually a young man came by. We were having a very pleasant conversation when I spotted Paul approaching. I terminated the conversation with the young man, and that was the end of my attempt at having lots of boyfriends. I did look for the young man from time to time when I went by the savannah, but I never saw him again.

Disrespected By Paul's Family

One day I met Paul's father. He said, "Young lady, I want to have a talk with you." Then he insulted me. "If you think, you are going to get my son in trouble so that he would marry you, you'd better think again." "Sir," I said respectfully and boldly, "I have no intention of getting into any trouble, but I have all intentions of marrying your son." I guess he was surprised at my fearless response.

Another time, I met Paul's grandmother. She called me a little red nigger and wanted me to leave her grandson alone. I didn't answer her. I had never seen her before that day. All the parents were against us.

Miss Andrea Palmer, Working Woman

At seventeen my school days were over and I went about applying for work. I admired nurses, but my stomach was too easily upset for that profession, and besides, I didn't have the time for years of training, I had to make money immediately. I sent applications to the Catholic Teacher's Board, and to the Civil Service. From time to time, during the summer, I stopped at Holy Name Convent to inquire about job opportunities. Just before schools were to re-open, Mother Bernadette asked me if I would be interested in a temporary position as a teacher in the Montessori School. A teacher was going to be absent on maternity leave for three months. Of course I accepted the position.

With two blouses, a skirt, and a dress, Andrea became Miss Palmer, the working adult.

I was overwhelmed and frightened, and I didn't believe I was able to teach the children. I was so stressed and felt so inadequate, but I did my best. The pay was $90.00 a month. I brought my first pay-packet straight home to Mama. She took sixty dollars, gave me thirty and told me to buy a skirt and a blouse and keep some money for my toiletries, transportation, and incidentals. The end of the next month I would be able to purchase a pair of shoes. However, at the end of October, when I was presented with my pay-packet, I was informed that the teacher for whom I was substituting, was returning to work and I was relieved of the position.

But God was in my corner. On arriving home with the disastrous news of my termination, I was greeted by a letter from the Ministry of Finance, advising me to report to the Trinidad House, for an interview. Without missing a day, I was once more employed. I went to work in the Pension department, Widows and Orphans section, in the Treasury Building. The pay was $110.00 per month; more money for Mama and me.

While working at the treasury, I was surprised by something. There was a man about twenty-six years old, my immediate supervisor, who gave attention to me. Actually, quite a few guys attended me. I didn't even have to do my own work. Timothy, Narinesingh, and Sealy, were more than willing to do it for me. I took all the attention for granted, not because I considered myself special, but because I just thought that that was the way it was in the work place. I was only seventeen, and I was glad to find that people were so considerate.

Mr. Samuel Price was different. Everyday he strolled by my desk and said good morning. Invariably, he paid me a complement, and went about his business. Sometimes, if it was raining at lunchtime, he would invite me to sit with him at his desk, (it was not a private office) and he would chat with me. At times when I was bored, I would ask to leave early and Mr. Price would allow me to go. He never recorded my tardiness or absences. It was all very pleasant.

Soon, it was time for the Treasury Christmas ball and I couldn't attend because I couldn't afford the price of the ticket. Most of my salary went to my mother. After my expenses, I was usually left with a little pocket change that had to be stretched to the end of the month. When Mr. Price discovered that I would not be attending the ball, he pried into my financial situation, and as a result, he bought me a ticket, and arranged transportation for me to get there. I felt like Cinderella.

One day before the Ball, I met one of the girls crying in the ladies lounge. When I asked her what was the matter, she blurted out, "How I wish Sam Price would look at me, the way he looks at you." I was astonished by her remark, discounted it as nonsense, and went about consoling her. Mr. Price did have a girlfriend, a very sophisticated woman. In fact I felt rather gauche in comparison to most of the women who worked at the Treasury. I thought that Mr. Price was a very kind man, like a nice big brother. I did not ever consider him as a romantic possibility. He was never fresh, in fact he was every bit a gentleman. I did not notice that he singled me out. I was totally in love with Paul, had been from age fifteen, and never had any desire for anyone else.

The Christmas Ball was wonderful. It was my first grown up function and Paul was a little upset because he would not be my escort. He came to my house to appraise me before I left for the ball and presented me with a gold chain, which was my Christmas gift. He put it on me, expecting that I would wear it to the ball. But the pink dress, which I was wearing, was better accessorized with pearls, so I thanked him with a kiss, put it back in the box and went off with the person who had been sent to escort me.

I danced all night. Everybody seemed to want to dance with me. My 'game leg' did not hinder me at all. I had never felt more alive and beautiful than on that night. I chatted and laughed, was brilliant and witty. I believe that I actually lived in my fantasy world for a few hours.

The week between Christmas and the New Year was filled with parties at the homes of my work mates, some of which I attended, to Paul's annoyance. On New Year's Eve, we all got together after lunch and were treated to drinks by the leadership. People toasted each other, and in the joy of the spirit of the season, wished each other health, happiness, and prosperity in the coming year.

On 2nd January, 1966 when I returned to work, something had changed. Sam Price did not come by to say good morning and pay me my usual compliment, and I missed him. He never asked me to sit and chat with him anymore, and I missed that. I noticed that he did give attention to others, and that a tall beautiful Indian woman sometimes sat with him instead of me. And I was jealous. And I couldn't understand my own feelings. I did not want him. Of that I was sure. I was so confused that I actually told Paul about my feelings.

On my eighteenth birthday, my work mates bought balloons and made a big fuss over me. I was the youngest among them and I felt quite special. Even the manager, who was a very stern middle-aged woman, and Mr. Forgenie, the very feared comptroller came by to wish me a happy birthday and many more. I hadn't broadcasted the fact of my birthday, yet even people from other departments had somehow discovered that the Treasury's baby had a birthday, and sauntered by to tease me and wish me good health and long life.

Everybody seemed to take delight in my becoming eighteen, except Sam Price. He never looked in my direction. It was as if he wasn't there. Before I clocked out, I approached him, "So aren't you going to wish me a happy birthday?" I asked. In an off-handed way, he replied that he didn't know it was my birthday, but happy birthday anyhow. What a crock!

After that, I used to catch him observing me, as I flirted with Mr. Sealy, who used to tease me good-naturedly about how I had lost my place at Sam Price's side. I pretended it didn't matter, but it did, for a short while. One day Mr. Price looked at me and began to sing, "It's easy, like taking candy from a baby." I was furious. So that's what he thought about me. I was just a baby. Later on when I heard all the words of the song, I concluded that Sam Price had fallen in love with me and had deliberately cut me off, because he knew it was a hopeless case. The song was "A, B, C, falling in love with you was easy for me—— it's easy, like taking candy from a baby."

I Could Have Been A Judge

During this time I met a man that I wished could have been my father.

When I began to work at the treasury Mr. Pierre, a mild mannered man was in charge. About a month later the veterans in the office began to whisper about a Mr. Forgenie who was appointed to replace Mr. Pierre. Everyone who knew Mr. Forgenie seemed terrified of him. Ours was a pretty undemanding and casually run office, but everyone seemed to expect things to change drastically. I could not imagine why grown adult people should be so uneasy over one ordinary man. In my youthful ignorance it seemed absolutely preposterous. What could he do?

The anxiously awaited day arrived. We were called to a meeting at which Mr. Pierre introduced Mr. Clive Forgenie, said his goodbyes and left. Immediately Mr. Forgenie began to explain his principles, policies, and expectations. His speech afforded no opportunity for query. It was a dogmatically presented "I, and Me" address. Everyone listened, and without comment or questions, said "Yes Sir," to whatever Mr. Forgenie had stipulated. I was flabbergasted by the cowardly silence and submission of my co-workers.

The mood of the office changed significantly after that. There was no tardiness, no walking about and chatting, no laughter, no fun. Everyone worked diligently. No one did my work for me anymore, and I dared not ask to leave early on account of boredom. From time to time, Mr. Forgenie, who seemed to keep a watchful eye on us, would emerge from his office to single out someone for a private audience. Each person entered that room with apprehension and exited with a grave and humbled expression.

At the Christmas ball of which I spoke, Mr. Forgenie requested that I dance with him. My friends looked at me as if I were being invited to my own execution. I was not afraid of the man. As we began to dance, he mentioned that he had specially requested the particular tune that was being played. It was a slow waltz and for a moment, I was a trifle uneasy. In the course of the dance Mr. Forgenie asked me what I thought of him. With the candor of fearless youth, I told him that I thought him to be an arrogant and egotistical man. At this he tried to appear quite austere, but there was laughter dancing in his eyes.

Having thus expressed myself, I was glad when the music ended and I could get away from him. But immediately the band struck up another slow tune. Mr. Forgenie did not release me, and so we resumed dancing. He continued to inquire of me, what was the basis for my negative assessment of his character. I explained, that at the meeting at which he was introduced, his speech had consisted solely of his own thoughts, rules, and expectations, and that he had not even considered that someone else might have had something to say. To which he replied that he did not think, that anything anyone could have had to say would have been important.

The dance ended, another started, and still he did not release me. I began to feel like a mouse being toyed with by a cat, and pleaded with my eyes for some one to 'cut in' and rescue me. If I had been dancing with anyone else, someone would already have cut in, but no one wanted to cut in on Mr. Forgenie. At last, however Mr. Price came to my aid. He had not had the pleasure of dancing with the prettiest girl before.

Everyone wanted to know what Mr. Forgenie and I had conversed about for three dances. When I told them what I had said to him, they were amazed at my courage and wondered what would happen to me. Well, I couldn't rewind the tape of time. What will be, will be.

The next morning Mr. Forgenie stopped at my desk and said good morning. He commented on the lively freshness of my countenance, which he thought remarkable for one who had danced till three in the morning. And that was all.

At the beginning of March, I received a letter from the Catholic Teachers' Board inviting me to an interview. A new door was opening. I was offered the post of a primary school teacher at Nelson Street boys R.C. School, effective immediately. The pay was $120.00. I decided to accept the position, but not tell Mama about my extra ten dollars. I was gaining wisdom. I was sorry to leave my friends at the Treasury but I was bored there anyhow. All I did was add figures. Besides Mr. Price no longer spoke to me, except for a cordial "good morning", if we happened to cross each other's path. It was time to move on.

I wrote a letter of resignation and requested an audience with Mr. Forgenie. Having been invited into the office to which everyone had been called at some time, that is, everyone except me, I took the proffered chair facing him and handing him my letter, waited for his response. He asked if I wanted to be a teacher, and expressed sorrow at my leaving, but was glad that I was offered the opportunity to discover if teaching was to be my vocation. Having accepted my resignation, he proceeded to chat. He told me that he was married and had two teenage children. He lived in Belmont, as did I, and he invited me to visit his home. He really liked me. He liked my bold and innocent honesty.

I had a question. "Sir," I said, "I have noticed that at one time or another, you have called everyone into your office to be reprimanded for some reason. I know that you've seen me breaking your rules, walking around and chatting, when I should be sitting and working. You have even reprimanded people to whom I was speaking, but you have never called me to account for my behavior. Why is that so, sir?"

Mr. Forgenie laughed a hearty laugh. "How old are you?" he asked. "Eighteen, Sir." "Well Miss Palmer," he replied, "I did not reprimand you because I knew you were only acting your age."

Some time later I did visit his home. He talked with me, sounding me out, gauging my intelligence and potential. Then he announced, "Miss Palmer, I think you ought to be a judge." That was the moment when I wished that Clive Forgenie had been my father. I believed that I could have been a judge, if I had him to give me direction.

However, under the circumstances that was just a dream to

add to my fantasies.

I actually enjoyed teaching the infants. They came to me with no academic knowledge and whatever they knew and understood at the end of the school year, was what I had taught them. That gave me great satisfaction. I made new friends and was quite comfortable. My next step would be Teacher's Training College.

At the end of August of that year, before I returned to work from summer vacation, Paul and I were formally engaged in the presence of his parents and my mother. Paul's father mentioned the conversation we had had a couple of years before, and observed that I was not pregnant. We were engaged for a year. We needed time to prepare financially, and I needed to prove that it was not a marriage necessitated by pregnancy. We had remained virgins by choice, for we certainly did not lack opportunity. Everybody probably took it for granted that we were sexually active.

Even though I was eighteen, engaged, and earning my own money, I still asked permission to go out. Some friends, boys and girls, planned a weekend beach lime. I had never done anything like that before and I really wanted to go, and I wanted Paul to be there. I went to Mama with my request and opened the whole plan, boys and all, before her. "Go if you want to," was her uncharacteristic response. How I prayed that Friday evening would come before she changed her mind.

It was an absolutely wonderful weekend. We had rented a house with three bedrooms, kitchen, drawing room and dining room. We carried food to cook, sunglasses, and bathing suits. We behaved ourselves decently, each keeping an eye on the other to ensure that no one got into trouble. We bathed and went canoeing by day, and by night we sang and danced by the light of gas lamps. Except for Shirley, we were paired off: Valerie and Arthur (not Paul's brother), Ann Marie and Monty, Paul and I.

Unknown to me, Valerie and Ann Marie, who were sisters and still attending school, had told their parents that they were going on a class trip. Only I had told the truth. So when they were found out, they surmised that I had let the cat out of the bag. Valerie, who was my very good friend, stopped talking to me without an explanation. For a few months I tried to make an appointment to talk to her to find out what was wrong. I phoned her almost every day, but she was always busy. Eventually, hurt, puzzled, and miserable because I missed her friendship sorely, I gave up.

One day she phoned and asked if she could see me; she had a confession to make. Two years had passed. I was married and had a baby, I didn't want her friendship anymore, but I was curious, so I invited her to my home. I felt very angry and cold towards her when she explained why she had cut me off. I forgave her but the friendship was finished.

Why I Continued to Believe That Mama Hated Me

I'll never understand why Mama wasn't proud of me. I had stayed in school, got an education, had a decent job as a primary school teacher, and didn't get pregnant. I thought that, being the first daughter to get married from the home (Marcia had gotten married in London to her childhood sweetheart), Mama would share in my joy. Why should I have thought that? Nothing had changed. Instead immediately after the engagement, she stopped speaking to me completely.

Every morning I'd say, "Good morning Mama." And she would look at me as if I were a piece of filth, and grunt. When I came home I would say, "Good evening Mama," and I got the same grunt. When I got paid, I would give her money and she would say, "Put it down there." She offered no help, no advice. Every month I bought something towards my trousseau. My friend Margaret's mother agreed to make my wedding dress, which I designed. Each purchase I brought home and put in full view of everyone, but nobody seemed to care. I was happy and sad. Each day I cared less about my family. I learned to sleep a lot during that time, just to block Mama out of my consciousness.

A month or so before the wedding she broke the silence, "So

you're getting married," she stated. "Yes Mama, on August 20th." "And who is taking you to the Church?" "Nobody." "And how are you getting there?" "I'll take a taxi." "You have no shame. Why don't you ask your brother to take you?" "Okay Mama." "And why don't you ask your cousin Pam to go with you?" "Okay Mama."

I spoke to Linda, my big brother's wife, and she spoke to him. I suppose that Mama also spoke to Gregory. He reluctantly agreed to take me to the church. I spoke to my cousin Pamela, and she agreed to be my one attendant, my maid of honor. As the day approached, I asked Mama if she could do me the favor of preparing a wedding lunch for ten people. She said, "That will be thirty dollars." I couldn't believe it. I was the main financial support of her house and she charged me for my wedding lunch. I felt that I was nothing more than a convenience to her. Like a stove or refrigerator, useful but unloved.

After four years of loving Paul and absorbing Mama's acid words of condemnation, I married my wonderful boyfriend. His father and his best friend came to the church with him. His mother said she wasn't well. She had wanted us to postpone the wedding; but I thought that it was just a ploy to stop the wedding altogether. I knew she didn't like me. I was not a suitable addition to their great and precious family. I told Paul, "If you postpone this wedding, there'll be no wedding later."

My brother, his wife, and my cousin as well as my friends Cheryl, Margaret, Juliana, and Junior came to see me get married. No mother, no sister. It never occurred to me to ask my father. He probably would have got all decked out in his white suit and proudly walked me down the isle. But even though I used to speak to him, I had shut my emotions down where he was concerned, and hadn't given him a thought.

Mrs. Andrea Nurse, Married Woman

On Saturday August 19th, Paul and I went to confessions, a necessity before receiving any sacrament, and marriage is a sacrament. He had his hair cut, and I had my hair done. He picked up his suit from the tailors, and took my trousseau to my cousin's house. I couldn't care what was happening in the world or in Mamą's house for that matter. I was about to be married and nobody could do or say anything to affect me negatively.

It was a glorious Sunday. We went to the Five o'clock morning Mass and received communion. The last banns of our forthcoming marriage were read that morning. Banns are announcements to the congregation of a couples' intention to marry. They are read at every Mass on the four Sundays preceding the wedding. Banns are also posted in the Red House for one month, so that everyone who cared to know could find out who was about to be married. No one had come forward to dispute the legality or religious impropriety of our marriage.

I dressed at my cousin's home. As prearranged, my brother and his wife drove us to the church. Paul was already there, nervously smoking a cigarette. Strange as it seems, I don't remember one word of the wedding ceremony. But I remember the bells ringing. We couldn't afford a choir, but had paid twelve dollars to have the bells rung as we exited the church. As I stepped out of the church on the arms of my husband, into the brilliant noonday sun, I smiled to myself and thought, "Andrea, you are a woman now". I was free from Mama's tyranny. Free to live happily ever after.

After the delicious lunch which Mama had prepared and served, I changed into the simple blue after-wedding dress that I had had made for the occasion, and Paul's father drove us to our home at Reid Lane.

The boat that would take us to Tobago for our honeymoon didn't sail on Sundays. We actually had about thirty-six hours before sail-time.

Sad to say, two weeks before the wedding, when our mattress was delivered, we had yielded to curiosity and temptation, and clumsily tried out the forbidden fruit of sex. I was truly sorry that we hadn't waited. After all we'd been waiting for four years. With just two weeks to go, we had spoiled it.

Nevertheless, it was as if that first time hadn't happened. We hadn't been naked that time. I was very shy about exposing my body, because ever since one day when Paul had remarked on the smallness of my breast, I had felt physically inadequate. To be perfectly honest, that first time had been disappointing. Our normal limited lovemaking had been more exciting and pleasurable than our quickie illicit sex act. I think I was too tense and too afraid to give myself to the experience.

However, the ring on the third finger of my left hand made all the difference. Our love-making was slow and sweet as we lost our shame and began to learn the art of pleasuring each other. We consummated our marriage with multiple orgasms.

Our honeymoon in Tobago was wonderful. We stayed at a small guesthouse, where the proprietor, Mr. Charles was also the tour guide and cook. We enjoyed the change of scenery, the beaches, the fresh fish dinners, the light from the lighthouse at the fort that we could see from our room as we lay in each other's arms, and the freedom to have sex. We laughed a lot. We had taken a pack of playing cards with us, and we spent a considerable amount of time in the room playing the games we enjoyed. What was funny was that the other guest and Mr.

Charles all thought that we were having sex all the time. I suppose that was what we were expected to do.

My Husband Or His Father's Son

I was pregnant immediately. Being Catholic, we had tried the rhythm method of birth control. We must have done something wrong. I did not have a period after I got married. Instead, three weeks later, I was sick as a dog. I did not want to be pregnant. After being under Mama's strict thumb, I wanted to spread my wings, go places, and do things.

I was not lazy, but I was weak from constant vomiting. Besides that I went to work everyday. Sometimes I vomited in the street because the smells of the market, which I passed on the way to the school, made me nauseous. I also suffered from acid heartburn and leg cramps constantly. There were times when I couldn't make it through the whole day. Being so sick, I needed my husband's help around the house.

At Christmas time housework is usually doubled with all the baking, cooking, and cleaning to be done. Early in the morning, on our first Christmas Eve as husband and wife, Paul's father phoned to say that he needed his son to assist him in his house. I needed him at our house and he chose to complete all his chores before responding to his father's request.

On Christmas Eve night, we both arrived at his father's house to find him in quite a disagreeable mood. I was embarrassed by way he spoke to my husband, as if he were a wayward little boy. "Is now you reach, since morning I calling you." My husband said nothing, but I said, "Sir, Paul had things to do in his own house." To which his father replied, "This is not your business, I am talking to my son." "Well," I said, "He may be your son, but he is my husband, and he didn't choose to be your son, but he chose to be my husband." His father replied, "He will always be my son." I suppose that I was in Mama's word, insolent. But I had had it with them. They always behaved like I had no significance.

Allan was born while I was on Easter/spring break, so that my three months maternity leave ended at the beginning of the summer vacation. Consequently, I had five months at home with my baby, before I had to consider the problem of a baby sitter. The natural choice was my mother. Before we were married, Paul understood that my mother had no income and I felt an obligation towards her. He said that it was one of the things that he admired about me. My salary had increased and it was not a hardship. He and I divided the household expenses between us. Since I was paid monthly, the rent became my responsibility while the food and other bills were his. We saved a little, and we each had a little spending money. We lived within our means and were quite content. But I could not afford to pay a sitter, while continuing to support my mother.

I Felt Like A Motherless Child

During the months of my pregnancy when I was so sick constantly, my mother had totally ignored me. I used to visit her, but she never asked me how I was doing. One day, it was at the end of the month, I went to take her some money. I had had unscheduled doctor's visits and because of the un-budgeted expenses, I had to decrease her usual allowance. The morning sickness, that had begun even before I had become aware that I was pregnant, continued for the duration of my pregnancy. The scent of food, soap, toothpaste, smoke, dust, my husband's perspiration, and everything else made me nauseous. Nothing stayed down in my stomach. Most people did not even realize that I was pregnant because I had lost so much weight, that I never even needed to wear maternity clothes.

Mama appeared not to notice my weakened condition. My collar-bone looked like craters and my eyes were sunken. Yet, Mama seemed not to see me. I stood in the kitchen, leaning against the refrigerator, feeling faint and about to fall. I explained my condition and the reason for the reduction in her allowance. All she said was, "Put it down there," referring to the money I had brought. She didn't even offer me a seat or a glass of water. I steadied myself and walked away, leaving as soon as I was able to get a taxi. I never felt more like a motherless child than on that day.

Nevertheless, when Allan was born, she came to the hospital to see me, admired my handsome son, and said to me, "Now you know what a mother's pain feels like". She even went to my home while I was hospitalized, offered to clean the house and did our laundry for us.

I had hoped that now that I was a mother, Mama and I would become close, but that didn't happen. However, I approached her and explained that I had to return to work and we would appreciate it if she would take care of Allan for us. To my amazement, the woman said "no". She had raised her children and she wasn't about to raise mine. I did not plead with her. I had no time to waste. I had to find a baby sitter immediately.

Throughout the years, my husband and I had maintained a friendship with Beade's family who lived just one block from our marital home. Mrs. Boucaud was a wonderful gentlewoman. She had always liked me, and agreed to take care of Allan. We settled on a price for her services and although it worried me, I resigned myself to the fact that I could no longer assist my mother financially. Our fragile and shallow relationship was ended.

Mama must have been doing some thinking. Perhaps she had

been expecting me to beg for her help. If I had done that, she probably would have asked for extra money, as she did when I asked her to prepare a wedding lunch for me. On the Sunday night, which preceded the Monday when I had to return to work, she sent my sister to tell me that if I wanted, she would take care of Allan for me. I wanted, because I was very much concerned about her finances.

Happy At Last

Despite those few situations, Paul and I were very happy. We loved each other and were comfortable with each other. We had no inhibitions. Our sexual life was excellent. When I was on vacation from school, Paul would come home at lunch-time to make love. There was never a time when we refused each other. During my pregnancy, despite my illness, sex was the very best. In my mind there was never the suggestion of a thought that I could ever have sexual feelings for someone else.

I was a wife, a mother, and a teacher. I had been chosen and was cherished. I had a man who was my husband, my best friend, and my lover. Our son was handsome and brilliant. And we had dreams. What more was there to life?

I did not enter Teachers' Training College as I had expected. Instead, I decided that my husband's career was more important than mine. He desired to study Electrical

Engineering in The USA, and we made plans to migrate.

No Grief, No Tears. Something's Wrong With Me

On July 20th 1969, my husband, my best friend, and lover, left Trinidad. He went ahead to New York, USA, to prepare for my coming.

We had been together for six years and I expected that I would be devastated by his absence. According to all my books, I should have been inconsolable. I waited for the grief and tears, but none came. What was wrong with me? I actually went to a church and knelt down and tried to feel bad and sad. I didn't. I moved back to my mother's house and for a week, I walked around quiet and pensive as I supposed I should be. Eventually, my mother said that I should go out with Deborah, who at eighteen had a lot more freedom than I had ever been given. Freed from depressive inactivity by Mama's approval, I gladly joined Deborah and her friends.

It was an exciting time when the people of Trinidad joined the black people of America in the proclamation of "Black Power." We wore afros and dashikis and greeted each other with the sign of Peace, Love, and Power. And the country was getting ready for a coup. It was also the year of Aquarius, marijuana, and Soul. There was magic in the air. I was free and tireless, and I surprised my sister by the way I embraced the magic of the moment. I didn't drink or smoke, but I was constantly high on the music, the dance, the people, and the atmosphere.

I was supposed to take a course in typing and shorthand in order to prepare myself for a secretarial position when I arrived in New York, but I could not absorb any new knowledge. I realized that I had never been free before, and after a few months of being intoxicated with license, **I became afraid of myself.** I did nothing wrong, did not compromise my principles, but I just didn't understand the me that was emerging. Therefore, I did not know what kind of behavior I was capable of. This had never been a part of my fantasy life. I couldn't handle it. I no longer knew who I was. A couple of friends were also worried about me.

When my husband returned at my request, I was relieved. I could return to being the proper person he and I knew. I felt stable and solid once more. Two months later, I said goodbye to my two-year old son, my family, and all that was familiar without tears or fears. My husband who had returned to the United States a month ahead of me was waiting to receive me.

-14- New York, Where Heaven Meets Hell

From Bright Lights To Bewilderment

The excitement of looking down on the millions of lights that was New York on Sunday 12th April, 1970 at midnight, as the Pan Am Jet descended into Kennedy Airport, was displaced by bewilderment when I arrived in the Bronx; A bewilderment that intensified when I looked out on the street next morning. Tall concrete brick apartment buildings were never in my picture of the land of plenty. A studio apartment, which my husband shared with his brother and cousin, was not my idea of home. The metal smell of the New York air, and the strange taste of the water, made me nauseous. The shaking of the building as the #4 Woodlawn train rumbled by, awoke the fear associated with the memory of the earthquakes, which occurred occasionally in Trinidad. New York was not my cup of tea. I wanted to go home.

Nevertheless, I was with my husband and I was quite clear about my duty and my place. The very next evening when Paul arrived home from work, we went apartment hunting. We were overjoyed to be directed to a large one-bedroom apartment in the same building where his aunt, brother and cousins lived. They were on the fourth floor, while we would be on the third. We could occupy the apartment immediately.

Apartment 3F was in pretty decent shape. We cleaned, painted, and wall papered our home, and furnished it cheaply. We made lists of the things we needed, and little by little, starting with the essentials, our house became a home. I quickly adjusted to the smell, water, and rumbling and went about being a good wife. Paul and I both missed home terribly, but we were happy to resume our love life. We had a five-year plan. We had a focus. We had a perfect family to raise in the dream house which we would build when my husband, the Electrical Engineer and I returned to our son in Trinidad. We were prepared to make the necessary sacrifices to hasten the realization of our dreams.

By the end of the week, my aunt-in-law offered to take me job hunting.

Grace was the only one who had said to me, "Welcome to the family." On the day we were married, she had phoned from New York and without knowing her, I loved her for that kind gesture. Paul was her favorite nephew, and it was she who encouraged and helped him to migrate. He had shared her apartment at first, but when they had had a disagreement, he had moved in with his brother and cousin. But aunt and nephew remained on friendly terms. So it was that Grace took me to Martin Sneiden's paper company, where I was offered a job as a girl Friday. The salary agreed on was $60.00 per week.

Hired To Be a Mistress

Mr. Sneiden gave me a key to the building when I arrived there the next Monday morning. I worked in his office answering the phone, which hardly rang. That was good, because my ear was not yet attuned to the New York accent, and I couldn't quite understand what the callers were saying. Anyhow, it was soon obvious that there was really no work for me to do. Mr.Sneiden used to hang over my shoulder, and touch me as he passed by, speaking words of encouragement. I was not suspicious of his behavior. I just thought that New York people were very touchy.

Thursday was payday and Martin Sneiden came to re-negotiate my salary and work requirements. 'I am sure you realize," he pointed out, 'that there is no real work here for you to do. I really do not need an office clerk. I need a mistress. Now, if you agree to be my mistress, I will pay you three hundred dollars a week. I understand that you've just arrived in New York. I will furnish your apartment. You can tell your husband that you've bought the things on term and will be paying for them monthly. I will not need you all the time. I do have a wife and two children. No one will have to know that you are my mistress. So what do you have to say to my proposition?"

I was sick. I had been eating a green apple, which I had bought for lunch. I ran to the bathroom and vomited. I developed a dislike for green apples, which lasted for many years.

Mr. Sneiden needed a reply before he wrote the personal check that was my salary. I informed him that I was truly taken aback by his proposition, and that I needed time to think. I said that I would appreciate it if he paid me the amount on which we had previously agreed. I further said, that after thinking things over during the weekend, I would let him know of my decision. I indicated that I was leaning towards accepting his new offer. He wrote the check out for forty-five dollars. I then inquired of him where I may cash the check immediately, since I was entirely without even lunch money. He sent me to his bank. With my money in hand, I got on the train and went home. That was the last I saw of Mr. Martin Sneiden.

I went directly to Grace's apartment. As I leaned on her door waiting for her to answer the bell, I became overwhelmed by what had transpired, so that by the time Grace opened the door, I was trembling. I explained to her what had occurred, expecting to receive sympathy and good advice; or at least some expression of the same disgust that I felt. Imagine my astonishment when she said, "I don't see what you are so upset about. You could hold on there until better can be done." I couldn't have heard what I thought I heard. The world was upside down.

When my husband came from work, I told him what had

happened and what Grace had said. He didn't believe me. He said either she didn't understand what I had said, or I didn't understand what she had said. But later on I came to believe that she had set me up, and that she was looking for a way to prove that I was an unfit wife for her nephew. She used to speak ill of me, remind him of my parents' illegitimacies, cast doubts on my fidelity, and instigate thoughts of my potential to be bad.

My First Taste Of Racial Discrimination

The following Monday, I went by myself to Forty-second Street, which was lined with employment agencies, to seek a job. And I was introduced to racial discrimination.

I was offered a modeling career, but of course I did not entertain such ambition. The man who attended to me proceeded to telephone several businesses that used the services of his agency. I was willing to accept a job as a receptionist, math-clerk, file clerk, or girl-Friday. That day I went to several interviews, but never was in time for one. It seemed that, always, just before I arrived at each office, the position had been filled.

It only occurred to me that I was facing racial discrimination, when I was sent for an interview at the Bowery, a bank that was on Forty-second Street, just half a block from the employment agency. There was absolutely no way, someone else could have been interviewed and accepted, in the two minutes it took me to get from the agency to the bank. And yet, when I arrived at the door, the position had just been filled. I was angry.

I did get a job that day. And for four and a half months I was employed by Luminiere Corporation, a lamp factory. The pay was $65.00 per week. The people were very friendly, except for Herb and Florence, who were the bosses. Tardiness was punished by one's paycheck being docked. If one was five minutes late, one was docked for fifteen minutes. No one was allowed to stop working until exactly 5:15. I was an office clerk. I don't remember what I did there. But no one propositioned me.

It happened that one of the senior clerks was ill for a considerable length of time. Because the work that she did was more important than mine, I sometimes neglected my duties to attend to hers. One day, Florence reprimanded me for not completing my assigned tasks. I explained to her that I had been doing May's work, and angrily enumerated all that I had done. The following day I called in sick and went to find another job.

I Boldly Walked Through Opportunity's Door

I was heading for the Lexington Ave train station to go to an interview, when, at the corner of Madison Ave and Forty-second street, I saw a sign that read, "New York Telephone Employment Agency". I opened the door and a cheerful voice asked, "Are you here for the test." "Yes", I replied, having absolutely no idea what test the lady was referring to. I sat down and was given a test to determine my employable status. When I was through, the lady said I should hear from them soon. By then, I was too late to proceed to the interview, so I went home. It was a Wednesday.

I went back to Luminiere Corporation the next day, having made up my mind, to do only what I was hired to do, and to take a day off the following week to continue my search for another job.

It so happened that while I was manning the phones so that the operator could get a break for lunch, a call came through for me. It was the phone company calling to advise me that if I so desired, there was an opening as an accounting clerk that paid $88.00 a week. I needed to report to 330 Madison Ave the following morning. I immediately went in search of Florence to inform her that I was leaving her employment. I had received a better paying position. She offered me a $5.00 raise, which I politely declined. Even if she were prepared to match my new salary, I wouldn't have stayed.

At about two-thirty that afternoon, there was another phone call for me. The Phone Company informed me that there was another position, that of an engineering clerk, that would be available on the following Monday. The salary was $110.00 a week, and if I could wait the extra day, that position would be mine. Of course, I could and would.

And so it was, that for the next twenty-six years, until I retired, I worked for New York Telephone Company.

I found out later that 1970 was the year of Affirmative Action. In New York, Blacks were hired as never before. The public serving companies, such as the telephone company, had a quota to meet, in exchange for being allowed to raise their rates. After I was hired, I was given applications for my family and friends. Before long my husband was also an employee of NYT. The money was good, the benefits were great, and the people were friendly.

The group, to which I was assigned, consisted mostly of women. There were Whites, American Blacks, West Indian Blacks, and Puerto Ricans. Contrary to the opinion of some who think that women cannot work well together, we all got along fine, although I did discover that American Blacks did not take too kindly to West Indians. They felt that we were usurpers, taking jobs that should be theirs by right of birth, and that we were snobs, thinking ourselves better than them.

The Ambitious West Indians

I think the difference was one of dreams, purpose and possibilities. West Indians, like other immigrants, came to America with dream-driven time-slotted purpose that kept them focused. We were prepared to work hard and make sacrifices, to get an education, and/or become wealthy. We were not used to apartment life. We bought homes, which gave us stability, permanence, and a piece of America. The relationships that we had had with white people had been different. Our countries were populated with a majority of colored people, who governed themselves. Independence in the early sixties, had put colonialism to death, and introduced sky-limited possibilities to those who were willing to pay the price of study and hard work.

Trinidad, my homeland is known as the most cosmopolitan island of the West Indies. There, the people range from darkest black to un-tannable white. There, races mix and intermarry producing beautiful blends of colors and features, as well as cultures and religions, that create the happy people called Trinidadians. The mood is relaxed. The people work, worship and recreate. Carnival is the highlight of the unsaved Trinidadian's life. Cricket, football, dances, fetes, beach parties, house parties, club parties with plenty of food and alcohol characterize the weekends and holidays. When things go wrong, whether personally or nationally, Trinidadians tend to expect troubles to pass and life to return to ease and pleasure.

Our education system guaranteed every child a very thorough elementary education. At about age sixteen, those who were not academically inclined were given apprenticeships in trades for which they displayed skill. Children who demonstrated scholastic aptitude were encouraged to go as far as circumstances, money, and scholarship grants permitted. As a people of varied colors, the children of Trinidad encountered lawyers, doctors, teachers, nurses, athletes, entertainers, musicians, government ministers, religious ministers, merchants, agriculturists and scientists of every color, race, and creed. Role models were there to encourage every child to dream of becoming someone of significance. The discrimination factor was primarily one of money, rather than race; and social status and education rather than color. Consequently we were not as intimidated by whiteness or felt as limited by blackness as some black Americans were.

Life At Telephone Company

Working at NYT in the early seventies was pleasant. We worked and we partied. Every occasion was a reason to have a luncheon. Birthdays, pregnancies, a period that signaled no unwanted pregnancy, marriage, or any personal success and we were having two hour lunches at some of Manhattan's interesting restaurants. The bill was always divided equally among us. It didn't matter that I only drank coke. I contributed the same as the boozers. And that's why I began to drink.

Except for Neutrice, another West Indian woman and I, everybody drank alcohol: Black Russians, Bloody Marys, Brandy Alexanders, Singapore Slings, Gin and Tonic, Vodka and Orange juice, Whiskey and Seven-up, Tia Marias, and Amaretto. Everybody had a favorite. So I made up my mind to experiment with each person's drink. Soon I had my own favorites: Brandy Alexander, Gin and Tonic, with Tia Marias as my after-dinner liquor of choice.

Confidence, Embarrassment And Success At Work

As the years passed, the company introduced the "Upgrade and Transfer program". It was a promotion system whereby people who were ambitious, and desired to climb the ladder in a department other than the one in which they currently worked, could apply for available positions in other departments. They were tested and interviewed, and if successful, upgraded and transferred.

Believing that I had the ability to communicate and persuade others to buy, I began to apply for sales positions. My co-workers, who were content to remain where they were and crawl like snails to the next level, both admired and laughed at me when I turned up for work, dressed in my one good suit with matching shoes and handbag, little cotton gloves, my afro replaced by pressed and curled hair, and an air of expectant success. They knew that I was off to an interview.

I first applied to be a business representative, which is the lowest entry level into that field. I did very well on the test and interview, and was advised to wait six months then apply for the sales representative position. That I did. Again I so impressed the interviewer that she recommended that I apply for a special representative position. Although one of the requirements was that applicants possess a college degree, which I didn't have, I was encouraged to submit an application. A driver's license was also a plus, but I didn't allow that to be a deterrent. Where there's a will, there's a way.

I did a written test, which I aced. Two weeks later, I was interviewed. That went quite well. The final step was to be a simulated job situation. I was both confident and anxious. Confident because I knew I could do the job; anxious because I couldn't drive.

One day I received a phone call and was instructed to appear at 1290 Avenue of the Americas for an interview. Expecting to be examined in reference to the special rep position, I dressed in my interview suit and with my usual air of "I am in control, I can do anything, but fail", I was ushered into a large waiting area. The first thing I noticed was a sign that said, "College Degree Applicants".

After a short while I was shown into a grand executive office and invited to sit. Mr. S. asked me what my interests were. I proceeded with great zeal to sell myself and my ability to sell the company's products. I was so impressed with myself, that I was ready to sell ice to the Eskimos. However, after I finished speaking, Mr. S quietly said, "Would you like to be a computer programmer?"

I had no idea what a computer programmer did, but I replied, "Well actually that is my first love, but I didn't know that the opportunity existed." He explained to me that the company trained people for the position and that a class was about to begin the following week. He said if I could get my present manager to release me, I would be put in that class. I would go from being a non-management grade two clerk to a management grade six. My salary would be equal to my present salary plus all the overtime I had been working. If I failed at the end of eight weeks of classes, I would return to being a grade two clerk.

Ecstatic and apprehensive, I returned to my unit and went straight to my District-manager, who, when he heard my story, agreed to release me immediately. The non-management clerks from the engineering department were green with envy. Granted that a few people rejoiced with me, but others, especially the women that did not work directly with me, made catty remarks about my mini-skirts, which I enjoyed wearing when I wasn't dressed for success. They said that I had worn my mini-skirts to flaunt myself before Mr. B, the district manager, and that I'd probably worked on my back for my promotion.

I was aware that the position of computer programmer required at least an associate degree. However, I was ignorant of the fact that besides the interview, there was a qualifying test that one must pass, in order to be eligible for the programmer's training program. Subsequent to my un-tested entrance into the class, an unprecedented number of my co-workers applied for the position and were tested. None succeeded. Later on I concluded that the company had had to meet a quota of Blacks and Latinos for the class and needed a black female. I had come to their attention because of the positions for which I had applied, the tests I had taken and passed, and interviews that I had had, through the venue of the Upgrade and Transfer program.

I didn't care what people said. I never cared if people said bad things that were untrue. I did care if people who were my friends or family believed the jealous lies. I never attempted to disprove any lie. I just went about my business saddened if people I trusted thought ill of me, and laughing at those who didn't count.

When I was just an ordinary grade two clerk with a union behind me, I dressed in whatever I felt looked attractive. It was a time when women were just beginning to wear sensible tailored pants suits. But I was young and bold and to some degree naïve. I wore sporty pants, mini-skirts, and when hot pants were in vogue, I graced the office with my black satin or hot pink shorts. They were not tight and of decent length and looked quite chic. No one complained. Some wondered at my daring. To me it was inconsequential. I did enjoy walking down Broadway and being complimented by the men who admired me. They called me Pretty Lady and I smiled and wished them all good evening. However, commonsense dictated that as a manager, I should dress appropriately; therefore, I discarded the miniskirts and hot pants for more business-like attire.

Finding myself in a room full of people who boasted of bachelors and masters degrees in computer science and suchlike, I felt somewhat out of place. However, I realized that the average American was unfamiliar with the English system of GCE. I hit on a plan. Our final high school exams were set by Universities of England. Therefore, I bluffed my way through the embarrassing introductions, by talking of my Certificates from the Universities of Cambridge and London. Nevertheless, despite my confident appearance, I was very intimidated by the scholarship of the members of the class. I began to be very shy. I didn't socialize. I kept to myself.

I found the coursework fairly easy, but as we neared the second set of exams, I began to be afraid that I would forget all that I had learned, as I had done just before exams in high school. I was frantic with worry. My husband was distressed to see me so troubled that he suggested that I quit the program. I sought a second opinion from a very good friend who advised me to approach the teacher and let her know of my fears. What did I have to lose? Heeding his counsel, I asked for a private audience with Mrs. Mctique who was extremely understanding. She tested me in a very casual non-stressful manner. I did very well.

At the end of eight weeks, we all expected to be assigned as assistant programmers so that we could put into practice what we'd been taught. There were not enough positions available, and it seemed to me that those with the highest level of college education were placed, while a few of us were sent to work in computer rooms, where we were required to read cards into one machine and remove paper from another.

I was the last person from my group to be given a programmer's assignment. What made me believe that I was discriminated against was the fact that months later, a new group of programmers received programming positions, but I was left to read in cards and pull paper in the computer room. I was a grade six manager, receiving grade six pay, doing grade three work that a grade two non-management clerk could do.

Eventually to my great joy, I was given an assignment to modify and complete a program that had been left unfinished by someone who was no longer there. Enthusiastically, I set to work to prove myself worthy of the title I had.

It was a large and complicated program. I believe I was expected to fail, but failure was never an option in my mind. I was given no due date which eased the pressure, allowing me to work at my own pace. I spent two months reading the unfinished program and the original specifications in an effort to understand what had been accomplished so far, and what needed to be done. I concluded that the previous programmer created an impossibly problematical mess of code that would never achieve the stated purpose. Of course those who had given me the assignment already knew that. I decided to take on the humongous task of re-coding the whole program. I discarded the mounds of spaghetti code, and proceeded with the specs and flowchart to create a working module.

No sooner was I ready to begin testing my program, than the assignment was taken away and I was reassigned to another group. I was asked to write a program that would change the rates of every piece of service equipment that the company used. This was an extremely important assignment because it affected the company's revenue. I was told that if I failed to produce acceptable results, I would be sent back to the engineering department as a grade two non-management clerk.

It was so unreasonable to give an un-tried assistant programmer an assignment of such magnitude with such an unjust threat.

I believe that I was again expected to fail. I did not. I delivered the program on the due date and the results were good. From then on I became the Service and Equipment Rate Change programmer.

Miserable At Home

It was about this time that I began to be very unhappy at home. It seemed to me that my husband considered the needs of his parents, brother, and sisters, more than he did those of our children and I. He seemed unable to deny them anything, and they showed me no respect as his wife. I knew that my family background made me a less than desirable daughter-in-law, but their son had wanted me more than anything in the world. Paul had gone against them in marrying me and that made me feel like I mattered. But soon I began to feel unimportant, helpless, and hopeless. And, after nine years of marriage and two children I couldn't trust the love I no longer felt was mine.

We had had dreams to fulfill, but it seems to me that his purpose in life was to help his father, mother, brothers and sisters fulfill their dreams. Ours took a backseat. Nobody extended a hand to help us, or cared about our plans. We were young, just starting a family, and needed to build a foundation.

There was a time when his mother moved out of her husband's home and my husband was asked to supply the money for her furniture and rent. And he was unable to refuse. Yet, when I became pregnant again, his mother, who had had fifteen children, wanted to know why I would allow myself to be pregnant, seeing that I was so very sick. I was making life hard for their precious son. Their intrusion on our lives never stopped.

I remember the cold/hot anger I felt as they discussed what my husband should do with our money. His sister needed two thousand dollars per semester for college fees. And what about him? Hadn't we migrated to the USA so that he could become an electrical engineer? Didn't we have a five-year plan? Weren't we going to move back to Trinidad after he got his degree, build our dream house and raise our children? We couldn't meet their demands and fulfill our plans.

I was angry because none of our plans were coming to fruition, but they were sure enjoying his money and their lives. I had no voice in their family discussions. I didn't belong, and he seemed to need their approval and affection, while taking mine for granted. He voiced no objections.

Not Happily Ever After - The End Of A Dream Of A Future

It seemed to me that my husband was plotting with his family against me. We had bought a house and I had wanted us to have a fresh start. I wanted us to christen every square inch of the house with our love-making. Then I wanted to bring our children from Trinidad so that we could be a real family. I did not want my sister-in-law living with me. She had lived with us from time to time and I thought that if she were not in our new house, we would have a better prospect of improving our marriage. It bothered me that she could lead an expense free life and fulfill her ambitions, while our dreams and family life were sacrificed. The five years had passed and there seemed no likelihood of our dreams being fulfilled any time soon. I wanted the opportunity to establish some roots without his family.

When I expressed my unhappiness and frustration, my husband accused me of infidelity. He couldn't understand. He felt I had no cause to be unhappy. He didn't drink, gamble, or hang out. He paid the mortgage. He worked hard to give me security. But he was insecure, and I was insecure. When I asked him what reason he could have for suspecting me of infidelity, to my horror Paul explained that he didn't trust me because I was a bad seed. I was expected to be unfaithful. My mother had had eight children by five men, and my father had sired twelve children by three women. I believed that I was being judged by my parents' past behavior and I realized that my husband was therefore likely to receive any information that proved my infidelity.

From the time Paul and I had decided to be a couple I had told him every thought I'd had, everything I'd done, every discovery I'd made, whether good, bad, or indifferent. And he was fully acquainted with my whole family. I should have been more secretive. I should have hidden myself. My innocence damned me. Realizing that I would always be suspected of immoral behavior, I despaired.

Could things have been different? I don't think so. It seems that we both suffered from low self-esteem and consequent insecurity. He needed his birth family to stand with him and approve him, and I needed him to stand with me against them, and make our dreams come true for us, not them.

When my husband went to her for advice and comfort, my own mother, told him that I was too hot for one man, and that he had not been first with me. She of all people knew nothing about me. I was able to speak to my mother and ask her what was her reason for saying such a thing. She said, matter-of-factly, that it seemed so to her.

Many years later I learned that one of my half sisters had poured fuel on the fire of Paul's suspicion and insecurity, by telling him that I had a habit of bringing men home when he was at work. That was preposterous, but he believed it, because unknown to me then, the trust had already died.

When I became aware of these destructive lies that my sister had told against me, I was thrown into a pit of bewilderment. My mind exploded with pain that I tried hard to suppress. I didn't shed a tear, but I bawled. I had already become a Christian and the knowledge that I had to forgive my sister, plagued me for weeks. I was unable to broach the subject to her. God knows I tried. I started conversations to bait her, but she didn't bite. I wanted revenge, but about ten years had passed and she had probably forgotten the whole incident.

God is so wise. It was at that time that my sister asked me to pray for her as she was having marital problems. I was a Christian. What could I do? I had to forgive her and pray for her marriage. Suffice to say, that by the grace of God, I have forgiven her.

The low self-esteem that had developed during my childhood and early adolescence, overwhelmed and convinced me, that I could not win what I perceived, as a battle to restore myself to the preeminent place in my husband's affections. Paul and I had never had a quarrel. We didn't fight. We didn't deal with negatives. He didn't express his fears and dislikes and I didn't mine. We both had always avoided hurting each other, and had tried to dismiss or at least ignore pain-producing situations. Neither of us knew how to handle something this big.

We went for counseling. The Catholic priest offered us no help or hope. After listening to my story, for I did all the talking, he told us that it seemed that our marriage was dead. He advised my husband to move out and suggested that if he cared to, Paul could try courting me for about three months, to see if he could regain my love. But, he didn't think it would work.

At first Paul said he was willing to try the suggestion, but before we arrived back home he changed his mind saying, "If you are unhappy, you leave."

Consequently I sabotaged my marriage, destroying my family, bewildering my husband, and damaging my children's fragile emotional health.

The divorce, which I initiated, left me fragmented, bewildered, and completely lacking in confidence. Unable to believe that I could adequately parent my children, I sent them to live with my mother, causing my eight–year-old son to believe that they had been abandoned by me, and that he and his little brother were responsible for the divorce. Thus I perpetuated the legacy of emotional damage.

Recently, as I spoke to Paul of my journey, he told me that a key factor in his readiness to believe that I neither cared about him or our marriage was my missing display of emotion, especially the absence of tears. Under the traumatic circumstances of our break-up, I should have been crying miserably. I didn't know how to do that. My abnormal indifference and ability to shrug and move on branded me as a heartless monster.

I wrote this poem to express how I felt about my husband and his family.

THE ULTIMATE BETRAYAL

There sat I, an alien, a stranger in their midst,
Invisible, contemptible, ignored,
Excluded from their august family,
My husband, no, their son, their brother,
The center of attention.

There sat I, and listened, voiceless, as they spoke,
Necessity demanded the invisible be dumb,
And deaf, and even blind,
And so remain unheard, unseen,
And immaterial.

There sat I, and listened, and anger swelled my heart
And clutched my throat,
And filled my neck,
And flaring hot exploded in my head,
Destroying all intelligence
And maximizing fear.

There sat I, and trembled, cold with terror,

And burning now with hate,
Impotent against their collective strength,
The cold and heat combined and tears rained down
Flooding me with pain.

There sat he, who'd made the solemn promise to leave them
And to cleave to me alone,
Till death did part,
Betraying our love, forgetting all our dreams, leaving me
Empty and alone.

There they sat, arrogant and imperious,
Killing all my dreams, my hopes, my aspirations.
With every word they cut away my present,
With every plan my future sacrificed,
Redeeming him.

There he sat, salvation paid in full, accepted son,
Restored to their good graces,
Saved from an unwise choice,
And watched me stripped, and robbed, and wounded,
Left to die.

And there I sat, and cringed, and shrank,
And hid myself within the tomb they'd dug,
Naked I came, and naked now I went,
Without a dream,
No hope, no joy, and loveless,
Into their created hell.

But they hadn't created my hell. My hell began long before the day when my husband's grandmother had called me a red nigger. It began before they considered me unfit. It began when I realized that mothers and fathers were married and that they and their children have the same last name. It began when I understood brothers and sisters resemble each other, but we all looked different. You see I was born at a time when illegitimacy was a social crime. My birth certificate branded me, "illegitimate girl child". Coals and depth were added to my hell when my siblings and other children called me "broko foot"; when Daddy and Mama fought and cussed and were dragged away by the police; when Daddy threw us out and "Uncle Freddy' sexually molested me; when Mama called me ugly names and said she could disown my sister and me any time because she was black, but we were red; when she scoffed at my excellent grade and called it a fluke; when she threatened to throw me out of her house; when two of my big brother friends almost raped me.

The Past Has Lost It's Power

Lest you think I'm still an emotional mess, let me assure that I'm not. I am not perfect, but I've been healed significantly. And the healing continues. The memories evoke no pain, and even the memory of the pain has left. The old past has lost its power. I am being reconstructed by God's truth. God is awesome.

Three years after the divorce, the Lord Jesus saved me. I was born again by the Spirit of Almighty God by His Grace, through faith in the vicarious death of Jesus Christ, the Son of God. It had been a long journey, but God had patiently pursued me until I understood my need and received His free Gift of Salvation.

-15- Rescued On The Path To Hell

Life After Divorce

No one would have believed how sad and lonely I was after the marriage was over. I wore a very convincing skin-tight mask of strength and I seemed very sure of myself. It was that I just refused to dwell on the past or consider the future. I had learned the secret of living one day at a time. I understood that to look into tomorrow when I belonged to no one, and was loved by no one, was to entertain fear and sorrow.

I was the life of any party I attended. I drank, smoked cigarettes and marijuana, and danced. How I loved to dance, but most of the time I went home to my lonely apartment, made emptier by the momentary escape into a fantasy world of laughter and flirtation.

Oh I always attracted men, but it was hard to believe their words of love for the simple reason that I felt bankrupt. I had nothing to give. I could give my body, but without the intimacy of joined souls, the giving took what I had and left me empty. I did enjoy sex, but it was different from when I was married. It was never total. And when it was over, I turned my back, not even wanting to be cuddled. I did have two male companions during the two years before I was saved. The first lasted five months, until I found out that he was in another relationship. I ended the second relationship when I discovered that his marriage that was supposed to be over was still bearing fruit.

The man of the second relationship, whom I shall call George was heart-broken. I was not. I never really gave my heart to anyone, but I knew how to show love, and so it appeared that I was in love. Soon after I terminated our relationship, I began attending a Bible study group and a strong spirit of conviction so worked in me, that I was glad that I was not having sex anymore. However, a few months later, George's wife who had only then been made aware of my existence, incurred my wrath. She phoned my house, and finding my eleven-year old son alone at home, said some nasty things about me to him. I didn't get mad. I got even. I invited her husband to move in with me. He jumped at the offer. He became a good friend, but we never resumed a physical relationship.

It seems that I am what men consider wife material, and I had many marriage proposals, but I always wondered what those men wanted from me. I always felt I didn't have what it took to sustain a permanent relationship. So I pushed the-would-be husbands away. I could trust no man's love for I was not worth loving.

I was a failure. I had done my utmost best. My husband had said we had a perfect relationship. We had been taught that a woman must be a cook in the kitchen, a lady in the drawing room, and whatever her man wanted in the bedroom. And I was all that. I wasn't a busy body, knockabout, spendthrift. I was wise. My material needs were few. His clothes were always clean and ironed, his meals were well prepared and presented, and I was the best social companion and sexual partner he could desire. All my ambition was for his success. I was jealous for his well-being. He knew I would have gotten between him and anyone who attempted to take advantage of him. We had been together from my age fifteen to twenty-eight. I had borne him two sons, and when he expressed his un-readiness for another child, I had had an abortion. But I could not make him put me first in his life.

Having identified with Paul for so long, divorce left me feeling insecure, not knowing who I was. I felt like a little girl in a woman's body. It seemed that in order to find myself I had to go back to who I was before Paul became a part of my life, and that seemed too long ago to travel backwards. So I chose to go on taking one day at a time, not thinking to deeply about anything, not even about my children. Having absolutely no confidence to raise my children in a system that was foreign to me, I was content for my children to belong to my mother. I worked and provided for all their material needs, and consoled myself that I was doing the best I could, because they had a mother in Mama and their father had moved back to Trinidad.

Nevertheless, it was hard not to feel sad at Christmas when people brought their children to the workplace for the Santa Claus gift-giving. And New Years Eve was the loneliest night of the year. But the practice I had had in immediately putting myself to sleep to escape Mama's indifference and acid tongue certainly helped. I would lie in the bed and cover myself from head to toe and not move till I had to. Some times I was tempted to end it all, but I was afraid of hell, and besides, I had to provide for my children.

I joined a spa because I wanted to make friends. I imagined myself engaged in intelligent conversation, but I didn't know how. I did not seem able to converse with new people, although I did very well with people I already knew. Two years at the spa, participating almost daily in every activity that my crippled leg would allow, bought no new friends. But my body was slim and strong, and I could stand on my shoulder and relax.

I lived in a large apartment complex and as many do, I came and went without ever knowing or caring who lived next door. One day, my neighbor Betty knocked on my door and invited me to a Tupperware party at her house. Apparently she had invited every body on our floor, and we all accepted. When we arrived and were seated expecting to be given a demonstration of Tupperware, Betty revealed an ulterior motive for her party. She was lonely. She was divorced and lived with her two children Maria and Cosco. She came from Greece, didn't work, was intimidated by the New York culture, and went nowhere. She didn't care if we bought her Tupperware, just please, could we be friends. We all agreed to befriend each other.

We were quite a group. There was Mary, divorced with two daughters; and Linda, divorced with two boys and a girl. There was another Betty, a stay at home mom, with five children; Beverly who never married and had no children; and yours truly, divorced with two sons.

Thanks to Grecian Betty's desperation, I made one of the best friends of my life. That was Mary Burton. She was my first best friend in New York. We were good company for each other. Until I accepted the Lord we eased each other's loneliness. We remained friends for twenty-four years. She died last year.

God Begins His Courtship

The Lord introduced himself to me through a wonderful man, an accountant who also sold insurance, named Watson Duncanson. He came to prepare my tax returns, and sell me life insurance. He stayed to tell me about Jesus and Life Assurance. I couldn't hear a word he was saying. He was tall, and handsome and even as I listened without hearing, I knew he was pure and un-corruptible. I didn't know he was a

Christian. I did not understand the concept of Christianity. However, when he invited me to a weekend retreat in the Poconos, I accepted the invitation

As a Catholic, I used to attend retreats. I remember times of withdrawing from the humdrum of life into a place of quiet meditation. I thought that it would be great to enjoy a weekend away from the city, to be left alone with my thoughts in the fresh spring mountain air and natural beauty of new wild foliage.

I was disappointed, angered, and saddened. I was not left alone. I was invited to participate in various seminars and workshops. It was all about Jesus. Then they showed two movies called "Thief In The Night" and "Distant Thunder." It was all about the rapture and the tribulation. It was quite frightening.

I had never heard of such events. I knew nothing about the book of Revelations. Watson Duncanson and Brian tried hard to persuade me to be saved. Brian, an ardent, young teenager, stood before me with tears flowing down his cheek, but I stubbornly refused. I was disappointed in the retreat's agenda, angered by the fright of the film, and saddened because I could not be saved.

Without being told, I knew that to turn my life over to Christ meant a changed lifestyle that included giving up sex. I couldn't see how I could do that. Not that I was having unlimited sex, I didn't even have a boyfriend at the time, but I had come to realize that I could be turned on and enjoy physical sex without marriage and I wasn't sure that I would ever risk being married again. I was no longer a good Catholic.

The Dilemma Of Being A Catholic

Catholicism, more than any other religion, can be for some, a religion of despair. It's claims of being the only true church produces hopelessness, in those whose circumstances of life reveal the truth of unregenerate man's natural bent towards sin.

Those who live in convents and monasteries and have taken vows of perpetual chastity, voluntary poverty, and entire obedience, can sometimes deceive themselves into believing that they are righteous and acceptable to a holy God, especially by means of the penances that they do, the novenas that they pray, and the indulgences that they buy. Their needs of food, clothes, and shelter are met, and they do not necessarily have to concern themselves with the day-by-day pressures of life. There is a built-in protection from the occasions that lead to sin, and even the exposure to temptations is somewhat limited.

Catholics who marry early, enjoy a good marriage and family life, and earn a decent livelihood, may be protected from yielding to the temptations that the un-married, the lonely, and the poor, find difficult or impossible to resist. Lack of opportunity and lack of need often constitute the only deterrent to sin. Given opportunity and need even good Catholics discover that they lack power to resist temptation. They further discover that the sacrament of penance becomes a place of facing one's sinfulness and guilt, but offers no means whereby the evil desires are removed. So the sin-sick Catholic is caught in a helpless circle of hopelessness and fear. His only chance of redemption is the hope that there will be a priest present at the hour of death, to grant the absolution, he so desperately desires.

Why I Became Disillusioned By Catholicism

My faith in Catholicism had begun to unravel after my second son was born. Marriage counseling for Paul and I was done by a priest whose only concern was that we understand that the use of un-natural methods of birth control was mortally sinful. We were introduced to Rhythm Method, which necessitated the taking of temperature every day, and looking for that small increase in temperature that signaled the onset of ovulation. The next four days were unsafe; the rest of the month was safe. This method did not take into consideration the possibility of low-grade fevers that might be present due to infection, or sudden changes in the menstrual cycle, due to stress. Consequently, before I was ready to be a mother, before I had learned to be a wife, I had found myself pregnant.

After Allan was born, I started taking birth control pills. I had spoken to the priest about it. He had declared that my only options of birth control were Rhythm or Abstinence. I was a twenty-year-old married woman with a twenty-four year old virile husband. Together, after almost five years of resisting temptation, we had discovered the greatest pleasure outside of heaven. Abstinence was not an option. We had also experienced the flaw in Rhythm called pregnancy. We loved our baby, and planned to have two more, but at present, Rhythm/pregnancy was not a practical option. Consequently, we were excommunicated and consigned to hell fire.

One night, about a year after I started taking birth control pills, there was an earthquake. I woke up in terror of hell. The possibility of dying in my state of sin and excommunication seemed imminent. If my life was spared, I knew I would throw the damned pills away. It was, I did. My husband and I went back to confession and make a good act of contrition. We became good Catholic communicants again. But we did not abstain.

One night, on the way home from a walk around the savannah, I began to feel nauseously ill. Remembering the nine moths of sickness of my first pregnancy, I immediately concluded that I was pregnant. We were in a quandary. Paul was set to migrate to America in a month's time and, I would be left to care for our year old son by myself. I could not go through a pregnancy without my husband. We couldn't afford to have another baby so soon.

The next day I went to the doctor who confirmed that I was pregnant and offered me an immediate abortion. Later, when I thought about the whole fiasco, I wandered if I had really been pregnant. I had felt ill one day and panicked. I had not missed a period. I believe the unscrupulous doctor had assessed my fear and responded to it. Later on, as Paul and I considered the facts, we remembered that he had bought a shrimp roti that night when we went walking. I had ordered chicken. It was possible that shrimp had inadvertently been put in the chicken roti and my nausea was an allergic reaction to the shrimp. I do suffer from such an allergy. Nevertheless, fear is more powerful than death. For three hundred and fifty dollars, I had a D&C at the Community Hospital. This was 1969.

True to form, my soul being once more in jeopardy, I went to confession. I was given a penance of six Hail Marys. I could not comprehend the inappropriateness of the penance to the sin. Whether or not I had been pregnant was not the issue. I had deliberately done this worst of crimes in my heart. How could it be that, for using birth control so that no baby would be conceived, I was excommunicated, but for murder I got six Hail Marys? It just didn't add up. But I was a Catholic in good standing again.

After my second son was born in 1972, I once more went through the fear of an immediate pregnancy. Again I made an appointment to see the priest. "Father," I said, I've just had a baby, and I also have a four year old who doesn't even live with us at present. We can't afford to have another baby right away and it is not fair to ask me to abstain." "Well," replied the priest, "Why don't you use birth control pills?" I was floored. How long had I suffered the tormenting fear of hell because of birth-control pills, and now it was OKAY? It wasn't sinful anymore? Truth should be a constant, regardless of place, time, or circumstance. I was glad, but I was confused.

A year after the divorce and for two years before I became a Christian, I continued to attend Mass, but never again did I go to confession or communion. I was living a sinful life. I realized that I had no power over sin, so why fight it. It didn't make sense. We used to say, "What's the use of getting sober, if you know you will be drunk again?" Because of the indoctrinated fear of hell, some Catholics keep trying to live morally upright lives, but others eventually conclude that they cannot possibly gain heaven, so they give up the fight and yield totally to sin. Such was I.

Wooed And Won By The Grace Of God

But God did not give up on me. He pursued me for almost three years. Sometimes it seemed as if He was right there protecting me; like when we got in the accident in Canada and everyone was hurt except me; or when my appendix ruptured and a co-worker who never came to my house got there just in time to take me to the hospital. Then there were times when I felt as if God took His restraining and protective hands off me so that I could learn how degenerate I would be without Him.

Without Christ the flesh cannot be crucified, and un-dead sin-sick flesh continues to deteriorate. And all that I thought, good Catholic as I used to be, that I would never do, I did.

Then I met some wonderful Christians who invited me to study the Bible with them. I had no intention of joining the group. I only wanted to find out what they knew that I didn't know. Their love for me was unbelievable. They behaved towards me as if I were as righteous as they were. That made me feel guilty. I was also moved to jealousy by their peace and obvious joy. I called Watson Duncanson, who had stayed in touch with me and in prayer for me, and told him about the Bible study group. He came to check it out. He was happy that I had found Christian friends with a Bible-based perspective.

I kept going to the Bible study every Tuesday night, and I began to want desperately to be saved. However, because the members of the group were all young inexperienced babes in Christ, nobody invited me to receive Jesus as my Lord and

Savior. I didn't know what to do. I was too shy to ask the question, ***What must I do to be saved?***

The weight of my sin grew every time we got together until I could bear it no more. I identified with Paul. Somehow I understood that the power to live righteously came with the Savior. And He was mine for the asking. ***" O wretched man that I am! who shall deliver me from the body of this death? I thank God through Jesus Christ our Lord. So then with the mind I myself serve the law of God; but with the flesh the law of sin."*** Romans 7:24-25.

And so it was that one morning with a weight of sin, guilt, and shame that was too heavy to bear any longer, I slipped onto my knees and simply prayed, "Lord Jesus, they say you can take burdens, please take mine."

Immediately, I felt the weight lifted out of my life and a song, that had lain forgotten in my soul from my Gospel Hall Sunday school days, sprung into my heart, and I began to sing. "Jesus took my burden, I could no longer bear, yes Jesus took my burden in answer to my prayer."

My joyous singing woke up the man who was in my bed. Bewildered, he wanted to know what was the matter. I confessed, "Jesus took my burden." My friend Margarite who was temporarily living at my house woke up. "What's happening?" I told her, "Jesus took my burden." There came into my heart a peace, which passed my understanding. My circumstances had not changed, but I felt as if all was well with me.

The lease on my apartment was almost up and I began to look for a larger apartment so that when my children came for summer vacation they could have their own rooms. I asked God for direction, and He led me to a three-bedroom apartment in Brooklyn.

Three weeks after my desperate prayer, my sister Ann Marie invited me to an Assemblies of God Church. I had wanted to go to church, but I had not known where to go. As Pastor Bher preached, it dawned on me that I had asked the Lord to take my burden, but I had not given him my life. I had one need and that was to get to that altar and surrender to Christ.

And so it was that on a September Sunday in 1979, I gave Jesus my life, and He gave me His.

Even before I gave my worthless life to Christ, His Spirit had convicted me of sin, and with the conviction came guilt and sorrow. I did not want to sin anymore. Even though my boyfriend stayed at my house, we could have no sexual relationship. He liked me a lot and so stayed around even without that pleasure. He saw and felt the change in me and knew that it was over between us. Eventually the day came when I told him he had to go. He meekly packed and left.

-16- The Restoration Begins

Christmas that year was different. Suddenly I understood the reason for Christ's coming. And, even though I was alone, I did not feel lonely and miserable, but hopeful and happy.

One thing I realized I wanted more than ever was a relationship with my mother. I thought that now that I'd been changed, and she too had been saved for a number of years, we could enjoy each other's company.

After my divorce had become final, I had gone home for a visit. I desperately needed for my mother to embrace me and tell me everything would be alright. I mean there was no reason to believe she would do that, but I needed it that badly. Every night I would sit by myself on the porch wishing she would come out and say, "Andrea, why don't you go to bed?" and I would throw myself into her arms and cry my heartbreak out. But it never happened. She was embarrassed by my divorce and all she said was, "You don't have to walk around telling people that you are divorced."

Now, because of salvation, I had high expectations. I planned to visit her for mother's day. It would be a double treat because my children were still in her care. I anticipated such pleasure.

I Hated My Mother

I was shocked to find that my mother had not changed and even more shocked to realize that I hadn't either. I Discovered That I Had A New Spirit But An Old Soul. We were still unable to communicate at a positive emotional level. In fact things were worse than ever. My children were being neglected and abused. With all the money I used to send her, my elder son who was then twelve years old, was wearing shoes that were too small for his feet, and sneakers with holes in the soles. He had two pair of pants, which he washed at nights and hung behind the refrigerator to dry. He hadn't been attending school because he had got into some trouble and the principal had instructed him not to return to school unless he came with his parents. Mama had informed him that he had no parents. She refused to go with him, and so, tired of being physically punished for turning up at school without his parents, he had stopped going. He was also severely beaten and verbally abused by my mother. He suffered from headaches and cried himself to sleep at nights.

My younger son was allowed to go to school if he pleased; consequently, at age eight he hardly knew his alphabet. The teachers had been told by my mother, that he was a delicate child and that madness ran in his father's family, so they were not to put any pressure on him. Mama kept him in the company of her elderly friends, so that he talked like an old woman, and actually walked with his back bent.

My mother explained to my children that they were better off with her because I didn't want them and that I was a cruel person. My older son had known me and he knew I wasn't cruel, but I had given him away to hardship and abuse, therefore, he concluded that it was probably true that I didn't want them. My younger son who had not spent much time with me was actually afraid of me.

All the money and things I used to send to my mother were used to help her family in her hometown, where she went for vacation every year. She portrayed herself as wealthy, carried large barrels of gifts to her sisters, their children, and grand children, while my children suffered deprivation and neglect.

The way I had reasoned it out was, that Mama had treated her own children badly out of the frustration of poverty, but that if she had no financial lack she would be happier, and life with her would be good for my children. Besides that, grandparents were supposed to love and pamper grand children.

When I questioned my mother about my findings, which I observed for myself, and which were confirmed by my sisters and the children's teachers, (and also years later by my son), my mother became angry and offensive. I hated her. I never hated her before. I had stopped loving her. I had felt disconnected from her, but I hadn't hated her. Now I hated her. I knew I had to take my children away from her. But I was troubled. How would I manage with them? I decided to speak to God about it.

God, Our Father, Restored My Children To Me.

One day while taking my children for a walk, and pondering my next step, I said to the Lord, "Can I do this? Shall I take the children? I have no one to help me." Suddenly, I heard voices singing, "What a friend we have in Jesus." Immediately I knew that I could take my children and God himself would help me. I was confident. (They were not angelic voices, but voices from a nearby church).

I asked my older son if he would like to live with me. He could hardly believe his ears. He wanted to be with me, but his concern was what about Mama? I knew that Mama wouldn't want them to leave. She would be afraid that her money would be cut off. I told Allan that we would keep it a secret, that when I sent for them to come for summer vacation, he must pack anything that he didn't want to leave behind, because he would not be returning. He must not tell his brother about the plan, because his brother couldn't keep a secret. With that hope my son was able to make it through the next three months.

When my sons first came to live with me, they were always fighting and I was unhappy. Eventually I was advised to take them for counseling. I don't know if that helped, but eventually they seemed to settle down and life was normal. Later on I understood the area of conflict between Allan and Ian. While they lived with my mother, Allan, to protect his brother from the brutal beatings, which he himself received, accepted the blame for all Ian's wrongs. Now that they lived with me, Allan no longer wanted to take the blame, and so Ian had to take punishments for his own bad behavior. This made Ian very angry. He thought that Allan was reneging on his big brother duties.

Anyway, we became a family. God's hand was in our lives. My children accepted Christ as their personal Savior. My younger son, Ian said that he wanted Jesus because he saw how happy Jesus made me. Allan accepted Christ one day when he'd come to the end of his rope. That day he came to me and said, "Mummy, I want to get off this earth." It seemed to me that he was insinuating suicide. He sat there crying, not explaining, and I didn't know what to do. But God who sees the end from the beginning, had provided my cousin Nolene, a veteran saved woman to be visiting at the precise moment. She took him in hand and led him to the Lord. I still don't know what was going on. I think the cultural shock of the New York school system, with fighting, cursing, gangs, and the lack of discipline, was one factor. Another factor was the missing father.

My children's father had migrated back to America and I had reached out to him after I had received salvation. I had informed him of my decision to have the children with me, and had suggested that it would be great if he could have a relationship with them. I had given him financial help to get himself a place to live. His parents had also migrated and he was presently living with them. I knew that they did not like me, or my children, so I wanted him to have his own place where the children could visit him. He had agreed to everything I said, and so my children's joy was full when I advised them that they would be spending time with their father.

But their father had not kept his promise. After they'd been with me for three weeks, Ian asked, "When are we going to see our father?" I gave him his father's phone number and told him to call, figuring that if he heard the child's pleading voice, it would soften him. When Ian came off the phone, I asked him when was his father going to come by. The little boy was in a rage. He said, "Some time. What does some time mean?" I think after that he stopped expecting to see him and no one mentioned him any more. I subsequently learned that Allan used to roam the streets of the village where he suspected his father lived, hoping to run into him. But he never did.

Nevertheless, the children and I were moderately happy. The

Lord led us to a Pentecostal church three blocks from where we lived, and as he had promised, I was able to raise them in a satisfactory manner. Not wanting to ever be like Mama, I did not quarrel or make negative statements to them. I did not spoil them. I taught them to be strong and self-sufficient, expecting help from no one but God. God demonstrated His care of us and they came to expect His intervention in their lives. They did not always receive the things they wanted, but they never went without what they needed (that's what I thought at the time). On occasion I felt that corporal punishment was warranted for misbehavior, but on the whole life was pleasant. We shared the chores and the fun. At first my boys went everywhere with me. When they began to have their own social life, I missed our times together terribly.

The Things I Didn't Give My Children

There was much I would have liked to do with them but fear of poverty prevented me from spending money on non-essentials. I wish I had taken them on vacations. Gone with them to Disneyland, seen the great sights of America, and made forever memories. But I had had no one but myself, no income but my own, and was always afraid of being broke. There were also things that did not cost money, which I wanted to give my children and could not.

I had a friend, whose attitude and behavior towards her children I envied. She addressed her children in loving terms like, "sweetheart" or "darling". She smothered them with hugs and showered them with kisses. She continually expressed her love for them. I wanted so desperately to display such affection to my sons. I would sit at work and plan in my mind. "When I get home I would hug them and kiss them and tell them I loved them. I would say, "Sweetheart, you're the best son a mother could have." But when I arrived home I found I didn't even know how to start.

My Father's Kiss Purchased My Forgiveness

In the summer of 1981 my father came to visit. During the years I had kept my promise. After I was married, while I was still living in Trinidad, I used to bake bread every Saturday. I would give my father a loaf and say "This is for Olympia and the children, not you." He never said a word of rebuke. I suspect he remembered the conversation I had had with him, and I don't know if he ever ate of the bread. I had never spat in his hand, for he had never asked me for anything. Olympia was the lady with whom he lived after he left my mother. She had six children for him. They lived together for thirty-six years, until she turned to the Lord and left. They seemed, by observation and by report, to have had a happy life, without the violence that we had experienced. Olympia is still a sweet, simple, loving woman, who embraced all Daddy's children as her own.

Whenever I needed company to go to the cinema, I invited

my father along. He it was, that introduced us to the pleasure of movies. In my mind, that and the love for comic books were the only legacy he left us. Mama used to become very angry when he would send a message to her by Deborah or me, saying, could she have us dressed for such a time so he could take us to the movies. She would cuss and carry on about how he didn't know whether we had clothes to wear or food to eat, but he was spending money on theatre shows. Nevertheless, to our joy, she would have us ready and allow us to go.

It was therefore my vengeful intention, never to give my father anything more than the pleasure of my company at a movie. Even when I would return from New York on vacation, I took presents for Olympia and the children. My youngest sister was also my goddaughter so I always gave her money. But Daddy I took to the movies.

In 1981, Daddy sat in my living room in Brooklyn, chatting about the fact that when he had last seen me my hair had been cut so short, as if I had been scalped, and now it seemed like I was wearing a wig because my hair was on my back. When I used to visit Trinidad for the Carnival festivities, I used to cut my hair so that I didn't have to bother about styling it. My father hated it. To my astonishment, my mother had said it looked good. Previously, I had not worn a short haircut because my mother had said that I had an ill-shaped head.

"Daddy," I said, "this is not a wig, I just haven't been cutting my hair since I got saved." Daddy was overjoyed. He pulled me unto his lap, ran his hand through my hair, and kissed me. In that moment all the animosity I had felt towards my father melted away. Before he left, I went into my bedroom, took fifty dollars out of my purse and gave it to him, explaining that it was for him, nobody else. I think he understood that he had been forgiven.

A couple of years later when I went to see him, Daddy asked me, "How are you making it, with the two boys and no one to help you?" He couldn't help me and I knew that. But he was the only person who had ever asked me how I was making it. I loved him for the concern.

How could I love my father who had not participated in my life except negatively, but feel no emotion for my mother who sacrificed her life to house, feed, clothe, and educate me? Dr. Rev. Rattray explained that it was because he gave me approval and showed concern. That's what I needed.

The Only Way I Could Love My Mother

One day while at prayer the Lord revealed to Cindy that I hated my mother and she confronted me. "You hate your mother." Not any more. "Yes you do." Okay, I don't feel any hate, but if you say so, what can I do to love her. "Love her."

I had never stopped supporting Mama financially, but I realized that I really had no heart for her at all. I remained emotionally detached from her for the rest of her life. But love is action, not just feeling. So I set out to perform acts of love. Not living within physical reach of my mother made it impossible to do things for her. I started writing letters.

Each month, I would search my memory for something positive to write to her. I realized that the Christian hymns I knew were the ones she used to sing while doing her chores. I wrote about that. I remembered when I had asked her for the piece of material she had been given by a friend to make a skirt for herself. She'd said it wasn't enough and I had said it was enough for a straight dress. She had said nothing, but some time later she had surprised me with my first grown up dress made of the same mustard collar material. I wrote her about that. Then I started sending her information about my boys.

It was almost a year before she replied to me. "Dear Andrea, I received all your letters but I didn't feel like writing." And I laughed with pleasure. She knew she had been forgiven.

In 1983 I sent the boys home for the summer. She was pleased. She had not thought she would ever see them again. In 1986 I invited her to come for their graduations. Ian was graduating from Junior High and Allan from High School. It was the last time she would see them.

When Mama was dying I took my turn to take care of her. I used to sit on the bed, put her head in my lap and sing her favorite hymns as I stroked her hair. Nevertheless, no emotional feelings accompanied my work of love.

-17- Becoming An Ambassador Of Jesus Christ

Not long after I gave my life to Jesus, they Lord began to draw the Christians who worked at NYT together. We formed a group and met every day during our twenty-minute coffee break to read the "Daily Bread" devotional booklet and discuss the suggested scripture for the day. First there were five of us: Leo Fher, Vernon Grant, Cindy Valentine, Ingrid Ramos and yours truly. Like wild fire the news of our meeting spread, drawing all who loved Jesus to the cafeteria at ten-fifteen every morning. And we grew in grace and love and knowledge, until we became an obvious threat to the kingdom of the world.

Eventually, as if by an agreed arrangement, our several bosses began to complain about the length of our coffee breaks, which was a privilege not a right. We tried our best to keep it at twenty minutes and a few times when someone had a great testimony or a great trouble, we stayed a little longer. Suddenly we were all so busy, we had no structured coffee break time, so that we could no longer all meet at the same time.

But it was summer and we were full of the Word and wanted to do something positive. When Leo excitedly told us of Street Evangelist Dick Richards, who frequented the Fifth Avenue side of Rockefeller Center, and encouraged young people to share tracts while he preached the Gospel, we took a decision to spend our lunch hours doing just that.

That was when I realized that I had no confidence to approach strangers. I would offer a tract, but if the person did not accept it immediately, I quickly withdrew it. I did not feel too good about myself.

Then Dick Richards began to encourage us to testify and share the Gospel. Leo first accepted the challenge, then Cindy. Others were happy giving out tracts and talking one on one with passers-by. Nobody knew, but I felt like an absolute failure. I wanted so much to participate in the evangelistic ministry. Each day Dick Richards urged me. Each day I shied away. I was on the verge of giving up altogether and running away in shame, when I lost my voice to laryngitis, which lasted three weeks, rendering me quite dumb.

Called To Be An Evangelist-Anointed To Preach.

One beautiful warm and sunny Friday morning, I boarded the Long Island Railroad to go to Massepequa to check on a job. Seated on the train among total strangers, I felt a compelling voice inside of me that said, "Get up and speak." Before I could know what I was doing, I was on my feet preaching the Word of salvation to a captive audience, who closed their books, folded their newspapers and gave me their undivided attention. Words and scriptures tumbled out of my mouth to my amazement. I felt high, elated, and powerful. When I was through, the people clapped as I exited the train. It was unbelievable. All I could think was that I needed to get to Rockefeller Center before I lost whatever I had. I didn't know about the anointing.

At noon, I was back in Manhattan. I hurried to Dick Richards. "I am ready now." I informed him. From that day, everyday, until it was too cold, from 1:00 to 1:45pm, I entered into the high of the Holy Spirit and ministered the Word to the world who passed by. Without a permit to use a mike, the spirit of God and the natural acoustics of the area took my voice and carried it into the ears of many. It was a glorious time.

Then somebody discovered Street Evangelist Donald Spitz on Forty-second Street. And so for an hour every afternoon before going home, we joined him to minister to a different sort of crowd.

At Rockefeller Center, Fifth Avenue, we were cursed and spat upon by Jews who put their fingers in their ears, offended by the name of Jesus. On Forty-Second Street, Times Square, we were cursed by black people didn't want a white Jesus and by those who believed that Jesus was black, and the devil white. We saw the power of God hold back a group of Black Israelites, a mob of Black Muslims, and rabble of Rastafarians, who became particularly incensed at seeing Leo and I together.

Had it not been for the Lord, I am sure they would have attacked and beaten us.

Appointed To Pray

Winter sent us indoors where Marva Johnson, Cindy Valentine, Evelyn Davella, and I started a mid-day prayer meeting, which expanded to include people who neither worked in our building, nor for the same company. Those who were unable to attend the meetings sent their request. Not one prayer went unanswered. The Lord had begun working the gift of Prophecy in Cindy's Spirit and at times He opened her spiritual eyes, so that she saw visions. The very first day when the four of us assembled to pray, Cindy received a vision of us being handed a flaming sword, with which to destroy the works of the enemy. We wielded it with great confidence and authority.

God used Cindy to encourage us, and we listened to her. She wasn't just a feel good prophet, but could be relied upon to administer a painful chastening Word or a warning reproof as we sought the Lord's will. We became best friends. We often thanked God for making sisters of a black woman from Trinidad and a white woman from the Bronx. We were amazed by how parallel our emotional lives had run. We understood each other's deficiencies. We could be brutally and shamelessly honest with each other, without fear of being reduced in each other's estimation. Cindy helped me to recognize, understand, accept, and express in words the normal emotional responses to painful experiences.

Anointed To Teach

The years passed. I outgrew the Tuesday night Bible study group, which I had continued to attend for three years. I entered Immanuel Bible Training Institute where I soaked up the words of Kenneth Hagin and Fred Price and studied subjects such as Faith, The Holy Spirit and His "Gifts", Prosperity, and Biblical Hermeneutics. I loved the Word of God and although I had never regained the confidence to participate in regular conversation, I could talk for hours about the Lord and His Word.

Even before I went to Bible School, my Pastor used to ask me to share a Word of exhortation on Sunday nights. One such time when I was asked to prepare a message, I felt in my spirit that I was being called not just to minister the Word, but to minister to the people. The thought was frightening. The Thursday before I was to minister, I went to my teacher, Phillip Gordon, and asked him to pray for me. He laid his hand on me and said, "Lord let the anointing that is upon me be upon her". I was really disappointed by his simple prayer, but I received it, thanked him, and feeling no less fearful went home.

That Sunday night I taught on The Baptism of the Holy Spirit, then with trepidation of heart, I asked who would like to receive the baptism with the evidence of speaking in tongues.

Five people put their hands up. I was concerned that I was about to embarrass myself in front of the whole congregation, so I asked them to follow me into a little room, laid my hands on them and they began to speak in other tongues as the Holy Ghost gave utterance. I was relieved.

After two years Bible school ended.

Bernard Jordan had been a teacher at IBTI and his prophetic ministry had drawn a crowd. People were more anxious for a "Word from the Lord", than for the "Word of the Lord" Bernard Jordan would teach for ten minutes and then he'd get a "revelation" or start prophesying. I was not interested in his revelations or prophesies, much of which did not line up with the Word of God. I went to Bible school to grow in the knowledge of the Word. I was a Berean scholar. I searched the scriptures and questioned all the inconsistencies, but Jordan could never give me a satisfactory explanation. He didn't like me.

When Bible School re-opened in the fall of 1984, Bernard Jordan did not turn up to teach. The money that President Pastor Barratt could afford to pay him was not enough. He had decided to start his own school and EBTI was left minus a teacher. The President and the Dean agreed to ask me if I could sub until they were able to get a teacher. They would give me guidance. I agreed. When the students saw that instead of the prophet, they had me, half of them quit. But the half that remained was not disappointed.

The classes were taped. Phillip Gordon, who taught the second year class, took my tapes home so he could listen to them, and give me the guidance I needed. It blew his mind to discover that I taught exactly like he did. He said it was like listening to himself. Then I reminded him of the prayer he had prayed. It had worked. I was a teacher. ***Not by might, not by power, but by the spirit of the Lord.***

All Ministry Doors Closed

After a year EBTI closed its doors with a promise to re-open at a new location, but it didn't ever happen.

About this time my pastor, Pastor Ricketts decided to relocate to Florida because of his wife's health and Pastor Paul was installed as Pastor. Pastor Ricketts had spoken of me to him and had advised him to ordain me as a minister of Pentecostal Circle Tabernacle. He had asked him to observe me, and Pastor Paul had agreed to carry out Pastor Ricketts wishes. But he didn't. I discovered that Pastor Paul had a monumental problem with jewelry and makeup. This was after I had gone to London with him for a convention, had been refused the opportunity to Minister, and had been made to feel very unwelcome. A church that Pastor Paul had previously pastored hosted the convention. The lady, at whose home I was housed, seeing my confusion at the way I was being treated, took it upon herself to explain the problem.

When we returned to New York, I confronted Pastor Paul. I was furious because I had supposed that we had had an honest relationship. We used to spend hours discussing scripture, and he'd never revealed to me his objection to my make up and jewelry. In response to my question about his doctrine of jewelry, he said, "Well now that you know, I hope you will help to influence the young people in my way." I was furious. I replied that I could not teach with my mouth that which I did not believe in my heart and since we had an insolvable problem, and since I believed in obedience to leadership, I believed I should resign my membership. A week later I tendered my resignation.

But Pentecostal Circle Tabernacle had been my home church for five years and I felt like a fish out of water. The people thought I had backslidden because Pastor Paul did not handle things in the accepted way. He should have called a members meeting, invited me to the meeting, and have me explain the reason for my resignation. He did not. Therefore, most of the people were not aware that I had resigned. They only knew I was absent from Sunday morning service; and they drew their own conclusions.

For about six months before I went to the convention I had

been helping some friends who had started a little church at Rogers Avenue. I taught the adult Sunday school class, ministered the Word sometimes and was active in evangelizing the area by street preaching. When I returned from London, I found that the Pastor, who was not a teacher, had taken over my class and I was never asked to participate in ministry of any kind anymore. Puzzled over the ostracism that I felt from people who had previously welcomed my assistance, I demanded to know the reason. I thought that I was at fault somehow. No one could give me an explanation. I wasn't wanted. So, after expressing my concerns I left.

About that same time Dick Richards disappeared from his Rockefeller Center spot and Donald Spitz of Forty-Second Street, Times Square, married my dear friend Cynthia Valentine, and they relocated to Virginia. A brilliant young woman with a definite calling to Street Evangelism took his place. At first Marva Johnson and I worked with her on evenings, but suddenly she developed some doctrinal disagreements, and politely asked us not to come by anymore.

Marva and I stepped into Train ministry, but after being so very active and involved, I felt rather depressed and confused.

About a year later Pastor Paul died and I reapplied for membership under the present Pastor, Pastor Annette Rose. A year later she ordained me.

-18- Lessons, Encounters and Revelations

As you continue to read I want you to bear in mind, that the self-understanding that I gained, and the conclusions that I reached, only came after my decision to humble myself, surrender my pride and strength and ask for help. My restoration only happened as I was willing to accept truth, forgive wrongs, and make changes. The practice of suppression and repression that, in response to emotional pain and damage, had begun in my childhood and adolescent years was my ignorant and subconscious method of protecting and defending myself. But when God allowed my subconscious to surface, it became my responsibility to consciously and deliberately apply the axe of truth to the root of error, and nurture the seeds of reconstruction by actively being the person that God said I could be.

Marriage Possibilities

As it had been before I was saved, so men continued to consider me to be desirable wife material.

In 1981, I had met the young man who had wanted to be my boyfriend when I was fourteen, and we had fallen in love. Perhaps our common roots and teenage friendship made it easy for us experience a unique closeness. I had realized that I had not allowed myself to truly let anyone into my heart after my marriage ended, and now that I was saved, I was determined to lose the fear of loving, and give one hundred percent. Harry and I were ecstatically happy. Soon we were spending every free moment together, discussing being married, driving around examining homes, and chatting about which one we would purchase. My children questioned Harry about his salvation and intentions. They were quite pleased with him and his answers. Nevertheless, somewhere in my heart there was a warning signal, but I had no reason to think that all was not going to be perfect.

Harry and I were intent on walking worthy of the Lord, hence our only physical contact had been holding hands and a kiss on the cheek or forehead. The one time when we were about to kiss as lovers do, Harry pulled back and began to bawl as if he was being beaten. I was taken aback. I could not imagine what had happened. When he was quiet, he told me, that my Father said that he must not touch me. I was His.

Subsequent circumstances proved that our desire to marry was not in accordance with the Father's will, and so with my heart breaking, (I couldn't tell about his), we parted. I felt like a wounded puppy, but I had committed my life to God and very soon He mended my heart.

In 1982-1983, another young man pursued me relentlessly and proposed to me daily. I had many objections to Gary.

Firstly, he was twelve years and five months younger than I. Secondly, I had two sons, who were only eleven and seven years younger than him and I wanted no more children. Thirdly, there was a bevy of teenagers that persistently pursued him. Fourthly, I had enjoyed the way I had felt about Harry. We both seemed to have had a mutual devotion to, understanding of, and admiration and respect for each other that went far beyond the physical. That had made our relationship exciting, yet comfortable and controllable. If I had felt the same way about Gary, I would not have hesitated to accept his proposal.

On the other hand, Gary's parents welcomed me and his mother simply loved me. I could not understand why a woman who was only six years my senior, would desire that I should marry her son, who was the apple of her eye. Nevertheless, I thought that it would certainly be a wonderful experience to be married into a family that approved of me.

When I became familiar with Gary's parents, I asked his mother why she would accept a divorcee with two children as a suitable wife for her son. I had more in common with her and her husband than with her son. Actually when I visited their home and the three of us got to chatting about the culture of our teenage years, Gary would become irritable and would invariably be in a hurry to terminate the visit and take me home.

Gary's mother explained that apart from my physical attractiveness (at thirty-five I was still slim and pretty, and appeared to be much younger than my age), she believed that her son loved me, that she had never seen him more alive and happy before he met me. More than anything in the world, she desired her darling son's happiness and she thought that he needed a settled, stable, mature woman to "make a man out of him".

When eventually I agreed to marry him, Gary, who had been a perfect gentleman all along, asked if he could kiss me. I thought I was about to be given a simple kiss by a shy young man. I was left speechless and shaken, when he demonstrated a depth of passion and experience that delighted and awakened the dormant desire in me. Our courtship drove me to my knees because of great temptation to fornicate. We were both in Bible school so Gary and I were in the habit of getting together to study the Word of God; but the memory of the kiss became a constant and irresistible distraction from anything spiritual. Our focus on the carnal tormented me. Each visit ended with me pushing him away, and he was very strong.

In frustration and desperate agony of soul, I consulted my friend and spiritual father, Watson Duncanson about the problem. I argued that since the "sin of desire" was as wicked as the "sin of deed", I should just go ahead and yield to the temptation. My conclusion being, that, "one may as well be hung for a sheep, as for a lamb."

Watson asked me if, as was obvious to him, I was so distressed about entertaining sin in my heart, could I chance the resulting misery of a deliberate sinful act. I couldn't bear the thought, so every night I pleaded with God for His strength and help. I had hoped that He would respond the way He did when Harry attempted to kiss me, but He didn't. I had to grow and learn to take responsibility for my own choices.

Apart from the disagreements over the lack of progress in our physical relationship, the pretty teenagers, who simply refused to understand and accept the fact that Gary and I were exclusive to each other, bothered and intimidated me. I wondered if he had made them aware of our relationship and I became angry and quarreled with him over what I considered their disrespect. I was amazed at my boldness as I addressed certain situations and demanded that both he and his admirers observe my rules of propriety. I wondered whether I felt free to express myself because Gary was so young and I was used to dealing with my sons, or was it that I didn't care enough about a relationship that was both spiritually and psychologically distressing.

After a while, I noticed that the special daily attention to which that I'd become accustomed, decreased. When I questioned Gary's sincerity and devotion, he explained that having prayed about the marriage he no longer believed that it was God's will for us. I became quite indignant, but I must admit that I suffered no broken heart. However, we did not part amicably and for a little while, we ceased to communicate altogether. Nevertheless, we eventually admitted that we did like each other and were happy to be great friends. I had learned an empowering lesson, that friendship could survive disagreements, quarrels and even a slap in the face. Love does cover the multitude of sins.

In 1984, a friend with whom I had a very easy rapport, phoned out of the blue and asked, "Would you marry me?" I said, "I'll pray about it," and I did. God did not say yes, so I said no. Today we are still friends.

One Sunday, in 1985, I was feeling very lonely and depressed, when a dear friend, a very sweet fellow, put a smile on my face with a serious proposal of marriage. Half serious and half in jesting response, I said yes. He was so happy. His family was quite pleased. I was disturbed and felt pressured by the pleasure and expectations of Ray and his family. Soon I was feeling quite uncomfortable. I brought the matter to my prayer group and as we brought the situation before the Lord, the word of the Lord was, "Get out of that boat, it's going to Tarsus." I terminated the relationship.

For a while, Ray was too hurt to communicate with me. I was

never so sorry to hurt someone as I was to hurt Ray. He had always treated me as a very special lady. Two years later he died from cancer. His parents said that at his birth there had been a prophecy of him being mightily used by God. On his dying bed Ray repented of not fulfilling his calling. He had headed for Tarsus when he should have sailed for Nineveh.

My Attempt To Restore My Marriage

In 1986, Paul came back into my life. Before my son Allan had graduated from high school, he had signed up to join the US Marines. His father heard about it, and, after having had no input in his children lives for years, had the audacity to phone to express his disappointment in what he labeled my son's stupid decision. My son was miserable. He still needed his father's approval. I phoned his father and invited him to undo the damage he had done. He agreed to visit Allan, talk with him about his career choice, and since Allan had already signed up, be understanding, optimistic and supportive. I wanted my son to leave with a good feeling about his plan. He believed that the Marines were the best and bravest, and was proud to be a Marine.

I myself did not agree with his decision. I had voiced my objections, which I had supported with facts. I had given advice, and even refused to sign the papers when he first requested. He was seventeen at that time and needed my permission. I asked him to carefully consider and check out all my objections and if, in six months time, he still believed that military life was a viable choice, I would sign. He did and I signed. It was Allan's life. It was time to let him go to make his own mistakes and gain his own victories.

In 1980, I had told the Lord, that I'd rather be lonely the rest of my life than be married to Paul again. I felt that I could never have the pure relationship of our early days, and I couldn't be happy with a husband who didn't trust me. But in 1986, I suddenly felt that I would like a chance to restore my marriage. I spoke to Paul and he happily agreed. I knew, however, that I could not be unequally yoked and I could not return to the beggarly elements of Catholicism. When I was first saved, I had witnessed to Paul. Feeling inadequate to the task, I had had Watson Duncanson witness to him. He had even visited the Assemblies of God Church where I used to worship, and had heard the invitation to Christ. At least twice, he had made a profession of faith in Jesus, but he really did not believe or receive Him into his heart.

With the idea of being re-married to Paul, I began once more to witness to him. He was a very self-righteous fellow who didn't drink, smoke, gamble, chase women, or in his lofty opinion of his own character, do wrong of any kind. Knowing the power of the Word, I thought that if he would only read the Gospel story, he would understand his spiritual bankruptcy and be saved. Consequently, I bought him a New Testament.

He refused to read it. He had a few things against some portions of God's Word. God had said, ***a man must leave his mother and father and cleave to his wife.*** God had said, ***If a man does not hate mother, father, husband, wife, children, and his own life, he could not be his disciple.*** He couldn't agree to those commands.

Whom The Son Of God Set free Is Free Indeed

I was shocked one day when Paul said that God seemed to be particularly interested in the scum of the earth, and he wasn't scum and neither was I. He told me that I was a good person, had always been a good person, and that I didn't need the church. He knew that he could fulfill the dream we used to have and make me the happiest woman alive. But the bottom line was, he didn't want Jesus. The spiritual lines were drawn. The desire to be with him died. The Sword of the Spirit, the Word of God, the only agent that divided soul from spirit set me free. I was sad, but I was free.

I Acknowledged Being Lonely

In 1987, I entered into a relationship with a newly saved man. Because of a dream I had had, I supposed myself to be in God's will. At first, Logan and I appeared to be on the same spiritual track. However, after three years of changes, I knew that we were poles apart spiritually. We no longer walked the same narrow pathway. My principles stood against his policies and practices. We were unequal and incompatible and this was not, as I had assumed, of God. The Bible clearly states, "Can two walk together unless they agree?"

In 1988, the year that my mother died, my son Ian, then sixteen, in his quest for independence became rebellious and unmanageable. I had hoped that his father would have supported my strict stance and help bear the parenting burden, since we were on speaking terms. To the contrary, he seemed to undermine my authority. I was at my wit's end and as a result, I sent Ian to live with his father.

With disappointment and depression for company, I found solace in sweet treats and I began to put on weight. I had never had a real weight gain problem and was quite unhappy with myself. Then, after an emergency hysterectomy in 1989, the weight gain escalated leaving me feeling ugly, old, undesirable, and miserable. In fact Logan, the man in my life at that time, very insensitively remarked in my hearing, and in the presence of his family, that he could never love a woman who couldn't have children. He proved it by having other fertile female companionship.

Because I had believed that I was in God's will, for almost three years I had tried to sustain the relationship with Logan, although at the end of the first year, we had already found ourselves at odds with each other. Desiring to please God, and Logan also, I had pushed and extended myself until I was stretched thin. The mutual ending left me confused, sad and lonely, but relieved. I was confused because I couldn't understand why God had allowed me to waste my life, unlike the times before when his direction seemed quickly clear. I was sad because I was hurt and disappointed in myself. I seemed to have gained no wisdom, despite my experiences.

I was lonely because I couldn't share my pain. I was embarrassed by my failure, and I didn't want to burden anyone. I had reached a place where I believed that I was expected always to demonstrate "The Joy of The Lord is my strength". Besides, just as in my earlier years when people loved the seemingly strong, carefree Andrea, and could not or did not want to deal with a troubled me, so I believed that people loved the strong, cheerful Andrea and should not be asked or expected to respond to my confusion and sadness.

I seemed destined for unhappiness. My life became stagnant. Even at church, apart from praying with people who came forward in response to altar calls on Sundays, I had no specific duties. If I could have immersed myself in ministry, I would have been able to bury my loneliness and need, in purpose. Being used by God, and useful to others might have brought me some measure of satisfaction and made me feel worthwhile. But I had no purpose. I was bored. I felt worthless.

Although now, as I am writing, I have admitted to loneliness, that summer of 1989 was the first time I actually acknowledged to myself that I was ever lonely since I'd been saved. Jesus was supposed to be enough.

I learned some excellent lessons through that last relationship. Firstly, I realized that even when there are dreams and prophecies, one must seek God more diligently for clarity concerning His will. Secondly, I understood the necessity of waiting for the manifestation of the fruit of the Spirit of God, which takes time to develop and mature. Thirdly, I learned that when I believe that I am in God's will, I must have the courage and the tenacity to stay and wait.

I must say that in hindsight, there is no one either before I was saved or after, that I wish I had married. Father knows best. Don't get me wrong. I believe that marriage can be the most wonderful and satisfying relationship this side of heaven, and if the Lord leads the person of His choosing to me, I would be delighted to receive the blessing of a husband, especially since I have understood myself somewhat.

I understand now, that had I been able to capture illusive happiness, or fill my life with work, my growth and development would have been aborted. I would have erroneously concluded that all was well with me, and that God was pleased with me. I would not have known how deficient I really was. And I would have had no concept of how beautiful and worthwhile a reconstructed me could be.

The Beginning Of Self Understanding

One summer's afternoon, while sitting on the step feeling sorry for myself, I was reading the Love Express, a Christian publication. I saw there, an advertisement for a Bible School that was just a bus drive away from where I lived. Desperate for something to fill my life, I registered for Bible School. It was one of the pivotal decisions of my life.

Classes were on Thursday nights. Having already gone through two years of Bible school as well as many years of personal study, I convinced the President, Dr. Austin, to put me in the Bachelor degree program. While in conversation he asked if I was free on Saturdays. He informed me that he taught a certificate class in The Psychology of Christian Counseling. Would I be interested?" I needed something to fill my Saturdays so I joined that class. And that's how I began to understand and appreciate me, and to recognize that I was a product of childhood traumas, a victim of low self-esteem with damaged and frozen emotions.

However, understanding is only the beginning of the solution. Where does one go from there?

Eventually, I became a teacher at the Bible School and taught

The Psychology of Christian Counseling course. With my increased understanding, I was able to help others to arrive at the truth about their attitudes, behavior and relationship problems and increase personality growth and relationship skills. I encouraged them to apply the lessons at home, and some gratefully acknowledged successful change, where there had been problems. Yet I had not been satisfactorily changed. There had been developmental changes, but I knew that deep in my soul, I was still a psychological cripple. At every opportunity I reached out to God for help, but for years I remained unchanged.

One of the things I realized about myself was that my tendency to run away from pain had become second nature. Even though I had proved that I could stand and wait on the Lord, the temptation to escape pain was not eradicated. I had run away from physical beatings, and even when I had stayed in bad situations I had involuntarily removed the pain from my heart by pressing it into my subconscious. Some people admired the way I seemed able to turn my back on the hardships of life, and move on without complaining. I didn't cry, didn't rage, didn't even ask, "Why me?" I just turned my back and moved on. They didn't realize, nor did I, that I just hadn't dealt with it. Part of the reason that I felt so lonely was that I didn't know if I could risk the pain of failure in intimate relationship anymore, and was afraid of being alone for the rest of my life.

Learning To Wait And Stay Through Emotional Pain

On July 3rd, 1993, I brought my first son Allan, who had been a veteran of the Persian Gulf War, home to die. He had cancer. He had returned from the war with excruciating stomach pains, which had begun in September 1990, while in Bahrain, after he had taken some drugs that were supposed to protect him from chemical agents. As with so many military personnel, he had been misdiagnosed with Post Traumatic Stress and treated with antacids. There was little that he could digest. He'd continued to lose weight and suffer agonizing pains, having to be hospitalized in the military hospital, yet he was honorably discharged as healthy in 1992.

To protect me from worry Allan had not let me know that his condition had worsened. June 19th, 1993, in the early morning hours, I dreamt that two men in white came to tell me my son was dead. I awoke immediately and prayed. Half an hour later, his girlfriend phoned to explain that Allan had made her promise not to tell me how ill he was, but now he was hospitalized and dying, she didn't know what to do. I assured her that all would be well. I would be there as soon as I got a flight. I had been taught to believe that when God shows something before it happens, it might be that he wants to prevent it, but needs the prayerful intervention of the saints. Like how He told Abraham about His plan to destroy Sodom, which gave Abraham the opportunity to intercede for Sodom, thus saving Lot's life.

Immediately I called on all the prayer warriors I knew and a great war was fought for my son's life. He survived, and two days later I arrived in Hawaii to find my tall, strapping, handsome son, emaciated and aged almost beyond recognition. I brought him home, took a leave of absence from my job, and spent the next five months taking care of him.

It was the toughest assignment of my life. One from which I could not run. I learned how to stay and wait. Crisis followed crisis and I could not run. My son needed me completely so I asked God for grace, which He gave each day, each hour, each minute, and each morning. Then one day I couldn't bear to see the ugly thing that had been my virile healthy son anymore, and I balked at going to the hospital. I ran. But three days later, I did return with the resolve to stay. I had the privilege of being with Allan as he passed into glory. I still feel badly about the three days I deserted my son, but I was still learning that I can stay. I can wait. I don't have to run.

During those five months Allan and I talked, settling many misunderstandings.

Learning To Show Love And Express Myself To My Son

The day the verdict and sentence of his true diagnosis was meted out, my son ran through the hospital, searching for a window from which to jump and end his misery. Finding no un-barred window, he returned to his bed where I was waiting for him. He began to cry. I held his bony frame in my arms and cried with him. Not much, just a little. Remember, crying was not my thing. He told me later that that was the best thing I could have done for him. He said that he had always considered me strong, but cold, because he had never seen me become emotional. He had never seen me cry. He cited the day, when I came out of the train station, to find him waiting with the news that his brother had been impaled by his rectum on the spike of gate, over which he had attempted to jump. Ian was hospitalized. Althea was with him. Althea was a pregnant nineteen year old that I had taken in.

My son said, that he'd expected like any normal mother, I would be upset, distressed, and run crying to the hospital. Instead, I took his hand, said let's go home so I can put down my bags, then we'll go to the hospital. He said he wondered what kind of monster I was. I wasn't a monster. I had trained myself to rationalize everything into categories of what I could change, and what I could not. Ian was in the hospital being cared for by those who knew what to do. I needed to be cool and strong. I had nobody to whom I could turn. It never occurred to me that I was needed at the hospital. It never occurred to me that my son needed me emotionally. I was doing exactly what Mama did. I provided food, clothes, shelter, education, and I opened the door to spirituality. That's all I had. I was saved, but not restored. That was still all I had.

We also talked about his jealousy over my involvement in Marvalene's life. Marvalene was a teenager I had been helping. He felt that the interest I showed, and the steps I took to help her, were far more than I did for him and his brother. He felt I could have done much more to help them to better educational opportunities. I explained that many years had passed and I had gained courage by experience and education. When they were students, I was utterly intimidated by the system that was so different from that in which I grew up, I had had neither the confidence nor the aggression that I needed to challenge the status quo on their behalf.

Testimonies That Encouraged New Expectations

Constant prayer was offered for a miracle for Allan. He had known the healing power of God all his life. My medicine cabinet had held no pain-killers. My children believed me, and they believed in my God. When they had chicken pox, I prayed for them and told them that it would neither itch nor scar them. It didn't.

When, at fourteen, Allan had complained of pain in his knees that had become so severe, that he could no longer walk the many flights of stairs to his class rooms, I took him to the doctor. He was diagnosed with a degenerative incurable condition, with prospects of a wheelchair in a couple years. I didn't accept that prognosis. As we arrived at the steps to our house, I stopped him, asked him if he believed God could heal him. He said he did. I laid my hand on his knees, prayed a simple prayer, and told him he was healed. He asked, "Can I run?" "Sure," I replied and he took off. He was healed.

When, at twenty-three, an accident resulted in a spine injury that left Allan lop-sided and he faced major surgery that could either cure or paralyze him, he phoned me. "Mummy, please don't let them cut me." "Okay Allan, there will be no surgery, Lets pray." So, I prayed and next morning when he went for the pre-surgery test, he was standing tall and straight, without pain. So Allan expected that I would pray and he would live.

Many crises were checked by prayer. He should have died two dozen times, but he lived. The hospital staff was happy to see him after each crisis. It was almost as if he could not die. There was a day when the doctor said he could not survive the weekend and recommended that he be taken home to be with his family when he died. He had gained twenty-five pounds of fluid in his tissues, yet he was dehydrated. They sympathetically explained that they could no longer hydrate him and his fragile heart, which had been already stressed by several heart attacks, would not bear the pressure of the extra fluid much longer.

That Friday night we came home. All Saturday he lay there too heavy and swollen to carry himself. That night he said, "Mummy, I want to testify in church tomorrow." My usual answer was, "Okay Allan, you'll testify." Sunday morning I awoke to the words, "Mummy look!" I looked. His bones were once more visible. He stood on the scale, twenty pound lighter than when he went to sleep. We went to church. He testified.

But he didn't get better. The tumors grew and sucked him dry. And I had no answers left for him. We went to Benny Hinn's Healing Crusade. We went to Morris Cerullo's Crusade. He was the subject of much prayer. As impossible as it seemed, he got worse.

The Greatest Lesson: As For God, His Way Is Perfect

The trip to Benny Hinn's Crusade in Niagra Falls was the most painful experience of my life. My dying son was in constant excruciating pain, but he had elected to take Demoral instead of Morphine, which was a better pain-killer. He wanted to feel the pain leave when he received his healing. He was just skin and bone; bone which hurt with every movement. His belly was swollen with the tumors and the fluids that filled his stomach. His spindly legs looked as if they could not support him and I pleaded with him to allow me to order a wheelchair but he refused. He was bent almost double and he looked like an old man. In July, the people we met assumed that he was either my husband or my brother. By September, strangers asked me how my father was doing. His eyes were wild with the pain as we boarded the little plane.

It was an extremely bumpy ride. As turbulent winds rocked the aircraft I watched the determined grimness of Allan's face, with a breaking heart, knowing that he was in agony that increased with every passing moment. All I could do was hold his hand. We had no conversation.

Allan had no strength to stand in line with the thousands of people who waited for the doors to be opened. When we arrived at the crusade, all seats were already taken and no one offered my son a chair. Not that he would have been able to sit. We stood together in silence waiting with desperate hope for a miracle. An insensitive person approached and enquired if Allan had AIDS. Perhaps that was why nobody seemed to have any compassion towards him. When the healing prayer was said, a worker approached and asked him if he believed that he was healed. My son said that he had felt a touch when the prayer had been said. Then the thoughtless worker hit Allan in his stomach to find out if he still had pain. My son almost keeled over. Then the person said, "I guess you are not healed", and walked away.

Allan and I left the crusade. He was going crazy with pain. The Demoral was inadequate. His calcium level was rising. He could not drink enough water to hydrate himself. He needed intravenous hydration. We went looking for a hospital. The hospital refused to treat him. We went back to the motel to lie down and wait until the next afternoon when we would fly home. He said, "Mummy, you know that I could die here." I knew. Without the intravenous hydration he could go into a coma and die. We lay together in silence, with me holding his hand and watching him breathe, fearful that each breath would be his last.

By the grace of God we made it back to the Veteran's hospital in Manhattan. He was hydrated in time. There was a new and deadly problem. Allan had not had a bowel movement in days and his breath was beginning to smell like feces. An X-Ray showed that his bowel was impacted and twisted. An operation was needed, but in his case an operation would mean certain death. The doctors advised me to stay the night, because they doubted that he would make it through to the next day.

We were in an empty ward, so I lay on the bed next to my son. About two o'clock in the morning, he requested more Demoral, but it had only been four hours since the last pill and he was scheduled to receive it every six hours. I had a bottle of morphine but my son strove to bear the pain.

As he felt the presence of death, Allan looked at me and asked, "Why Mummy, why?" I used to have plausible answers with scriptural support, but I'd run out of answers. "I don't know Allan, I don't know anymore."

As I anxiously observed him, Allan stood up on the bed. Impossibly, with agonizing effort, he stretched himself up to his full height, and raising his bony arms to heaven, he emitted a chilling primal scream. **"WHERE ARE YOU GOD?"** he roared. I was terrified. The journey had been long and hard but his faith had been unwavering. Had he at this last crucial moment lost his faith? That was my fear and concern.

Suddenly, Allan knelt on the bed with his face down. I sat watching. After a while he sat up and looked at me. In awe I looked into a bright, pure, serene face that was so beautiful, he appeared more angelic than human. He said softly, "I'll take the morphine now." I gave him ninety milligrams of morphine and he went to sleep. I continued to keep watch.

The next morning when he awoke I inquired, "Allan how are you?" He understood what the real question was. He replied, "Mummy, **AS FOR GOD, HIS WAY IS PERFECT**." His faith was intact.

About mid-morning, praying that my son would not die in my absence, I went home to telephone my sister Deborah in London, and his girlfriend Amanda in Hawaii.

When I returned to the hospital, Allan was sitting on the commode. The room reeked with the wonderful stink of feces.

God had un-twisted his bowels. We rejoiced.

Learning Forgiveness And Accepting God's Ways

All this time, his father had been a daily visitor. His father's family had requested permission to visit him, but Allan had refused to see them. It was at this time that he told me of the totality of the abuse he had suffered when he lived with my mother in Trinidad. He had also felt ill-treated by his father's people. He did not want to see them. Perhaps he was doubly upset because I had always felt that it was their influence that destroyed my marriage, and maybe he felt that they had robbed him of his father.

I began to minister to Allan about forgiveness and explain that un-forgiveness was a hindrance to prayers being heard and answered. He had depended on my prayers all his life, now he needed to take charge, and he needed to begin by forgiving. He agreed, and his grandparents, aunts and uncles all came to see him.

There was one particular aunt with whom I had been friendly before her brother and I were divorced. He had told me that she hated me for what I did to him, and that others might forgive me, but she never would. Having become a Christian, I had asked God for the chance to show her Christian kindness. I think I just wanted her to think well of me. But God amazed me.

While everyone was busy making up to Allan, I walked away feeling that I was in the way of their reconciliation. After a while, Pearl approached and asked me how I was doing, if I had any arrangements made, and if I needed any help. She said that I shouldn't worry about anything, she would help. Her genuine concern and kindness almost destroyed my defenses. She was a generous source of strength, which both Allan and I appreciated. Not many people could tolerate the sight of his gaunt skeleton and the evidence of his suffering. Not even his best friend/cousin or his brother came to visit anymore. Pearl was God-sent. She could look past his gruesome appearance and chat with him about ordinary things, so that he was still part of the life of ordinary people. I had never known how to receive, only how to give. Now I took all Pearl offered. I was learning. I was being restored.

I buried my son that December, after which I lay in bed without a word for a month. Immediately I thought that I would like to have a baby to replace my son. Then my mind was a blank. I didn't cry, I didn't complain. I was a living dead woman. My joy was gone and my condition seemed permanent. Everybody was waiting for me to breakdown and fall apart. But I didn't. My friend Stephanie sat at the foot of my bed every night and watched over me, not knowing what to say, she wisely said nothing. Just her being there was priceless.

Threatened with forced retirement, which I couldn't afford, I returned to work. I also returned to teach the psychology class at the Bible school where I had first began to discover myself.

Experiencing Peace After Pain

Mother Mc Neil, my dear friend, an elderly church mother, said that I needed to get away and would I like to go to Jamaica with her. Yes, I would.

About that time, I had been befriended by a young pastor. He was less than a year older than my deceased son. We had become Wednesday night prayer partners. When I explained to him that I would not be available for prayer the following Wednesday because I was going for a time of rest and recreation, he asked if he could come with us. Mother Mc Neil, a vibrant seventy- year old, thought that young company would add to our enjoyment.

Jamaica was beautiful, but the memory of my son's suffering was an ever-present barrier to a true appreciation of its charms.

One night, I decided that I had had enough of pain and sadness. Pastor Vaden Grant and I were standing on the veranda looking out on the ocean. Since we had arrived he'd been trying to explain to me that I only had one son and I needed to let go of Allan. I had been quite annoyed with him. How could he ever understand? What right had he to instruct me in matters of which he had no experience? However, I had given thought to what he said, and even though I could not agree with him, I did understand that I had to let go, if I were to have a chance of being happy again. Somehow I realized that holding on to the pain was my way of holding my child and that I was afraid that if I lost the pain, I would also lose my child. But my threshold for pain is low, and so that night, I said to Vaden, much like Allan would have said to me, "Please pray and ask God to take the pain away, I don't want it anymore. I am tired. I want my joy back."

Vaden was a man of prayer, but he didn't know what to pray and he was afraid of his prayer not being answered. He had felt my desperation, and was concerned about my response if my request was delayed or denied. While I waited for him to pray, he started to sing. As he sang, I lifted my weary hands to God, and pleaded my own cause, determined not to leave the veranda, and not to stop praying until my request was granted.

And then Vaden stopped singing, and I was quiet. Silently the painful emptiness of death seemed to dissolve. There was an awareness of renewed strength and a sweet peace. I desired something more, something deeper and less temporary. ***In his presence is fullness of joy.*** I wanted to know the fullness of the joy in God's presence. I wanted to experience hilarious liberating joy. However, since what I had was much better that what I had had, after a disappointing while, I anesthetized the desire and settled for the little I had.

Whenever I felt disappointed, depressed, or threatened, I'd say to God, "I want my joy, give me back my joy", but what I had lost at those times was my peace. The place in me where joy could abide had long been locked and I didn't know where to find the key. I felt that I was incapable of reaching the heights of joy that others seemed to attain. What I had labeled as joy was the sweet peace. It was the absence of anxiety, the faith that God is sovereign and good, and the hope in His ability to fulfill His promises.

Given A Place And A Purpose

Daddy had died in March 1992. He had been found dead one Saturday morning by my sister who had recently returned to live with him. All twelve of his children, five sons and seven daughters were at his funeral. As I stood in St. Francis R.C. Church to extend a word of comfort and hope in the resurrection to my family, I heard in my Spirit, "Andrea you are coming back here to minister." I knew then, without a shadow of a doubt, that Trinidad was where my destiny lay.

Before that moment I had never had the feeling of being rooted to any place, or any one. It was quite uncomfortable to have no sense of belonging, and after a while I had ceased to contemplate my future, because I could see no further than the present without becoming afraid. Now, that had changed.

I had place and purpose. That was good.

Preparation For Purpose Takes Time

After Allan died, I put my house up for sale. I did not wish to be encumbered by a house with a mortgage. I must be ready to leave New York at any time. I could not imagine that it would take ten years of waiting, restoration, reconstruction, and training, before I was prepared to move, before I was able to proceed with the call of destiny.

On December 5th, 1994, eight days before the first anniversary of my son's death, and just as I was about to get a buyer for my house, tragedy struck.

While working late that Monday night, I received a phone call. My house was on fire. I didn't get excited. I turned to my coworker and calmly said, "Steve, my house is on fire." He looked at me. I suppose that he was relieved that I wasn't hysterical. He knew that I was a Christian, so he replied appropriately, "I guess it's praying time." I sat at my desk and waited for another call from my devoted young friend Marvalene, who had phoned in a panic, and who I had asked to observe the fire and keep me updated as to what was taking place.

When she phoned the second time, She informed me that it

was a very bad fire. I asked her who was at the house, and she said that my church family was there. That was when I put on my coat and headed for the train station, making sure that I boarded the train that would take the most time to get from mid-Manhattan to East Brooklyn. I was in no hurry to face the crisis.

By the time I arrived at 343 east 34th Street, the firemen had done their work. All my windows had been destroyed; walls had been broken down; floors had been ripped up; furniture had been broken; and everything had been drenched. The fire had been unceremoniously put out. Only the pungent stench of smoke remained. All I owned was the clothes on my back.

I immediately put the matter in proper perspective by considering that my only son Ian, who would normally have been in the basement where the fire started, had been upstairs answering the phone, and was safe. I thanked God for sparing his life, especially because he was presently in a backslidden condition. I reasoned that it was better to lose a house that could be replaced than a son who couldn't. I regarded myself as blessed; and without a whimper of grief or a tear, I thanked my church family for their support, and went to my friend Stephanie's home, where I lived for the next seven months.

Reconciliation With My Bother Patrick

Given that the bank owned a greater percentage of the house than I did, it had to be rebuilt. If the insurance company had been willing to give me the money, I probably would have aborted my preparation for purpose process and returned to Trinidad, before God's fullness of time. It has become quite evident as I revisited the roadblocks and detours of my journey that God was pulling all the strings.

The rebuilding of my house resulted in reconciliation with my bother Patrick. Seven years previously we had, to my delight, begun to communicate. This resulted in a good relationship. He was a big bother on my father's side, and I was thrilled to have him on my side. Sadly, a misunderstanding that was fueled by some erroneous information that I'd been given, led me to behave very badly towards him, and he in turn, being angry, had responded in kind. But we were family and I needed help. Without resurrecting the ugly past, Patrick came to my aid.

It appeared that the insurance company worked with certain construction companies to rebuild homes as inexpensively as possible. The very morning after the house had been burnt, before damage could have been estimated, a building contactor approached with a contract for me to sign. He offered to rebuild my house, exactly as I wanted it, for any amount on which the insurance company settled. I had the presence of mind to refuse what appeared like a God-sent proposal. After the insurance company had determined the probable cost of rebuilding, the same man again approached me with the same offer. Insisting on knowing the exact specifications and details of his plan, I again refused to sign a contract, and asked my brother Patrick, who is also a contractor to investigate the matter.

Patrick went with me to the insurance company to sign some papers and who did we meet there, but Mr. Earlybird himself. My brother made an appointment with him to approve the plans for rebuilding my house, but Mr. Earlybird did not keep either that or two subsequent appointments. Eventually, Patrick, after studying the particulars of the insurance company's estimate, decided to extend to me the same deal that Mr. Earlybird had offered me. I knew my brother to be a man of integrity, who took pride in the excellence of his work, so with no further deliberation, I agreed to his terms.

Not waiting for the insurance to provide the money for the rebuilding, Patrick laid out his own hard cash and began the work. Obviously disappointed and angry that I did not succumb to the pressures of their own contractor, the insurance company eventually revised its estimate. They paid me far less than Patrick had expected, but I was happy to pay him with the money, which I had received to replace the contents of the house, which had been destroyed.

Without my brother, I would have been so distressed, I might have retreated to my former behavior and run away.

With my purpose and plan of relocation uppermost in my mind, my intention to sell my house did not change. However, there were many lessons which I had yet to learn; and I needed a few more years of preparation.

Seven years have passed since the rebuilding and ten years since I heard the call to Trinidad. I expect my house to be sold within the next four months. The time has come.

Much has happened in the interim.

-19- No Longer Hagar, My Name Is Rachel

About three months after the fire, while I was staying at my friend, Stephanie's house, my thoughts began to run wild. I had just returned from a successful evangelistic trip to Trinidad with my Pastor, when I became overwhelmingly depressed. Carnal desires shamed me; the devil accused me; and suddenly my whole life seemed like a series of tragedies. The devil, that accuser of the brethren, took me through the pages of my life, the ones where his activities were most evident, and showed me how nothing good had ever happened to me. Thank God that I was saved, but that was all. I couldn't remember a time when I had sunk so low. My case was simply disgraceful and I just couldn't get over it.

It seemed that I had made no progress as a Christian. My son who had been some measure of my success as a parent had died. If I had not left his father or if I had been a good parent he would not have gone into the military. He would be alive. My younger son, Ian and I parted several times. He proved me an absolute failure. My mother was dead. My father was dead. I had had a hysterectomy, was no longer a real woman. I was fat and felt ugly. I lived with the shameful stigma of divorce, which some Christians seemed to think is the unpardonable sin.

My parents had ruined my childhood with fighting, fear and shame. Poverty and ignorance had robbed me of a better education, and better career opportunities. I hadn't been promoted in years because I no longer attended the company's open bar parties. When I questioned the insult of promoting someone, whose work was inferior to mine, above me, my boss said, "Off the record, your name is submitted every year for promotion, but some one always mentions that you are more religious minded than company minded." My house had been destroyed by fire and the insurance company with its fraudulent schemes was holding up the money for the rebuilding. Murphy's law had been and was the operational rule of my life.

In times past when I was feeling desolate, I would sit on my bed with my Bible and hymnbook. Isaiah fifty-four, Psalm eighteen, and Psalm one-thirty-nine were the special chapters that I read. Then beginning with hymn #1, I would sing my way through the hymnbook. "Under His Wings", and "O Love That Will Not Let Me Go", were my favorite hymns for blue days. Then I would compose praises and offer them as a sacrifice to the Lord.

Always, after a few hours, the depression lifted and I felt better. But in March 1995, although Stephanie would certainly have wanted me to do it, I couldn't shut her out of her own room for an indefinite period of time, so that I could read, and sing my way out of the doldrums. Besides, if she heard me singing, she would automatically join in and exorcizing depression was, for me, a private operation.

After two weeks of wallowing in the devil's quagmire God proved that he remembered me.

The message that Sunday was about Jacob. Pastor preached about Jacob's background, Jacob's parentage, and Jacob's personality. Not a pretty picture. Then she preached about Jacob admitting who he was and God changing his name from Jacob to Israel. I had heard it before. It was the same message that she had preached in Trinidad. I sat there in the front seat listening, but not hearing. Depression had deafened me. Then Pastor descended the pulpit and said. "I am not going to call out any name. You are here. You have been abused as a child, physically, sexually, verbally and emotionally. You've been rejected and refused. You are disappointed in yourself, in man and in God. If you want help, stand up now."

That was me. There may have been others in the congregation who fitted the description, but I knew it was me. I couldn't be bothered to be embarrassed. I had no time to waste in wondering what the people would think about Minister Palmer, who always seemed to have it all together; who went through so much and remained strong and unmovable, always abounding in the work of the Lord. I was sick in my soul. I needed help. I didn't need to be coaxed. I stood up. I surrendered my impotent strength. "Help me, Lord. Please help me."

Just like on that day when I asked him to take my burden of sin and I knew that he did, so I knew without a shadow of a doubt that God was beginning a new work in my life. How would He proceed? I had no idea, but I was open. Whatever way He chose to heal me, I was ready. The depression left, but that was not enough. I had a lack. I wanted ????? I couldn't even voice what I wanted. Now I know I wanted wholeness.

After that I answered every altar call, hoping for what I didn't know. Then about two months later, when I was kneeling at the altar of my Father God, I heard the transforming words. "This is what the Lord says to tell you", said Pastor Rose, "**Your name is no longer Hagar**. **Your name is Rachel.**"

With the understanding of my new name I began to expect change and opened myself to receive changes. That was not easy. I needed help to become Rachel. Rachel was the beautiful woman with whom Jacob fell in love at first sight. She was a woman worth working for and waiting for. She was not loved for anything she could give or do. She was loved just for who she was. She was as loved as Hagar had been unloved; and as wanted as Hagar had been rejected. My mind had to be renewed to believe, accept, and receive the unconditional love of the Father-God, who loved and wanted me. The scripture spoke of Jacob's love for Rachel, never of Rachel's love for Jacob. I wanted to love, not just in the doing and the giving, but I wanted the emotional bond of love between my Father-God and I.

Liberty Through The Remittance Of Emotional Pain

Not long after my name change, Reverend Farley came to minister at Circle. He said, "Today, I come to bring you liberty." The text of his message was, "Whose sins you shall remit they are remitted." He began to testify of his discoveries during the time when he was recovering from a heart attack. He talked about remitting the memory of the pain of emotions. This went beyond forgiving people who had hurt you. This was about getting rid of the emotions, which resulted from the hurt. Grief, anger, and fear are some of them. Reverend Farley used scientific and biblical data to prove that the memory of emotions lodged in the body cause physical as well as psychological damage. He advised us to examine the hurts we had experienced, recognize the resulting emotions, and remit them by asking God to remove them from our memories and body tissues.

I believed that I had forgiven all who had ever wronged me and that I had no emotional baggage left. Nevertheless, as I sat at the kitchen table that night, I said one of my simple little prayers. "Father, if there is any emotion that I need to remit, you'll have to show me."

My ex-husband Paul had been in the habit of phoning me periodically, just to talk. Even though our conversations were limited by our spiritual difference, I didn't mind chatting with him. I had forgiven him and was prepared to be Christ-like and treat him as if he'd never hurt me. Besides, I had not wanted the burden of carrying him around in my mind.

It so happened that a short while after my simple prayer, Paul phoned with his usual chat. Suddenly I was surprised by the enormous dose of anger that flooded my soul. His small talk and inconsequential chatter infuriated me. I heard myself telling him that he had been the greatest disappointment of my life. How I lambasted him! He was utterly shocked. He couldn't understand what had changed me. All through the years I had been strong and nothing ever moved me. I had watched my marriage wrecked, but I had never once expressed anger, or sadness, or any emotional pain. I had seemed to shrug off my troubles and move on.

Now, after twenty years, I was enraged. I had something to say. I told Paul that I never wanted to see him or hear from him for the rest of my life and I slammed the phone down. Unbelief made him redial, only to be pounded by another storm of angry words. This was not the Andrea Eden whom he had known, admired, and envied for the way she handled life. He phoned again. Convinced at last, he left me alone.

I believe that Paul was the only person that had mattered enough, to keep a steady deposit of anger going into the suppression vault of my subconscious. Mama and Daddy were deceased and any expectations that I had of them had ceased long before their deaths. At one time I had killed Paul with indifference, but circumstances had brought him back into my life. Over the years he had continued to disappoint and infuriate me. He had never pursued a relationship with his sons. He had continued to verbally express love for me, but his actions always left much to be desired. He hadn't changed. Because we were divorced, and because I no longer wanted him, I had not thought that I had the right to that anger, nor did I have the time or energy to waste in emotional expression on him.

So there I sat at the kitchen table realizing that for at least twenty years, the memory of the anger and the subsequent deposits that had been added from time to time, had been hiding in me. Forgiving the person who hurt me had not remitted the suppressed emotion. I asked God to take it away. And he did.

Some months later, I was surprised by a phone call from Paul, who had continued to heed my request so that I no longer expected to hear from him. "Ann", he said, "I have something to say, I will just say it and hang up. Please listen." "I'm listening." I replied, thinking that perhaps he had called to say that he was terminally ill or something of the sort.

"I had a dream of when we were young and I remembered the promises I made to you. I realize that I never kept those promises and I also realized that I must have hurt you. I want you to know that I am sorry and I am asking you to forgive me."

Paul hadn't received the forgiveness I had extended before, because he didn't believe that he had done anything for which he should have been forgiven. I assured him of my forgiveness. Three weeks later he phoned to see how I was. I felt no irritability at the sound of his voice. Today we have as good a friendship as people who lead different spiritual lives can have. The truth is that he does love me as well as his damaged emotional and psychological self allows him to.

My walls were tumbling.

Soon other people were being shocked by my anger. I found that injustice, oppression, and betrayal triggered strong anger. I actually enjoyed expressing myself. People would tell me afterward how my voice was raised and my finger pointed at the source of my anger. That was good. I was becoming normal. I just had to learn how to ***be angry and sin not.***

I Wished Mama Were Alive

Cost effective recommendations on the job offered me early retirement in 1996. I was quite happy. Because of previous downsizing the work place had become a very stressful and unhappy environment. The pension wasn't much when compared with my salary. I refinanced my house at a significantly lower interest rate and was therefore able to pay my bills. Mama always used to say, "Take little and live long." That is why in 1997 when Mama Christie came to visit from Ghana, I was free to accommodate her. One day, before she arrived, I was sitting on the toilet and an amazing thought crossed my mind. *"I wish Mama was alive. I'd like to phone her."*

God sent Mama Christie.

Mama Christie was a very commanding individual, just like Mama; dark-skinned like Mama, but strapping and taller. Even though my mother was only about five feet, four inches tall, she strode about with such an imperial manner, that she always seemed much taller and much larger.

I tried my best to accommodate Mama Christie, but she stressed me out as I tried to make her feel happy and be comfortable. I was tired of hearing 'Rachel, come here, do this, fetch that."

One day, She saw me braiding my hair and decided that she wanted her hair braided as well. She had always worn a wig and I had never really seen her hair. As I stood behind her and started combing her hair, I was transported back in time. All of a sudden, I was a little girl and this was Mama's hair. It was the same thick, long, salt and pepper hair that my mother had had. I was overwhelmed with emotion. That was when I knew that I had loved my mother with a deep emotional love, and after all the years of indifference and hatred, just like the anger against Paul had surfaced, so the love for Mama emerged. God is amazing.

Emotionally Like My Mother

In 1997, Reverend Rattray ministered at a seminar on Parenting. She spoke about the parents' responsibility to nurture, and the importance of meeting the emotional needs of their children. She understood that some of us had not received hugs and kisses; some were never approved and applauded; some were told that they would never amount to anything. etc. However, Rev. Rattray believed, and many agreed with her, that despite the missing model of a proper parent, wc could all learn to give what we never had. It was an excellent seminar but I disagreed. I had known that I should have been demonstrative in my love for my children. I had wanted to desperately. Yet I had been unable to give them that emotional thing that every child needs in order to feel a sense of security and significance. I made an appointment to see Reverend Rattray.

A few years previously, when I had wanted to begin the process of restoration, I had begun to think of my childhood. I had approached a friend, a Christian Counselor hoping for the help of a listening ear, an understanding heart, and sound advice. I was extremely disappointed when she said to me, "Rachel, why do you want to go back there? You don't live there anymore." Her response and attitude discouraged any further conversation and investigation, and I had retreated into myself once more.

Reverend Rattray was different. She asked questions and allowed me to go back into my childhood. She helped me to understand why I couldn't cry. She said that sometimes we make covenants with ourselves. In my case, every time something occurred that would naturally evoke crying or anger, because of the negative responses I had received whenever I cried or became angry, I would suppress the emotion and its expression and tell myself, "I will never cry," or "I will never be angry." Words are powerful building blocks that can erect walls or bridges in our personalities. I had effectively shut in anger, pain and tears. The walls that imprisoned anger had toppled. Now I needed my tears to flow.

One important thing that Reverend Rattray helped me to realize was that, the traumas of my life had caused the shutdown of my emotional responses to appropriate stimuli. In the same way, Mama must have had some traumatic situations and experiences that shut her down, so that she was unable to give us the emotional touches and words that we needed. Un-natural circumstances give birth to abnormal behavior. That's how I learned that emotionally, I was very much like my mother.

That year, as December opened, I began to feel completely miserable, sad and irritable. The fourth anniversary of my son's death was approaching and I had no idea how to deal with it. Acknowledging the negative feelings was progress, but I needed to cry. I had handled Allan's death like a Stoic. I had even helped the master of ceremonies at his funeral. I had grieved silently. I had displayed no depth of emotions. I had only felt the weight of death, but I hadn't cried. It wasn't because I was strong, It was because I couldn't. The tears I should have shed had been frozen with the hurt, like all the other painful emotions of my life.

Mama Said: "Living Is Hard But Life Is Sweet"

People labeled me as a strong woman. I think that my mother was truly a strong woman. Her strength was born partly out of pride and partly out of courage. She used to say that living was hard, but life was sweet. I personally could not appreciate the sweetness of her life. I imagine that she had had some good times, and probably some great times, but overall, her statement had puzzled me. In retrospect, I suspect that the daily victories, which she gained in spite of her circumstances and pain, sweetened her life. She knew how to cry and rage and fight and talk to man and God. She embraced pain, dealt with it appropriately, and then moved on.

I later learned that my mother was well known for her acts of kindness to many. I was told that she used to purchase oranges and visit the hospital. She would observe the people who had no visitors. Those, she approached with her gift of oranges and small talk, helping to ease their loneliness and encourage them to have faith in God. She also visited those who were shut-in by reason of age or infirmity, always bringing them some home made treats to enjoy, as she spent time with them to liven their days. Many depended on her visits. It must have given her great satisfaction to be so needed. She had discovered her purpose and was well loved.

For a little while, I tried to accept the popular evaluation that I was strong. Yet, I knew that, in my heart, I never felt the strength I obviously portrayed. Unlike my mother, I could not describe life as being sweet. Life was bland at best. Before I was saved the only thing that made life preferable to death was, the awesome prospect of eternal hell and my responsibilities to others. My mother never wanted to die;

not even when she was wracked with the excruciating pain of cancer.

My son Allan had discovered a sweetness in living. He was not afraid to die, but death was an enemy against whom he fought valiantly.

Pancreatic Cancer is inoperable and incurable. Yet with several tumors in his liver and pancreas, Allan had refused to give up to the clutches of death. All that the doctors could do was keep him on escalating doses of morphine and intravenous fluids to hydrate him. Pancreatic cancer pulled the calcium out of his bones and into his blood. Whenever the calcium content of his blood was high, he became disoriented, hallucinated, and lost the ability to control his muscles. We were told that if ever the calcium became very high, Allan would go into a coma and death would quickly follow.

My son's conversation was always of what he planned to do after he was healed. He was in love. There was a woman in Hawaii, with a son that he adored, waiting for him to come home. There was a college education and cancer research waiting for him. He had love and purpose. Like Job he complained at the unfairness of fate, but unlike Job who looked for a resurrection, Allan expected a restoration to health.

There came another day when the doctors concluded that Allan could no longer be hydrated. His stomach was grossly enlarged. His tissues were water-logged and his liver could burst. They said he would die an unbelievably painful death if they continued to hydrate him. Their counsel was that I take him home, where he would slip into a coma in a couple of days, and die peacefully. The decision was Allan's.

My son agreed to come home. He called his father, his brother and I to his bedside to inform us of his decision. "But", he told us, "I am not going home to die. If I die, I'll go to heaven, but I want you all to understand, I haven't given up on living." So we brought him home. And I began the vigil. He could neither walk, stand, nor sit and had to be lifted and held. He was taking ninety milligrams of morphine, as needed; and trying hard to drink enough water and keep himself alive. Soon the hallucinations started.

One morning he didn't ask for water or morphine. As I laid at the foot of his bed watching him sleep, his breathing became loud and labored. As the day turned to afternoon his breathing quieted and his breath became quite shallow. I knew that he was dying. I telephoned his aunt and by evening the family had gathered around his bed to witness his death.

As we stood there silently waiting for his last breath, Allan opened his eyes. "Ma, I feel cold. I want to get up and walk."

"Allan you cannot walk." "Ma, lift me up and make me walk, I have no intention of lying here and letting death take me. Make me walk." He insisted. I had noticed the cold creeping up on him. His life was leaving. "Ma, make me walk." he commanded. We raised him up to a sitting position. We swung his bony legs around and raised him to a standing position. His father held him up, while I took his feet in my hand and moved them forward, making him walk. Warmth returned to his body. Eventually he said, "Put me to sit now." And we sat him down.

He laughed at death and said, "Auntie Pearl, I want some rotisserie chicken, mashed potatoes, and apple pie." We looked at him in happy amazement. His aunt asked. "What just happened here?"

About two weeks later, Allan said to me, "Ma, take me back to the hospital." He could no longer get any relief from the oral morphine, nor was he able drink enough water. He needed to have both administered intravenously. Whether he had been hallucinating or having divine visitations, I do not know. I think the latter, because, whereas he used to want me at his side constantly, lately he had been saying, "Ma, leave the room so that the angels would come." I would step outside, and after about fifteen minutes he would call me back. He never complained about the pain anymore, until that day when he asked to be taken back to the hospital.

The Saturday before he died, I cringed and screamed as I heard my son bawling, when the doctor put the intravenous needle in his groin. The doctor had given him the choice of having it in his neck or his groin. He had questioned the doctor about the side effects. Because he was so thin, there was a chance of the needle in his neck puncturing his lungs and causing death. The needle in the groin could cause an infection. Allan had concluded that an infection was preferable to death. When I heard him bawling I rushed into the room. "Allan," I asked, "do you still want to live?" "Yes Mummy, I do."

I Was A Practicing Buddhist

I was fascinated. What was there about life that was so precious, especially if one were suffering and one knew that death had no sting, but was only a doorway to life?

After I was saved, the fact of God's love and the experience of His grace had made life pleasant, yet there was a missing ingredient. As I sought for truth about myself, I came to the conclusion that I was a fake. I was the worst kind of coward.

I had been afraid to embrace life to the fullest, because that meant embracing pain. It also meant embracing love and pleasure, and to sacrifice one necessitated the sacrifice of the others. The degree of passion expended in loving, and the measure of pleasure experienced, was equal to the intensity of the pain produced when the object of love was lost, and the pleasure destroyed.

I have just finished reading Larry Crabb's *Shattered Dreams.* I identify with his observation. *"We Christians"*, he wrote, *"are often practicing Buddhists. We kill desire in an effort to escape pain, then wonder why we don't enjoy God."* While in my spirit I have been a Christian, in my soul I had since my childhood, practiced the four noble truths of Buddhism.

- Life is suffering.
- The cause of all suffering is desire.
- The way to end suffering is to end desire.
- Spend your life learning to eliminate desire.

Without understanding what I was doing, I had followed these principles. I had constantly and consistently killed desire. I consciously desired nothing. If some pleasure came my way, I took a little, never drank a full cup, never filled my soul, never experienced full satisfaction, never desired to have it again, never missed it when it was taken away or had to leave.

When Daddy left us homeless after years of beating Mama, I immediately killed the desire of having my parents living together. When Mama seemed not to care, I killed the desire to have a loving and understanding mother. I eventually killed the desire to have good, caring, protecting, nurturing parents. I divorced them and became an emotional orphan who had no claims on parental love. When I had to be temporarily separated from my husband and later on, my children, I had so well learned the third principle that the desire for them had been killed, the moment I realized that I wouldn't have them with me. By the time my marriage, the most important part of my life ended, I had already killed all my dreams and moved on. Even when my son died, rather than experiencing the pain of grief, I killed the desire that caused the suffering.

Why Was I So Afraid Of Pain?

Looking back to discover why I was so afraid of pain I have reached some conclusions.

My early childhood was replete with pain, fear, and shame. My mission from then on was to avoid the pain, hide fear, and cover shame. Witnessing the violent relationship of my parents probably caused in me, a determination to avoid all circumstances and situations that could result in physical or emotional or physical pain. I was never going to be like my mother. No one would ever beat me, or throw me out in the streets.

I avoided arguments and verbal fights. Mama and Daddy quarreled a lot and later Mama quarreled with us, her children. I hated quarreling. Daddy and his wife Merle never had physical fights; nor did Daddy and Olympia, his companion of thirty-six years. Merle and Olympia did not quarrel. When I realized this I began to consider that perhaps Mama's quarreling drove Daddy crazy, and that was why he beat her and eventually left us. I am not saying that that was so. I am just stating my conclusions and subsequent decisions. I determined never to quarrel. I believed that any expression of anger or opposition would result in a broken relationship. I didn't know that love could not be knocked out by disagreements. I was determined to risk neither pain, nor rejection, nor abandonment.

Whenever Mama punished us she used to say, "You will either do, die, or runaway." I was afraid to die, so I did what I was told, to prevent physical punishment and verbal abuse. I did my best, and when doing didn't bring happiness, I ran away. Firstly, I killed the expression of desire, and later the very desire itself, to prevent emotional pain. Consequently, my relationships were fight-free and passionless.

That December, on the anniversary of Allan's death when the grief threatened, I did not run from the feelings, but I did not embrace them. I was afraid. I let them happen and still not able to dissolve them in tears, they passed. I needed to break the covenant I had made with myself that said, "Andrea will never cry." It was the same covenant that tacitly said, "Andrea will never embrace pain." It was the same covenant that said "Andrea will not give her heart to anyone, so that no one will break it."

But how could I ever experience the pleasure of loving and being loved if I guarded my heart so jealously. How could I even enjoy God, who is love, unless I was prepared to surrender? I sought to prove that I loved God by keeping his commandments, and His favor and His Word declared His love for me. But I wanted a real relationship. I desired intimacy. I needed to know "*the length and depth and height and breath of His love, which passes knowledge.*"

As many times as I attempted to kill those desires they refused to die. We were made for God and love, and there is incompleteness that cannot be made whole, and longing that cannot be satisfied otherwise. In the quest for fulfillment, we develop harmful habits. Unable to understand that only the living water of God's love can quench our souls' thirst, like Solomon the wise, we endeavor to fill our lives with earthly pleasures and industry. We become workaholics, alcoholics, drug addicts, sex addicts, food addicts, risk addicts, power addicts and even charitable addicts. But after all the temporary pleasures have been tasted, and the day's work is done, if we are honest we would declare like frustrated Solomon, *All is vanity and vexation of Spirit.*

The Friendship Journey

Today I have many excellent friendships and intimate friends. However, from the time I met Paul and began going steady at age fifteen to the time I became a Christian at age thirty-one, there was only one person that I considered a close friend, and that was Mary Burton.

I had a few associates but they didn't count. No one knew the real me. They knew the pretty flirtatious untouchable woman who had it all together. I had a few female associates. Some of them thought I was a snob. They were all co-workers and the only time I mingled with them was at company functions. The truth was that I usually froze in the presence of strangers, so unless someone initiated and carried the whole conversation, the people with whom I socialized remained strangers. I did not participate in gossip and small talk At a party, one could stand in a crowd with a drink and a cigarette, listen to everyone and say nothing; or one could dance and say nothing.

Certain situations did invite some level of companionship. For instance, Neutrice Benjamin was the only other West Indian who worked in my group at the phone company, so we had a common culture and it was natural for us to stick together.

When our marriage was good, Paul and I became friendly with Joan and Ed Guthrie and enjoyed visiting their home in Monroe, Upstate New York. But when we went bowling with them, the other people at the bowling alley seemed uncomfortable; and when we went to a restaurant with them, somehow the waitress didn't seem to notice us. By the time we had a home to which we could invite them, our marriage was already disintegrating. It is usually very uncomfortable for couples to hang out with divorcees.

Carol Walsh and I appeared to develop a friendship, because we were both sent to work in the computer room, we both had sons, and when her boyfriend broke her heart and she needed someone to talk to I was there and listened. I was always a good listener. Every other word out of her mouth was an obscenity, which was very offensive to me, but I chose to overlook that. She invited me to her home and introduced me to my first bar stool. I really couldn't relate to her friends and lifestyle. She was Irish and all their social activities seemed to revolve around beer, wine, and whiskey. Not that I didn't drink, but that was too much for me.

Richard Savage was a friend to me. He was fascinated with me. He was absolutely incredulous that a beautiful, bright and classy woman like me would accept a lunch date with him. He was a streetwise, self educated, ex-convict who loved using new three and four syllable words. He was making the most of a second chance and was honored that I chose to be associated with him. Richard would have done anything for me, and he asked nothing of me. He introduced me to all his girlfriends. Before he got married, he brought his fiancée to me and explained to her that I was his friend and that if ever

I needed his help for any reason, he pledged to be available to me. As with everybody else I never let him know me. We never conversed about personal things. He was the person to whom I attempted to open up, but he couldn't deal with an Andrea, who had personal problems like the rest of the world.

Mary Burton and I met in November 1977, because of our desperately lonely neighbor Betty who had invited everyone on the fourth floor to her Tupperware party. This is how we became friends. Three days before Christmas, realizing that I had not seen Mary for quite a while, I knocked on her door. She had been in an accident that totaled her car and left her injured. She was alone with no one to care for her because her family lived far away in Long Island. I promised to look in on Mary the following night when I returned from work.

I had to break my promise. That evening I had been feeling pretty low. It was two days before Christmas and the world was filled with the excitement of the season. I had phoned my good buddy Richard, and wheedled him into stopping at the Hare and the Hound for a drink after work. Soon, in the spirit of the season everyone was buying drinks for everyone else. Eventually I stood up and realized that, for the first time in my life, I felt unsteady. I asked Richard to take me home.

I remembered that I was supposed to look in on Mary, but I just wasn't up to visiting. Consequently, I asked Richard to ring the doorbell at apartment 4b, and tell Mary that I was sorry; that I was in no condition to stop by, but that I would see her the next day. Mary was very impressed because I showed such consideration. We became great friends. She loved me dearly and she too, would have done anything for me. We shared everything, clothes, food, and money. I couldn't drive, but she and her car were at my disposal.

I enjoyed 'at home parties' with my brothers and sisters, or grand ballroom affairs. Mary introduced me to discos and clubs. She was flashy and flirtatious. I was usually very reserved in the company of strangers. After my divorce I had quickly realized that without the protection of a wedding band, flirting could be misinterpreted and dangerous. I had no wish to advertise myself and preferred to avoid unwanted attention, so most of the time guys did not flirt with me. Mary on the other hand invited so much attention, some of which was unwanted. When Mary's behavior resulted in unwelcome attention, she would extricate herself from situations by saying that she had to take her sister, who couldn't drive, home. Mary and I took some crazy chances and had great fun, until by the persistent grace of God, I got saved and immediately changed.

About a year after I became a Christian, Mary gave her life to the Lord. In 1983, Mary moved to Texas, hoping to provide a better life for her children. Hers was a rough path. She died in March 2001.

I lost track of Richard around 1981. He stopped by my work place ten years later to give me the glad new of his salvation and deliverance from drug addiction.

Richard Savage and Mary Burton were easy friends to have because 1) they needed nothing from me, except my being there. 2) They were both talkers and I was a listener. 3) They both were obviously proud and pleased to have me as a friend. 4) They both behaved as if I were the most beautiful, brilliant friend that they had. 5) There was never any physical display of affection that demanded any response.

Christian Friendships

After I became a Christian I was immediately blessed with new associates. I liked all the Christians that I initially met. The BQ Bible Study group was made up of the beautiful young people who shone with and extended the Love of Jesus. In 2000, while I was convalescing I was surprised by visits from members of the BQ Bible Study that broke up around 1984. I was glad to know that the grapevine was still intact.

The Christian group at work consisted of wonderful people whose greatest ambition was to serve and please the Lord. Out of that group which lasted six years, I gained four precious friends: Cindy, Marva, Iris, and Evelyn. There was an easy, caring, giving, equal love that developed between us. We understood that it was there. Words were unnecessary. It was a love that accepted and respected each other, demanded nothing, but could ask anything, with the assurance that we could depend on each other.

We shared in each other's lives. Cindy understood me more fully than anyone of my friends, past and present. Others may understand me now, because I share a lot now and am able to explain myself and express my feelings. But Cindy seemed to instinctively know the real me. We had a lot in common. When life threw us curved balls we ducked and stepped aside. We preferred to be independent of people, and deal only with what we could manage. We also didn't cry over spilt milk. We squeezed each other's hands and groaned, "Mm, Oh! That's too bad. I'm so sorry", and because we came from the same emotional pool, it was enough. On the other hand, I couldn't understand why Marva's heart broke over elements of my story, while I remained totally emotionless.

Fourteen years ago, believing that they were called by God to Virginia, Cindy and her husband left New York. God has similarly been changing us, and we continue to support each other, as He uproots, breaks down, plants and builds in our lives.

Eight years later, Evelyn, who was the youngest, married a wonderful man, moved to Colorado, and is busy working at her own business and raising her family.

God gave to Iris, who had suffered from spousal battery and other abuses until she was so fearful that we had to help her to runaway, (her husband later committed suicide) a loving husband. They keep busy with A Mission of Mercy which ministers to the abused and homeless.

In 1997, Marva, my train ministry and walking partner, relocated to Georgia, where she continues to use her secular talents and love for people in the service of the Lord.

When I began to attend Pentecostal Circle Tabernacle in 1980, I suspect that I was viewed as being different from the other congregants. That difference was illustrated in that the people always addressed me respectfully, by my surname. I observed that except for folks old enough to be my parents (I was thirty-two), everyone else was on a first name basis. Some people may even have thought that I considered myself better than them, because while I was respectful to all, I was reserved, and invited no familiarity. There were several reasons for my reticence.

My Catholic experience did not prepare me for the overfriendliness of a small Pentecostal church. My two boys and I attended the eleven o'clock morning service. We sat together, sang the hymns, read the scriptures, listened to the sermons, received the Benediction, wished those who were in our pathway, "Good-afternoon", then went home. At first we didn't attend any of the night services. Sunday evenings were a time for going to the park in the warm months, and having my friends from the BQ Bible Study group over for dinner during the cold. Being occupied, un-observant and totally lacking in curiosity, it was three years before I realized that the people of Pentecostal Circle socialized with each other on a very intimate level.

Little by little, as troubles came my way, I turned to the brethren at church for spiritual support. They wholehearted embraced me and stood with me through my times of sorrow and heartbreak. As I let them into my life, friendships developed and grew. Today, I know that I had not only their respect and admiration, but genuine love.

There came a time when needy people began to lean on me. At first I was very uncomfortable and reluctant to invite or accept such relationships. I believe that I have, for the most part, responded responsibly to life's necessary challenges, but to deliberately volunteer for responsibilities, especially if I felt inadequate to the task, seemed unwise. I always hesitated to receive confidences or make promises. I never wanted to be guilty of betraying a trust or not keeping my word. My fear was that I did not have the capacity, or may selfishly not have the desire, to meet others' needs. I had no wish to disappoint or cause grief to anyone.

When I was first asked to assist needy people, I set aside my fears and responded with Christian charity on the basis of the Scriptures. I desired to sow seeds in the kingdom of God and store up treasure in heaven. I shared my home, my clothes, my money and even my time; and as much as I was able to, I let then into my heart. My first "daughter" came in 1980 and lived in my home for two years. She was pregnant and homeless when she came. I was literally at her side when she professed faith in Jesus, had her baby, was baptized, and eventually got married. She had a lovely wedding in my living room and moved away. I long to see Althea and her children, especially Javon who was born in my arms.

My home became a house of refuge. People came and went. They didn't seem to remember me after they were back on their feet and moved away. They left with a "Thank you very much.' And that was it.

I wanted fruit that remained. I desired to see them grow as a result of my influence in their lives. I allowed myself to be mildly disappointed, because I could not bear the pain of deep disappointment. The fact was that each time I felt like a bigger failure. However, not wanting to respond negatively to others because of the ingratitude of some, I told myself that I should not anticipate results or desire gratitude, since what I did, I did unto the Lord. I continued to assist where I could. I progressed to the place where I didn't wait to be asked but extended my hand of friendship and love.

There is one woman who became my friend because I was there to help her through some very difficult times. Apart from being one of the most grateful people I'd met, she thought that I was wonderful and wise and had it all together. Our friendship developed and I tried very had to live up to her high opinion. A mutual acquaintance, who had knowledge of me from my pre-Christian days, was extremely upset and I think, envious, that Valerie should think so well of me, and she made it her business to destroy my reputation and our friendship. Valerie was so disappointed with the disclosure of my past that she stopped associating with me.

Of course, I was unaware of the reason for Valerie's disassociation. Before the Lord had begun His work in my life, I would have shrugged my shoulders, walked away without caring to know why, and assumed an attitude of indifference towards her. However, I decided that in this instance, I was not willing to walk away from my friend. Contrary to my usual response, I made a nuisance of myself until she agreed to explain what had caused the death of our relationship. Then, after thinking things through, I had determined that our friendship was worth fighting for and that my reputation, because of my Christian witness, was worth defending.

That was a very important step in my growth. I allowed someone and something to be important enough, that I left my comfort zone, expressed myself, and clarified the matters. I took a relationship risk. I lost my halo, but gained a more realistic friendship that took the pressure off my being perfect. Valerie and I are still very good friends.

In 1990, when sixteen-year old Marvalene first came to church, I greeted her with a hug and a kiss, and an "I love you," and gave her my phone number. From that day she showered and smothered me with her love. Over the years she remained faithful and pushed her way into my heart. At the end of 1999 when I needed someone to care for me, she moved into my home and took charge of my convalescence.

Between 1990 and present time, my family of faithful mothers, daughters, sisters, nieces, sons, nephews, and friends grew. I am blessed with the genuine love of people who think the world of me. I learned that I could stretch farther than I could see, and that although there were people who thought so highly of me that perfection was expected, it was all right to fail or come short. Forgiveness was always available, because they love me.

Have I ever been disappointed since? More than ever. I have hurt so badly. I took the relationship risk and sometimes my heart was broken. And I learned to cry.

-20- The Dilemma Of Giving And Receiving

My friend Connie likes to say, "You can give without loving, but you cannot love without giving." The apostle Paul said it this way, *And though I bestow all my goods to feed the poor, and though I give my body to be burned, and have not love, it profits me nothing.* People who love people cannot comprehend giving without loving, because to them they are both one and the same. The giving that includes loving includes the giving of self.

The tragedy is, that these wonderful loving people expect that those who are recipients of their generosity also receive their love. They tend also to believe that the reverse is true; and when they are given gifts, that cost either time or money, they suppose that they given love. The greater tragedy occurs when the givers are needy love-hungry souls, who believe that when they have given their substance, time, and devotion in Cinderella fashion, they deserve and expect love in return. The greatest tragedy is that when such people have nothing to give, or if what they gave was refused, they believe themselves to be undeserving of love.

I call it "The Dilemma of Giving and Receiving". Children are naturally giving lovers. No wonder Jesus said, *And said,*

Verily I say unto you, Except ye be converted, and become as little children, ye shall not enter into the kingdom of heaven. But children are guileless and unwise, so they expect a response equal to the largess of their unselfish gifts of love. A small child who, in order to pick the loveliest flowers, tramples down the flower bed and dirties himself, does not expect to receives screams of anger when he proudly presents his mother with the bouquet. He expects her to receive as much joy as he had in the anticipation of her pleasure.

A teenage girl of fourteen, who remembers her mother's pleasure in receiving presents from her when she was a child, expects that after she had lovingly cared for her sick mother and younger siblings, to be praised and loved more than before. She does not expect her labor of love to be ignored, far less, to be immediately punished for a small infraction.

I believe that it was then that I began to give without loving; to perform my duties and withhold myself. This was a preventative measure to protect myself from the pain of, what was in my perception, unrequited love.

When I fell in love with Paul, any capacity I had for loving and giving was directed towards him. It seemed to me that my love was completely requited. When I perceived that to have changed, I resorted to my teenage behavior and withheld my loving and so I preserved myself. Consequently, giving became difficult and was no longer natural and automatic, but studied and deliberate. I could give while hating; I could give and be indifferent.

I have a keen sense of justice, therefore, having no intention of loving, and being convinced that he who gives, anticipates an equal or loving response, I had also refused to receive. Perhaps it was because I was emotionally bankrupt. Or, was it that I was an emotional miser?

Actually, because I had forgotten the pleasure of lovingly giving, and I did not perceive myself as worthy of love, I didn't even ask God for any help, or anything unless I was driven to desperation. I couldn't understand why He, or anyone would want to give anything to me.

My father had nothing to give but himself, and needing so many things, I didn't want, or know how to take, what he offered. My mother was a giver but it seemed to me (It wasn't totally true), that she gave to others more than she gave to me. Perhaps it was because the others asked, and I did not. I don't know if Mama gave of herself to us, I only know that I didn't receive. My husband was a giver, who gave what I believed should have been exclusively mine, to people that he believed to be more deserving than I. That's what I thought. Maybe I was right; maybe I was wrong.

These were the most significant people in my life and my concepts and consequently my self esteem was formed from my perceptions of their perceptions.

To Know The Love That Passes Knowledge

In 1998, I made the acquaintance of a wonderful Christian man. I couldn't evict him from my heart and he began to crowd my mind. The simple sound of his voice in a mundane greeting warmed my heart and energized me. Conversation with him destroyed my appetite for food, and my days were brightened by the anticipation of a visit from him. When the smile that danced in his eyes told me that he derived pleasure from being with me, happiness flooded my soul, until the old fear of pain stepped in. I wanted to run back to the time before we met so I could be comfortable. Nevertheless, because I believed that this experience was part of my restoration, I did not run away. I really didn't want to.

In an effort to put things in proper perspective, I began to compare my relationship with God with the desire that had developed for this man. I wanted to be absolutely certain that God had the pre-eminent place in my life. I desired to experience the continuous presence of God. He should excite me. His voice should warm my heart. Conversation with him should destroy my appetite for food. Visiting with Him should be the highpoint of my days and the pleasure of my nights.

And so it was that I began to endeavor to keep God in my thoughts and talk to him continually. I am still working at it. It is not easy because I am both a daydreamer and a doer. When my mind isn't off somewhere, in the past or future, I often become distracted by things to be done. Praying is always a battle. However I won't give up. I have to develop the discipline of staying in God's presence. With all the needs that exist, often when I come before my Father-God, every thought flees my mind. So I sing. I am so glad that God does not criticize my voice.

The Cycle Of Abandonment And Rejection

Until 1999, it was always easier to address Jesus my Lord, than God, the Father. The non-relationship, that Daddy and I had had, left me with no real point of reference for expecting or experiencing the consistent love of my Father-God. The lack of a natural father's protection, provision, and positive influence in my life had left me feeling unworthy of God's attention. That's why every time I stepped forward and did not feel God's embrace, I quickly retreated, feeling rejected. Abandonment and rejection was what I'd received from my father, and I had rejected him in return. Daddy's embrace at the time that I forgave him could not undo the psychological damage caused by his ill-treatment. It only enabled me to accept him and removed the pain.

I now realize, that it was easy to believe that Paul had rejected and abandoned me in favor of his family, because that is exactly what Daddy had done, and that is what I had come to expect. I, in turn, had rejected and divorced him exactly as I had rejected and divorced Daddy.

Why Ask When There's No Help?

The difficulty with the Father God was compounded by my reluctance to ask and receive. Growing up poor and proud had taught me to ask only for that which was absolutely necessary and not to accept that for which I could not pay. I had learned that everything and everyone had a price, be it cash or kindness. Mama borrowed, lied and stole to provide bare essentials. I never knew her to be given any voluntary help by any man. That taught me to expect help from no one.

The fear of asking and not receiving translated into an attitude of not needing. When I discovered that I did need someone, I didn't know how to express it.

I remember the day that I was feeling utterly depressed. I honestly don't recall the cause, but I desperately needed someone to talk to. I was married and Paul was still my only friend, but he didn't believe me anymore. I socialized with my co-workers, but no one had any idea that I was not the happiest girl in the world.

Driven by the fearful thoughts that crowded my mind, I telephoned a few of the women with whom I used to work before I became a programmer. Not knowing how to express my pain and need, I casually said, "Hello Helen, are you busy?" She said she was. "Okay, I just called to say hello. I'll talk to you later." Every conversation went exactly like that.

That evening as I stood with my husband waiting for the train and feeling completely miserable, helpless, and hopeless, I could hear a soothing voice saying to me, "Jump on the train tracks and end it all and you will have peace." Almost, as if I was in a trance, I felt myself moving toward the edge of the platform. Suddenly I heard Paul's voice say, "Hey, watch where you're going." I came to my senses.

Another time when I was overwhelmed by the plunging runaway roller coaster that my marriage was riding on, I approached my good buddy Richard and said, "Richard, I need to talk. I have problems." He seemed scared by my uncharacteristic sadness that I had unmasked. "Not you, Andrea, not you", was his response. I simply enclosed my pain with a smile and said, "No Richard, not me."

•

I didn't borrow money or even buy things on payment plans. If I wanted something I saved. I never charged more on my credit card than I could pay. I never asked anyone to do me a favor for free, not even my family. What I couldn't pay for, I did without. Gifts and things didn't impress me. Nobody thought I needed anything or anyone. I was really pathetic and like everyone else I wasn't aware of my condition.

Perfect Love Casts Out Fear

Watson Duncanson loved me with a pure Christ-like love. I thought that Jesus must be like him. Interestingly, he was the one person that I felt free to ask for help. He never gave the impression that I was a burden to him, and he never disappointed me. I could share the most shameful information about myself with him, and he never made me feel un-redeemable. Whenever I was in trouble or had a serious decision to make, Watson comforted and counseled me. When I was wrong, he showed understanding, while gently reproving, wisely correcting, and sternly insisting that I make appropriate changes. I loved Watson. He was proud of me.

When I visited him in the hospital a few weeks before he died from cancer of the stomach, he beamed at me, and said to his other visitors, "Look at her. She was the saddest person I'd ever met." Then he said to me, "Every time I see you, I know that God is real, and that I haven't followed a cunningly devised fable." Those were the last words Watson spoke to me.

The Word of God invites, *"Ask, and you shall receive. You have not, because you ask not. Ask and you shall receive that your joy may be full."*

Asking is a sign of dependency. This has been a tough lesson to learn, a difficult change to make. Confidence in the giver's love is the thing that makes asking easy and receiving comfortable. The confident child understands that it pleases her father to receive and grant her request. This child does not wonder whether or not she will get her heart's desire. She realizes that if her request isn't granted, it must be because her wise and loving father knows that it will harm her. She even feels free to throw a tantrum and make unreasonable demands without fear of abandonment as a punishment for misconduct.

I am now able to ask a friend for a favor. I am now able to declare, "I need." It's hard to do, but because I feel lovable and worthy, I believe that I am loved. Therefore, I have confidence that if I am a burden to my friends to whom I turn in the time of need or trouble, I am a wanted burden.

The problem with asking God is that sometimes he takes so long to answer that someone like me, withdraws the request before the Father's *fullness of time.* The fear is that delay really means denied.

When I first became a child of God, I expected Him to answer all my prayers and He did. Later on when I believed that I should be mature, I did not immediately run to God and expect His intervention. Why was this so?

To me, maturity and adulthood meant being independent. Babies and small children were dependent. A baby's cry brought immediate food and comfort with hugs and kisses. In my family there were no hugs and kisses for older children. The cries of older children brought either no attention or negative attention. Praise and reward were hard earned and harder won. Disappointing or disobeying Mama, who for the most part was both mother and father to us, negated any previous distinguishing achievement or obedience, and incurred her wrath. It would have been foolish to approach Mama, and presumptive to ask for anything, when she was displeased. Her loud screaming voice always shamed me into silence.

Being disappointed in my stunted spiritual growth and work, I expected that the Father-God was disappointed in me also. Based on my experience, it was therefore realistic to withdraw open requests and refrain from making new ones, unless some deserving child was to be the recipient. This was also a ploy to escape pain, the pain of refusal and rejection that may expose unworthiness and lack of intimacy with God.

Over the years, I had studied the psychology of Christian

counseling, I had understood, written a wonderful thesis, and taught others all about childhood, adolescence, adulthood, marriage, parenting, etc. I had counseled many who suffered from damaged emotions, stunted personality growth, and low self-esteem because of abandonment, rejection, and/or abuse of all kinds. I had helped people to deal with loneliness, depression, anxiety, grief, and anger. Best of all, I had recognized my own damage and resulting low-esteem. But all that knowledge and understanding, and wisdom (some people call me a wise woman), did not bring about the changes that I desired to see in my personality.

Over the years I had read, believed every word, and taught the Bible. I was a newborn Christian when a young man shared Psalm 139 with me and specified that the Lord wanted me to personally know verses 14-17. *I will praise thee; for I am fearfully and wonderfully made: marvelous are thy works; and that my soul knows right well. My substance was not hid from thee, when I was made in secret, and curiously wrought in the lowest parts of the earth. Your eyes did see my substance, yet being imperfect; and in thy book all my members were written, which in continuance were fashioned, when as yet there was none of them. How precious also are thy thoughts unto me, O God! how great is the sum of them!*

I was still a babe in Christ when I opened my first Scofield Bible at Joel chapter two, verses 25-26, and claimed those words as a promise. *And I will restore to you the years that the locust hath eaten, the cankerworm, and the caterpillar, and the palmerworm, my great army which I sent among you. And ye shall eat in plenty, and be satisfied, and praise the name of the LORD your God, that hath dealt wondrously with you: and my people shall never be ashamed.*

I had had great expectations of great change, of great spiritual development and personality improvement. That's why I believed that Mama and I could have enjoyed a normal, loving, mother and daughter relationship. But it didn't happen then, and fifteen years later, I was even more dissatisfied and disappointed with myself. The lack of the progress, which I had desired and envisioned, had, time and again, provoked disillusionment and depression.

I had hoped that, one day, perhaps in the midst of a great convention, the power of the Holy Spirit, the mighty anointing that breaks and destroys yokes, would have slain me and in that moment, I would have been changed. The years that the locust had eaten would have been restored and I would appear as wonderfully and fearfully made as the Good God, the Father of our Lord Jesus Christ, and my Father had planned, before I was conceived in my mother's womb. At least I would have achieved normal emotional responses and spiritual heights and depths.

I now know, that to have had that hope realized, would have necessitated neither surrender nor struggle on my part. All my painful experiences would have been wasted, because I would have learned nothing. I would not have discovered the roots or consequences of my dysfunction. I would not have understood how my subsequent thought patterns, attitudes, actions, were dictated by the fear and shame, which were the dominant emotions of my childhood. I would not have recognized the pattern of running away that characterized my reaction to pain or the possibility of pain. I would not have seen the rejection/abandonment syndrome that prevented me from enjoying intimacy with both God and man.

The word of God is a reference manual, which contains God's blueprint and standard for man. It shows us what we can be and aught to be, so that, having a veritable and attainable model to which we might aspire, we can never be satisfied with what we are.

Until I began to grasp what I should be in God's Word, I did not know what I could be. Until I looked through God's Love and Calvary's blood, I was never free to ask for and accept God's gifts. If all I knew was the condemnation of His *"Thou Shall Nots,"* my constant thought when in need would always have been, *No good thing will He withhold from them that walk uprightly*, and I will always be judging myself as unworthy. I needed to assimilate the Scriptures that describe the God who Jesus revealed, so that I could accept His Gracious Love.

When I look into the lives of the Bible people who had intimacy with the Almighty I am encouraged. None of them were perfect. Abraham was a Liar; Jacob was a thief; Moses was a murderer; David was an adulterer. They messed up all the time. The important thing was that they believed God's record of Himself and approached Him in humility, on the basis of His Faithfulness, rather than their righteousness. They expected Him to do for them, all that was consistent with His Holiness and Love; and He did. God was pleased with them because they believed that *He is, and that He is a rewarder of them that diligently seek Him.* I too can be on intimate terms with God, if I diligently seek Him.

Before I close, I must testify of the miracle that God worked in my life.

-21- The Touch Of The Father's Hand

On December 26th, 1999, I was in church, standing in the front bench, worshipping the Lord, having just done an excellent reading of the scripture. As we sang His praises, my throat became dry and ticklish, and I coughed. It was an ordinary cough, but immediately my head exploded, and suddenly I had an unbelievably walloping headache. Somehow I knew what had happened. It had happened to others. Few survive. As I held my head and literally felt the blood pouring and filling my head, I prayed, "Jesus, Touch me, Jesus touch me, Jesus touch me."

The headache worsened, my neck began to stiffen, I began to feel nauseous and I knew that I was about to fall. I looked up on the pulpit. Minister Nurse was looking at me. I motioned to him to come. In a moment he was at my side. I said "Pray for me." Without question he laid hands on me and prayed, and as we said Amen, I sat down, unable to stand anymore.

Time stopped. Then there was Pastor kissing me like there was no tomorrow. There was Dr. Mark Watson, a member of Circle asking me what had happened. I explained to him. He asked if it was the worse headache in my life. I told him "Yes". He asked if I knew where I was. I told him "Yes". He asked if I knew the people who were with me. I told him "Yes". He told me that they would move me to the back of the church, that the ambulance had been called. I said, "Don't move me." He asked if I wanted to lie down on the bench. I said '"yes". Sister Joyce Spence, a nurse, sat down and put my head in her lap. Dr. Mark kept asking me how I was feeling. I told him, "Nauseous, but I won't vomit." Then I vomited all over his lovely, new, Christmas suit.

He later told me that he was frightened because he knew what to expect. Despite the headache and nauseous feeling, I experienced a sweet peace, so that I just wanted to shut my eyes and sleep. Sister Joyce kept hitting me and telling me "Andrea, don't close your eyes, don't go to sleep. If you go to sleep you won't wake up."

I understand that it was half an hour before the ambulance arrived. But my time had stopped. I was in eternity. I was completely conscious, aware of everything, able to answer all questions; but it seemed that only a few minutes had passed from the cough to the time the ambulance arrived.

Pastor offered to accompany me to the hospital, but I refused her offer, knowing that her place was at church with the congregation. Their love for me would have emptied the church and landed everyone at Kings County Hospital. Betty had to be held up, June totally lost it, and everyone was in tears as Pastor brought the church to order and they united to pray for Minister Palmer. Children and elderly, young men and women, joined in tears and prayers to God for my life. Love cannot fail.

In the ambulance: I was accompanied by Sister Joyce who stayed with me for twelve hours, until she saw me settled in the ICU. She is actually a nurse employed at the hospital where I was taken. I began to vomit and urinate uncontrollably. Joyce continued to advice me to stay awake. I was at peace. I had no fear. It was all right whatever happened. She knew, and I knew, that I was dying.

Again it seemed as though one moment I was at Church, and the next I was at the hospital. I was afterwards told that the ambulance went very slowly because they knew that shaking me was dangerous. At the hospital, they did a CT scan of my brain. The report states that my brain was "grossly bloody". Then they did a spinal tap to discover whether or not the blood was clotting. If it were, they would find clots in the clear spinal fluid. When, instead of clear spinal fluid, blood just poured out of my spine onto the floor, the doctors thought that they had compounded the problem by puncturing a vein. I understand that I bawled when they did the spinal tap, but I don't recall ever bawling or crying. Sister Joyce stayed with me. I told her we should continue with the service. Then I thought of hymns and choruses to sing, and we sang.

A miracle had happened. The was absolutely no logical explanation for why the blood that was loose in my head did not clot, why oxygen was still getting to my brain, why I was conscious and alert, why I had neither stroke or seizure, why I was still alive. Given my condition, I should have died before the ambulance arrived at the church. The doctors did not know it, but God had kept the blood from clotting and had emptied my head when they tapped my spine.

The flow of blood out of my spine rendered me stable enough to be moved to the Intensive Care Unit twelve hours later. It was 11:30 PM. It felt as if at most forty-five minutes had passed from the cough to the ICU. I was given codeine for the pain, injected with Heprin to prevent blood clots, and dressed in surgical stockings. My legs and thighs were also put in an automatic massager, which kept the circulation going. That was nice.

While in the emergency room, due to the input from the I.V, I needed to urinate. My poor bladder was bursting, but the effort to start the urination put so much pressure on my brain, I could not do it. The pain in my head had been unbearable. So they had catheterized me. What a relief.

I soon realized what I knew: that every action of the body originates in the brain. Therefore, coughing, sneezing, passing gas, and defecating were unwelcome bodily functions. I was given tagamet for gas and acid, as well as colace to keep my stool soft, but not enough to cause a bowel movement. I was also put on medication to prevent spasm of the blood vessels and seizures, which are expected when brain injury has occurred.

The operation was set for early the next morning. The doctors were sure that there was a ruptured blood vessel (aneurysm), and they announced that my condition was still life threatening. Before the surgery they needed to perform a very invasive, life-threatening angiogram of my brain, because they were unable to tell from the CT scan where exactly the blood flow originated.

The plan was to perform the craniotomy as soon as they could determine the site of the aneurysm. All this time the church was praying that there would be no surgery. When I say the church, I don't mean just Circle. I was amazed later to discover how the news of Satan's attack on me had spread around the world. Beloved, I am the most blessed person I know. Honestly, I was so peaceful and content, I didn't think to pray. I knew I was in the Lord's care.

The angiogram was scheduled to take two hours. Just before they put the catheter into the vein in my groin, the doctor told me of one other risk. He said that at my age, it was likely that there was plaque in my veins. There was always a chance, he said, that the catheter, as it moved up toward my brain, carrying the iodine dye, could cause the plaque to break off. It would then travel with the dye to my brain, and cause a massive stroke. For one moment, I experienced a small anxiety, but I committed my life to God, and peace returned.

During the test, I experienced excruciating pain and a couple of times my neck stiffened as if it would break. I did cry out then. I thought, "Here comes the stroke." Actually, I would rather have died than suffer a stroke. I had seen stroke victims. I didn't want to be a vegetable.

After extensive testing, the doctor announced that they could find no aneurysm and the blood had disappeared. There was no need for surgery. I was taken back to the ICU for observation. The doctor was very uncomfortable with the unexpected, illogical results of the angiogram. His plan was to do another in seven to ten days. If that also proved negative, he would do another in thirty days. Meanwhile I was kept on all medications and the IV. No food for me.

Tuesday night: The catheter was removed and I had to urinate for myself. It was terrible. For about five hours, I strove to relieve a full bladder. I was so afraid of the head pain. Eventually, the nurses turned on all the taps and placed a hot compress on my stomach. I peed. The IV was removed and the next day I was given food.

Wednesday: The doctor ordered another CT scan to assess the amount of blood in my head and to determine whether or not another spinal tap was necessary. "Please God, I prayed, "No more spinal tap." Now that I was alive in the land of the living, I had heard about how awful the pain of a spinal tap is, and also I became aware of the danger of spinal injury, especially in my case since my spine is curved. The CT scan showed no blood. So they did a Doppler test, to check the blood vessels to discover if they had been narrowed by the spasms. There was some insignificant difference between the blood vessels on the left and those on the right. He warned me that I would be experiencing bad headaches for a lo-o-o-o-o-o-n-g time, but that eventually all will be well.

That night I was moved out of the ICU to a ward. I still lay prone most of the time, except when the nurses raised me so that I could use the bedpan. I still wore my surgical stockings and was still enjoying the constant massaging of my legs and thighs.

Thursday morning: The doctor came by. "Miss Palmer, are you ready to go home?" I told him no, I was not. I had been told that the fifth to seventh days were very critical for that was the time when evidence of seizures appeared. It was not uncommon I was told for a re-occurrence of hemorrhage with deadly results to happen. One nurse had said I should stay in the hospital as long as they would keep me. But God had saved my life and the hospital had no definite diagnosis to give to my insurance company. The diagnosis remained "suspicion of aneurysm."

The long and short of it is that five days after suffering a massive sub-dural hemorrhage, I was discharged from the hospital, with codeine for pain, dilantin for seizures, and ducolux for bowel movement. I hadn't even sat up from that Sunday to then, but I walked out of the hospital. Praise the Lord.

From time to time, I experience slight feelings in my head and a little stiffness in my neck. These are just reminders that I've been given a new and precious opportunity to live and declare the works of the Lord. I am so glad. O magnify the Lord with me, and let us rejoice together. For the Lord is great and greatly to be praised. Life is sweet. Blessed be the name of the Lord. I have learned and taught that God is a good Father, and that truth continues to convince me that God the Father loves Rachel. I just want to love Him more.

The End

Poetry

MAMA

Mama was the prettiest lady in the tenement yard.
Some times she went dancing.
We watched in wonder at the transformation.
Mascara, rouge, and lipstick brightening her eyes and lips,
Replacing simple prettiness with awesome beauty.
And in a slinky dress accentuating swaying, rounded hips
The wide low back-line exposing fine smooth chocolate skin
The three-inch timble-heeled glass-slipper lending her majesty
She waltzed on Daddy's arm.

A child could never understand the desperate heartache
Of one too proud to borrow or beg, to be beholden.
One whose life, in a moment of youthful indiscretion,
Changed, then stopped and then began to wither.
Ambition aborted, yet alive, lay strangled in the noonday sun
A chill defied the heat, and fainted eyes blocked out the golden ball
And cruel buzzards waited for a feast.
Pride put his hand in hers
And strengthened with that crutch, she rose
A fixed smile hiding fear and shame
She dressed her ravished nakedness in courage
And with a mask of bold defiance,
Her head held high,
Useless tears dismissed, she stood,

And finding solid earth beneath her feet, she forward marched
The disappointed buzzards flew away.

Mama said that life was hard but sweet.
I could not fathom where the sweetness lay,
But now I know it was the daily victory of once more conquering adversity,
And looking back, and seeing progress made.
She laughed at thwarted fate and winked at God who gave her grace
And dared the devil do his worst
She looked him in his face and he backed down.
She was a winner
The neighbors never knew how poor we were.
She taught us how to hold our heads up high, and smile and never cry;
Mama said, Good manners, character, dignity, education, and a pleasant personality, would displace poverty
So we were never poor.

Those who remember her said, that she was a tall and strapping woman,
But she was only five feet five and never weighed a hundred and sixty pounds.
But when she walked, it was with dignified and purposed steps,
And when she talked her audience listened with respect.
Her words though sharp, that we were left in pools of blood, were wise.
Dominant and domineering,
Mama strode through life, falling many times
But never once did she stay down, give in, give up,

or lose her nerve.
Each problem was a challenge she could meet and overcome.
When she was stressed, she sensibly sat down to rest,
But not too long
Her intellect was constantly employed, planning her next activity.

Mama, an aristocrat at heart
Despite the lack of higher education,
Appeared quite learned.
Philosopher, economist, politician, psychiatrist, and lawyer,
She conquered hardship, confronting every opposition
To give her children that which circumstance refused to let her have, marriage, and homes, and high big-paying jobs.
She lied and bluffed, out-witting men of high degree, with such expertise
They never did suspect that they'd been had.

Then cancer came and with the same determined optimism
She went about her business,
Expecting him to finally concede defeat and leave,
But like a parasite he clung to her and sucked her life away
Until one evening Jesus called her home.
O death, where is thy sting? O Grave where is thy victory?

Rachel Andrea Palmer

DADDY

Tall, light-skinned, and handsome.
A fun-loving, lover-man with no ambition.
His literature was comic books;
An adult with a childish spirit.
He lived only for the moment, for the day,
He engaged the children in his games
And, with unashamed advantage, won each prize.
The booty in his pockets told the story.
Pretty marbles, water guns, sling-shots,
Small carvings of wooden boats, and spinning tops,
He claimed with boisterous laughter
Still the children loved to play with him.

Daddy built the best kites, some simple, some elaborate
With colored paper, string, scraps of cloth, pliable cocoyea and paste.
He made little chic-e-chongs for the tiny tots,
And gigantic supermen for grown-ups like himself.
Then, on Sunday evenings in the vale
We mounted our kites and watched them sail above the trees
And Daddy's kite went higher that the rest.
When the moon was full, and night was bright as day
The children gleefully followed the pied piper to the memorial park
Where we played every game we knew, and some that he invented.
Grown-ups sat and watched and shared each other's lives and gossip;
But Daddy ran, and jumped, and skipped, and hula-hooped with us.

He was the blind man's buff, and Mr. Wolf who ate the little pigs.
And he enjoyed the games as well as we.

In his spare time Daddy played pranks on the neighbors.
It was Daddy who put the frog on Mrs. Theresa's stoop,
And danced with glee when she screamed and almost fainted.
It was Daddy who spray-painted chickens pink and green and blue
It was Daddy dressed in Dracula's cape who emerged from the cellar
It was Daddy who bagged Miss Nora's cat and Mrs. William's dog
And used their skins to make carnival costumes.
That wasn't funny. Only Daddy laughed.

Daddy loved Carnival and so, when we were small
We all participated in the revelry that preceded lent.
It was the most exhilarating time, except for Christmas.
Once all the girls, portraying Spanish damsels,
were dressed in vary-colored, three tiered skirts and white peasant blouses
The boys were matadors and bandits
They wore red cummerbunds and flashed red capes,
Wielded painted wooden swords and gleaming silver guns.
As, accompanied by the calypso beat of steel drums and iron
We danced through the streets, led by a handsome troubadour.

Rachel Andrea Palmer

MY LITTLE SISTER

It's strange,
But I suppose one cannot know one's self,
Except in relation to someone, some place, or some circumstance.
So I remember her, my sister, my friend.
I named her Deborah, after my cherished doll
Rejecting it, in favor of my pretty baby sister.

I remember
When the hurricane came with pouring rain and screeching wind
Forcing us to stay inside the little house.
I frightened her with tales of bad witches,
Who viciously shook the wooden shutters, trying to come in.
Trembling with fear, wrapped in the sheets, we hid beneath the bed,
Hugging each other protectively.

She mimicked me.
And with the very same inflection in her voice,
Recited every poem that I learned.
And, straining to copy my falsetto,
She sang my songs.
And like a shadow followed me precisely,
Echoing my ideas.
Doing everything exactly as I did,
Never wondering if I were right,
Flattering and loving me completely.

But life grew hard,
And to survive the hardships,
Instead of pooling our resources

From Hagar to Rachel

Against the bitter cold that threatened to destroy,
Instead of hugging each other protectively
As when the hurricane attacked,
We went our separate ways,
And lost each other.

Rachel Andrea Palmer

BIG BROTHER

By the time I noticed him, Brother was a working man.
Everyone was proud of him, and awed by him.
He had escaped the tenement yard and was a teacher.
He came home at end of month, bringing money and chocolate
And Mama gave him twice the food that even Daddy got.
At night, he brought out his guitar and with us little ones,
A most appreciative audience,
He sang and entertained us.

When I was fourteen,
My big brother knew everything
And had a fascinating secret life.
His terylene shirts were always white
For a quarter I seamed his trousers
And for a dime shined his shoes so bright
It was he who showed me how to fix my make-up right
And tried to teach my clumsy feet to dance to dance.
One - two, One - two - three.
I wonder if he remembers that he read Edgar Allen Poe to me.

He never knew how much I loved him, for we never said such things
And once I almost kissed him.
But we didn't kiss in our family, nor touch nor hug.

From Hagar to Rachel

And then he went away and changed,
And I could no longer reach him.
I still miss my big brother.

SHAME AND BETRAYAL

Ashamed, I walked the streets to delay going home from school.
I could not let my friends come home with me.
Mama might be crying, or dead,
And Daddy might be in jail.

Sometimes there was not enough to eat
And Daddy did not sleep there anymore.
One day Daddy brought two children,
Our brother and sister.

Locked out.
Daddy gave the key to Mr. Brunton,
And left us homeless.
Mama sat in the yard and wept,
While we huddled around her,
Bewildered and afraid, too terrified to speak.

Daddy slept in a comfortable bed with a full belly
And our new brother and sister.
Why didn't Daddy care?

MY PLEASANT ROOM DREAM

The sunlight dimly filtered through the redwood forest
That canopied the ancient track,
Revealing elves and fairy folk and rain-deer.
My train rumbled to a stop outside a castle
Where wanderers and outlaws found sanctuary,
And food and wine and friendly company.
There my pleasant room awaited me.

Treading softly on a thick carpet of autumn leaves,
For it was always autumn there,
Feeling my way around the ivied wall,
I found the secret window,
Which opened at my expert touch and climbing in,
A sliding shute poured me into the secret chamber,
A thick cinnamon bearskin rug gently breaking the fall
Of my unceremonious entrance.

From deep brown polished mahogany panels
A mounted bear's head and large antlers,
Like a hovering angel watched over David's harp,
Which I, my fingers knowing what I did not learn,
Played skillfully.

Ceiling-tall rich cherry wood bookcases, with gold-edged books,
Lured me to a world of make-believe.
Seduced by Tennyson and Wordsworth,
My fantasies, made real
I married King Cophetua, mourned Hallan's death,

Rachel Andrea Palmer

Charged with the Light Brigade;
And tired from that misdirected battle,
I lay among the daffodils listening to the reaper's plaintive song.
And slept and dreamed sweet dreams, within my dream,
And woke to find the lamps had used up all their oil.

It was time to leave.

MY SEASIDE DREAM

The old wooden train rumbled on, ambling along wooden tiers.
The passing scenery proclaimed
The love and joy and peace of simple souls.
Picture perfect cottages with window boxes
Whose profusion of pink and red lady-slippers
Interspersed with white geraniums,
Smiled their benediction.

Little gardens enclosed in magenta and green hibiscus fences,
Protected rambling roses
Which offered up their perfume to the breeze,
That lazily flew by my nostrils
To share the gift of their exquisite scent,
And on the soft incline beside the track
Nature strew wild flowers
Just to delight me.

I watched the train reverse itself, leaving me in sacred solitude.
I stretched, inhaled, exhaled,
My tired lungs rejoicing to receive
The unpolluted salty air, whose restorative powers,
Re-energized my blood, removing toxic city waste.
Then, alone, unfettered and revitalized, I danced,
And clapped, and sang and worshipped God,
For sun and sea and birds and fish and peace and joy.
While gentle breezes made sweet love to me,
Whispering, God loves you, child.

Rachel Andrea Palmer

Alone in this serenity, caressed by nylon water, I swam.
The warm waves barely rippled as schools of pink and crimson fish
Played ring-around-a-rosy within the barrier reef
That formed this gentle lagoon.
The sun's rays sliced the translucent water,
Highlighting luxurious gardens of peach corals,
Floating beds of brilliantly colored anemone, and sea pinks.
Here in this divinely made aquarium,
I, graced suddenly with mermaid qualities,
Frolicked with flipper.

As shadows lengthened, the pearly gulls winged their way landward,
And the sun, his tour of duty ending,
Began his journey home.
I watched him trail his blazing cape across the darkening sea.
Then, standing on the edge of night, he turned,
And with majestic dignity, he bowed,
And smiled and kissed me,
Which kiss I blushingly returned,
And sighed and closed my eyes,
And when I looked again he wasn't there.
The moon, pale and ghostly,
Emboldened by his absence, came forth,
Replacing golden fire with silver beams,
And ordering the stars to add their lights,
God said goodnight and closed the day.

MY MOUNTAIN DREAM

Sometimes the train stopped at the foot of a majestic mountain,
Which I, a mountaineer of much experience, conquered with ease,
To stand enraptured by the sight of Paradise-regained.

A million points of light that glistened in the brilliance of early afternoon,
Laughed and danced and tumbled, into a pristine lake,
Around which stood gigantic evergreens like sentinels.
In the adjacent glade, deer played with antelope,
While lambs and lions slept peacefully in each other's arms,
And children blithely rode giraffes and elephants.

The lake, unable to accommodate the never-ending avalanche,
Emptied her overflow into a river, that wound its way
Through verdant hills and fertile valleys,
A nursing mammy feeding rivulets from which small creatures drank.
Then satisfied that all earth's needs were met,
Fresh water merged with salt and lost itself.

What of the flowers with hues so rich and pure?
Unpolluted earth, mineral mountain water and the energizing rays of sun
That filtered through the crystal firmament,
Nurtured vibrant greens, bold crimson reds,

blushing pinks,
Golden yellows, imperial purples, and royal blues,
Which fed sweet honeybees, butterflies and humming birds.

A cloud, ominous and duty-bound, moved inland,
Obscuring sun and sky, drenching this Edenic scene
With rain that fell in fat splats until the sun asserted its importance.
As the intoxicating fragrance of wet earth overwhelmed my nostrils,
A double rainbow smiling its benediction,
As proof that God kept Noah's covenant.

LOST DREAMS

When I lived in the happily-ever-after,
I dreamt great dreams of calm seasides,
Majestic mountains,
And rooms where I was safe.

Then the war came.
I lost my way and could not find the sea.
The mountain was insurmountable,
And when I lifted the trap-door,
The narrow shute refused to let me in.
So I stopped dreaming.

Rachel Andrea Palmer

STILLBORN DREAMS

Unrealistic expectations are infertile
Producing only futility.
Unrewarded labor pains expel the phantom.
Screams mock the silence with agony twice felt;
For in the lifeless face of dreams born dead,
A cruel punishment for unwise love,
The unrelenting hand of un-relieved despair
Deliver stillborn dreams.

ROMANCE NOVELS

The sleeping house sang and sawed in dreamland.
My adolescent imagination lived within the pages
Where sweethearts kissed and touched each other
And consummated love.
Youthful lust, exquisite, feverish, and restless,
Nourished by stories of passionate foreplay,
Awoke with screaming urgency, demanding satisfaction.

I lay on my belly, the dim night-light, a silent observer, watched,
As my lover first tenderly, then with increasing passion,
Caressed, and .kissed and sucked and drove me wild.
My body tensed and heated, arched itself, seeking release.
My mouth so dry,
My little nipples hard,
My belly boiling with a strange, exciting pulsing,
Forcing me to push against the bed till all was wet and drained.
I turned, and touched myself, and smiled a secret smile,
Desiring more.

Rachel Andrea Palmer

MAMA'S ILLNESS

Every Saturday morning Mama goes to market.
Today, she stumbles and falls and complains of dizziness.

I will mind Mama and make her well.
I am in charge, important and trusted.
I cook, and clean and take care of Mama,
Happy in anticipation of her praise.
For twenty days she's moved in and out of consciousness,
Never remembering one previous moment or activity.

Something is different today.
A ghostly silence summons me to her side.
No sound, no breath, no movement of her breast.
I touch her and feel the nervous pricks of cold sweat start.
Cold, she is cold, dead cold.
I freeze.
Unwilling to accept the understanding of my mind,
I remain transfixed and speechless.
She opens her eyes. "My grandmother sent me back, she says."
And falls asleep.

It is Saturday morning and Mama is well
And I am tired of being the adult,
I want to be a child again.
Visitors keep coming.

From Hagar to Rachel

I am not needed
So I take a walk and go to see my friend who lives around the bend of the street.
The streetlights come on.
Here comes my big sister to arrest and take me home.
And Mama shames me with threats of punishment.
Why isn't Mama pleased?
Why does Mama hate me?
I resemble my father.

Rachel Andrea Palmer

WHO NEEDS THEM?

Mama, I need a quarter.
Go ask your father.
Today I need one lousy quarter and Mama doesn't
have it.
What Mama has are six hungry children
By four different men
Who don't give a damn about us.

Who needs her?
All Mamma does now is curse at me,
She always thinks I went off somewhere with
some man,
Doing some wrong thing,
Whenever I'm not home.

She says that I'm a whore,
But I'll never be a whore.
I'll keep my virginity,
I'll finish high school,
I'll get a good job,
I'll get married.
I'll live happily ever after.
I'll show her.

Today, I need one lousy quarter and Daddy
doesn't have it.
What Daddy has are twelve children.
Six live with him, four live with his wife;
Then there's Sister and I.

Who needs him?
A grown man who spends his days reading comic
books,
Killing harmless birds with a sling-shot,
Going to the movies,
And playing with children.

From Hagar to Rachel

Mama was ambitious,
So she nagged him,
And he left,
Not caring to improve.

One day, Daddy,
You will ask me for bread
And I will spit in your hand.
He never asked me for bread.
He never asked me for anything.

Rachel Andrea Palmer

MY RETREAT FROM REALITY

When life inside my books is more appealing than reality;
When I possess no materials from which I may construct true dreams,
Then illusion is preferable to verity.
And so, within the unlimited realm of unrestrained imagination,
I leap across the chasm of confinement
Into a world where I am beautiful, powerful, wealthy, whole,
And in control.

With head held high, my back and shoulders straight,
Oblivious of the ordinary people, held fast by chains of wicked circumstance,
Who, degraded by life's brutal switch,
Struggle daily to defend themselves against the cruel and relentless
Tides of poverty, made strong by hopelessness,
I relocate soul.

I will not feel the heartbreak of despairing women,
Whose voided breasts mockingly decry their motherhood;
Nor will I see the vacant stare of men,
Whose manhood, coffining stillborn expectations,
Lie buried in unacknowledged graves.

I will not hear the cruel words with which the women,
Weary of the piteous cries of empty-bellied children,
Emasculate discouraged men;
Nor will I listen to their whimpering cries
When they've been struck, knocked down, abused,
By men made angry by the taunting truth of their impotence.

From Hagar to Rachel

I will not see the ugly rooms where bugs and mice, and roaches,
Un-paying tenants, claim territorial rights;
And children scantily clad, huddle, five in a bed,
Have early lost their childhood to worry, want, and fear.
I will not feel the cold tongue force my silenced lips,
Nor the gnarled hand that spread my virgin legs,
To mutilate and rob me,

And threaten me to tell no one, or else.
The circumstantial chains that hold my people fast
Fall at my fleeing feet;
As I escape this desperate, dying sphere,
Where beauty, peace, and love are mysteries;
Where anger, fear, and shame, imprison hope and joy;
And death, a welcome thief, steals babies from their cribs.
Into my books, into a dream, into a safe and comfortable home.
Come, see my home, visit a while, enjoy the elegance
Of my mahogany paneled walls, and cherry wood furniture;
My Persian rugs that accent polished parquet floors;
My gleaming silver cutlery, and long-stemmed crystals,
And chandeliers that light cathedral ceilings.

Come, see my Victorian four-poster bed,
Dressed in gold satin sheets and shams, and fine silk curtains;
And my white marbled Roman bath with golden fixtures
Where I sip champagne while I unwind
After a day of sun and surf and sand.

Agatha pours freshly brewed aromatic tea
And serves those dainty pink and green sandwiches.

Rachel Andrea Palmer

While we describe exotic places,
Where nature's naked beauty transports us to
The paradise of Eden
Afternoon tea ended, we lounge languidly on the veranda,
Remembering our first romantic steps;
And planning future rendezvous with handsome men
Decked out in coat and tails
And elegant young ladies,
All beautiful with satins, lace, and timble-heeled glass slippers.

The palm trees bow and laughingly engage
The twilight shadows in a dance accompanied by
The rhythmic music of the waves,
Which gently lap upon my private beach,
As peacock-like Osiris struts across the evening sky,
Taking the warmth and sending us inside
To dine on pheasant, candied carrots, fresh green garden vegetables, and aged wine.
While, Beethoven, Bach and Straus lift the souls of
My sophisticated company.

When life inside my books is more appealing than reality;
When I possess no materials from which I may construct true dreams,
Then illusion is preferable to verity.
And so, within the unlimited realm of unrestrained imagination
I leap across the chasm of confinement,
Into a world where I am beautiful, powerful, wealthy, whole, loved,
And in control.

THE PRISON OF MY SOUL

Beneath a calm exterior,
Imprisoned in a lonely soul.
There beats a heart that rages, weeps, and groans despairingly.
A warden named Self Discipline keeps the key.
The chambers of the heart are full, "No Vacancy;"
There anger, grief, and fear keep company
And strengthened by pride reside.
A lifetime sentence, unjust judge,
The jury had no pity, justice denied,
Neither God nor man showed mercy,
Condemned to live in dying pain.

Too much abuse.
Physical, mental, emotional, spiritual.
Daily disappointment is the whip that chastens,
Keeping me in check.
No more, please.
Enough.
Too much.
Compressed and concentrated,
The potent poison of bitterness,
Finding no exit from the prison of my soul,
Recoiled upon itself.
Did I die and is this hell?
Yes, that must be it.
For here,
There's neither love, nor light, no beauty, faith, nor hope.
And still I long to live, to laugh, to care, to love.
I must escape, for yet,
I am not dead.

Rachel Andrea Palmer

EMOTIONAL CRYOGENICS

To halt the confusion that exists when hurt, anger, pain, and love
Keep wrestling for the right to dominate my mind;
To terminate the feelings of betrayal and eliminate the grief
That seeks to overwhelm my heart;
To stop the self-destroying hate,
That threatens to create a me that's hateful to myself,
I've learned that there's a place beyond my conscious soul,
Wherein a cryogenic vault was carefully erected
To house abuse and pain.

In this secret place, this undead world,
I hide all my emotions.
Fear bolts the door
Pride turns the key
And I emerge a shallow shell,
A barren oyster.

Now all I have is loneliness –
For not to love, be angry, hurt, or hate,
Is to be empty.

MY WALLS ARE TOPPLING

Everyone said, "How strong you are."
And I piously replied "God's Grace is Sufficient."
'Twas true,
But while I was grateful for the strength of Grace,
I resented the need for Grace.

I stayed but would not bend , would not break.
My walls were thick and high
And offered more protection than ***You*** did.
Then ***You*** changed my name.
You said I am no longer Hagar
Pain precedes conception, accompanies birth, and heralds life.
I am Rachel.

The hiding time is past, for Rachel peeks out.
I see her looking through the cracks,
Helpless, hopeful, pleading to be allowed to live,
She wants to fly, to soar.

Hagar wasn't lonely,
She occupied herself like Martha.
She filled the days with activity
And slept the sound and dreamless sleep of the laborer.

But Rachel, she is idle,
Dreaming only of being loved and becoming pregnant.
She is lonely; Barren, desperate, and unfulfilled.
For though Rachel peeks out, love is not consummated.
She waits to experience the destruction of the walls that keep her barren.

It was Hagar who erected the prison,
But she died giving birth to Rachel

Who longs to be free,
But the cracks are too small
And she is too weak to break down the walls.

She has been struggling against the giants that guard the fortress,
But she has not prevailed.
I need someone to destroy the giants and the walls.
I need protection and security
I need someone to shield me from the loneliness that frightens me.
My walls are beginning to wobble.
Please don't let them topple on top of me.

UNQUENCHED THIRST

I want to come near.
I feel like an orphan who receives a check and a letter of support
But never meets her benefactor.
Like the heroine in the movie "Daddy Longlegs."
Or like the "Poor little Rich Girl", who has everything and yet nothing,
Because she lacks love.

Here I am standing so far off, yearning to come near.
I watch the other children climb into ***Your*** lap,
I see ***You*** hug them and kiss them and tell them sweet words.
I want to run to ***You*** and feel ***Your*** love
And love ***You*** with my whole soul and heart and mind,
But I seem to be rooted to this spot,
So far from ***You***.

Many times I peeked through the cracks in the wall that stands in my way
I called to ***You***; but my voice was timid and I thought ***You*** did not hear.
Then I reasoned that ***You*** owed me nothing.
You gave me life, ***You*** provided for me.
I should be content with my situation.
So I withdrew and continued to watch from afar,
Not knowing how to change things.
I tried to be content with what I had,
Knowing I did not deserve anymore.

But I am discontented, because I need and want more.
I do not really know what it is that I so desperately

need.
I know the other children have it.
It's like never having tasted ice-cream,
But seeing other children enjoying it,
And wanting that enjoyment also.

I know intellectually, that ***You***r giving has nothing to do
With the receiver deserving the gift,
I know it has to do with ***You*** loving the one to whom ***You*** give.
I know so many things intellectually and
Once in a while I do know something more deeply,
But I seem unable to keep the deep things.
I feel so shallow and empty,
Yet I am like a dark deep well,
That still wasn't dug deep enough
To reach water.